iClone 4.31 3D Animatio
Beginner's Guide

Animate your stories and ideas to create realistic scenes with this movie making application geared towards new and inexperienced film makers, video producers / compositors, vxf artists, and 3D artists / designers

M.D. McCallum

BIRMINGHAM - MUMBAI

iClone 4.31 3D Animation
Beginner's Guide

First published: October 2011

Production Reference: 1171011

Livery Place
35 Livery Street
Birmingham B3 2PB, UK.

ISBN 978-1-84969-178-9

www.packtpub.com

Cover Image by Rakesh Shejwal (shejwal.rakesh@gmail.com)

Credits

Author

  M.D. McCallum

Reviewer(s)

  Guy Langlois

  Susanne and Joe Pass

Acquisition Editor

  Chaitanya Apte

Development Editor

  Reshma Sundaresan

Technical Editor

  Pramila Balan

Project Coordinator

  Shubhanjan Chatterjee

Proofreader(s)

  Kevin McGowan

  Linda Morris

  Aaron Nash

Indexer

  Rekha Nair

Production Coordinator

  Arvindkumar Gupta

Cover Work

  Arvindkumar Gupta

Foreword

First and foremost, I would like to thank Mike (M.D. McCallum) for the idea and inspiration that has taken to create such an endeavor. This is truly a noble cause that will undoubtedly inspire many throughout the years.

This all started a while back when Mike contacted me about his idea of writing a book about iClone. From the get-go, we were completely ecstatic that iClone would finally get the personal treatment direct from the mind and hands of a true production industry veteran.

From its inception, iClone has been an untamed breed of 3D software designed especially for creative users without prior 3D backgrounds. A software that, even though was jam-packed with the latest features and technology, was always missing something. Apart from its heavy feature-based manuals and tutorial videos, iClone always lacked a proper guide to personally lead and inspire users to nurture an entire project from scratch.

I am deeply grateful that M.D. McCallum, the author who has contributed so much of his enthusiasm to the iClone community, has now volunteered to make this book. M.D. McCallum is the first featured iClone professional who is honored with several iClone movie awards, along with being one of the first users to set up the iClone Wikipedia page. His kindness and generosity has always permitted him to share his knowledge through the iClone Revolution website, which he started as a need to address so many iClone inquiries. Being a senior iClone Content Developer has also allowed him to push the limits of creativity not just of himself, but also of the entire animation community.

As most of you know already, iClone is not just a collection of years of heartbeats and oceans of fervor from the Reallusion team, but it is also a chest of dreams and collaborated efforts from dozens of worldwide content contributors who over time have made the world of 3D production so much more accessible and inspiring to all of us.

Thanks to Mike's gamut of iClone animation knowledge, readers can now get a comprehensive view of what an iClone production platform is, including, how to master tools, access fast growing content libraries from talented developers, and how to make the most of being a community member. His work not only holds the hands of beginners who yearn to explore iClone in a structural way, but it also lends itself as an enjoyable must-read for any iClone veteran.

This galvanized book has been long overdue and awaited by many users who have spent hundreds of thousands of man-hours figuring out how to get the most out of their iClone, not to mention those who have hungered to enter the world of independent film making with a great self-taught companion.

This piece of work is also a great reward and humbling reminder to the iClone development team that has witnessed their software being used across every continent and industry on the planet. There is so much that our words cannot express... Thank you.

Charles Chen
CEO and Founding Partner of Reallusion, Inc.

About the Author

M D. McCallum, aka WarLord in the iClone community, is an international award winning Commercial Graphics Artist, 3D Animator, Project Director, and Webmaster with a freelance career that spans over 20 years and includes over one hundred individual and team-based awards. M.D. has worked as a freelancer for animation companies, 3D application companies, game development studios, indie film and animation studios. His experience with computers dates back to home-built kits in the late 1970s.

M.D. is the author of eleven whitepapers for the Reallusion iClone Developers Center and has been selected two times as a Reallusion Featured Developer. M.D. has been a loyal user of iClone since version one and is a Certified Content Developer and Reallusion Director. M.D. was previously published as an outdoor writer in national magazines before turning his attention to full time digital freelancing.

M.D. operates a freelance production studio in partnership with other highly skilled freelancers across the world to provide web and television-based commercials, product presentations and visualization. He also creates and provides quality iClone props including his innovative Destructible line of props and iClone freebies and tips at www. iclonerevolution.com.

I would like to thank Charles Chen and Jason Lin at Reallusion for their unwavering support of the book project. I would also like to thank Shirley Martin who helped me work out the kinks early on and the technical reviewers for their time and generosity. I particularly want to thank Guy Langlois (BigBoss) for taking the time out of a very busy schedule to help. And of course, I want to thank the incredibly patient team at Packt Publishing for guiding me through the writing and shaping this book in a way that no words could adequately describe. And last, but certainly not least, my wife Rosemary and stepson Zac. Two people that go out of their way every day to make sure I have the time to complete my various projects, meet my deadlines, and otherwise get to have fun doing what I love all day and long into the night.

About the Reviewers

Guy Langlois is a Computer Engineer with a Master's degree in Business and Administration (MBA). He works as an Executive in an engineering firm specialized in the development of high-end audio/video and 3D equipment and authoring tools for the Film and Broadcasting industry. Aside from work, Guy plays in a rock band and is a recognized Reallusion Certified Content Developer, Director, and Trainer who excels in the creation of specialized iClone characters and other derived iClone products.

Guy is known in the iClone industry as "*Bigboss*". He also manages the "*Bigboss's Treasures*" Theme Store in Reallusion City, which features his personal work as well as the work of other excellent Certified Content Developers, each with their own special aptitude for creation and design; http://city.reallusion.com/store/BigbossTreasures

I would like to thank the iClone community who so gracefully support my work!

Cheers!

Susanne and Joe Pass discovered their passion for animation, 3D modelling, and image editing. Susanne and Joe Pass worked in different jobs, she came from the social sector and he was a workman.

Joe concerned himself more and more with graphic art. His work has been presented in several exhibitions. Susanne was interested in photography.

The couple began to learn how to work with image editing programs like Photoshop and made their first flash animations. In 2006, they completely switched and offered, under the name digiMagic, services in the field of Animation and Web Design, shortly after they bought the first Reallusion products: CrazyTalk5 and iClone3.

They were directly thrilled by the new possibilities that opened. They expanded their service by content development and training courses for iClone or CrazyTalk Animator in Germany.

Susanne and Joe are Reallusion Certified Content Developers, Trainers, and Directors. You can find their content packs in Reallusion Content Store and Marketplace.

They count themselves lucky that they found a job they enjoy and can work together.

www.PacktPub.com

Support files, eBooks, discount offers and more

You might want to visit www.PacktPub.com for support files and downloads related to your book.

Did you know that Packt offers eBook versions of every book published, with PDF and ePub files available? You can upgrade to the eBook version at www.PacktPub.com and as a print book customer, you are entitled to a discount on the eBook copy. Get in touch with us at service@packtpub.com for more details.

At www.PacktPub.com, you can also read a collection of free technical articles, sign up for a range of free newsletters and receive exclusive discounts and offers on Packt books and eBooks.

 PACKTLiB®

http://PacktLib.PacktPub.com

Do you need instant solutions to your IT questions? PacktLib is Packt's online digital book library. Here, you can access, read and search across Packt's entire library of books.

Why Subscribe?

◆ Fully searchable across every book published by Packt
◆ Copy and paste, print and bookmark content
◆ On demand and accessible via web browser

Free Access for Packt account holders

If you have an account with Packt at www.PacktPub.com, you can use this to access PacktLib today and view nine entirely free books. Simply use your login credentials for immediate access.

Table of Contents

Preface

Reallusion's iClone is an animated movie making application that allows hobbyists, machinimators, home-based animators, and professionals to visualize their story or an idea by seeing it in action. Years ago, creating animations and single images would require a team of trained artists to accomplish. Now, iClone real time rending engine empowers its users to instantly view what is loaded into the 3D workspace or preview it as an animation, if you have the precise instructions.

The iClone 3D Animation Beginner's Guide will walk you through the building and animating of a complete scene and several one-off projects. First we create a scene with sky, terrain, water, props, and other assets. Then add two characters and manipulate their features and animate their movement. We will also use particles to create the effect of a realistic torch and animate cameras to give different views to the scene. Finally, we will see how to quickly import images to enhance the scene with a mountain, barn, and water tank. It will cover some fun stuff such as playing with props, characters, and other scene assets. It will also demonstrate some advanced topics such as screen resolution, formats and codecs but mostly, it will deal with doing hands on animation with precise instructions.

What this book covers

Chapter 1, Installing and Configuring iClone, goes through the installation and configuration process for iClone and discusses the Reallusion iClone community, where to get more assets, how to use the Content Store and City Marketplace, bringing outside content into iClone with import and drag-and-drop features, and exploring the iClone interface.

Chapter 2, Creating Your First Scene, we will explore the 3D workspace, create a basic scene with sky, terrain, water, and props, use Live Plants to create vegetation, work with standard, animated, and interactive props. We will build a gazebo prop from 3D building blocks and texture it, then we'll light the scene to get the mood right.

Chapter 3, Adding and Customizing Characters, we will add characters to the scene and customize these characters by altering their clothing and type of hair. While doing this, we will learn how iClone works with external image editors to modify the characters' clothing.

Chapter 4, Animating the Characters, this is a very important chapter in which the timeline will be discussed using key frames to animate our characters. We will work with interactive props, load and time the dialog between the characters, how to use paths, point-and-click and director mode for movement, and finally blending and editing motions on the timeline, which can create custom motions from existing motions.

Chapter 5, Enhancing Animation with Particles, this chapter is devoted to fun and eye candy. We will explore iClone's particle system. We will learn how to deploy the particles, attach or link them, and modify their settings. Each particle effect such as fire, rain, and dust have their own control panel with settings that can be modified for a variety of uses.

Chapter 6, Working with Cameras, a critical chapter in the iClone learning curve. This chapter devotes itself to the iClone camera system. We'll create cameras, name them, and deploy them as both animated and static to suit our needs. We will discuss clipping, depth of field, and the important camera switch that allows us to setup a long running shot between cameras of our choice as the scene plays out.

Chapter 7, Enhancing Scenes with Images and Videos, this is another fun and exciting chapter in which we will discover how we can use two dimensional planes, billboards, and objects with channel maps to create low poly backdrops and props for our scenes. We will learn to drag-and-drop video onto objects and why some objects don't want to work properly when dropping video or an image on them. We'll learn to enhance our scenes with imagery using opacity maps and other channels.

Chapter 8, Rendering our Work, an often overlooked but extremely important aspect of our journey in animation. We will discuss various types of renders for both still images and video. We will cover what video works best for our needs. We will learn what a codec is in comparison to a container file like AVI, WMV, or MP4, and what container files might fit our needs.

Chapter 9, Animating Outer Space, this exciting space scene challenges our skills and puts to use what we have covered in previous chapters. We will learn to plot a path for our spaceship that explodes as it crosses the screen, but not before we learn to animate a shuttle craft escaping from the exploding debris. We also learn to setup two dimensional planes to create a scene that is alive compared to flat background only starfields.

Appendix A, Using Personas, iProps, and Helpers, takes a close look at the Actionscript driven personas, AML templates and helpers. The section starts with a basic overview of AML after which we explore character Personas, AML driven templates, such as Sit Here and Grab It, along with helper objects like cars and planes.

Appendix B, Animating with iClone Physics, covers the basics of iClone physics, discusses rigid and soft body objects, their parameters and how to use them. Knock down, over or drop objects. Set up impact between objects. Impart energy to start a simulation and discusses physics as a simulation tool that enhances and helps our animation.

Appendix C, Exploring New Features, explores and discusses new visual enhancements, such as ambient occlusion and toon rendering. Looks at new performance improving features. Explores the new range of Post Effects such as Blur and Color Adjust. Also, takes a look at time saving features, such as the Multi-Duplicate dialog box.

Appendix D, Discovering New Animation Tools, discusses the MixMoves animation library along with the Motion Puppet and Direct Puppet features introduced in version 5. We will install and use the new Mocap Plug-in that allows us to use the Kinect sensor to pass simple motion data directly into iClone for animation. We will also be cleaning up that data for use, discuss and use the new Prop Puppet and Prop Look-At features, explore the newly licensed Human IK technology and its impact on animation with its bone control system.

What you need for this book

For this book, you will need the following:

1. iClone 4.31 or iClone 5 for Appendices.
2. Downloadable code bundle from `http://www.PacktPub.com`.

Who this book is for

This book is aimed at film makers, video producers/compositors, vxf artists or 3D artists/ designers that have no previous experience with iClone. If you have that drive inside you to entertain people via the internet on sites like YouTube or Vimeo, create a superb presentation video, showcase a product or create a movie, or get a fast start on the iClone program, this Beginner's guide was written with you in mind.

Conventions

In this book, you will find several headings appearing frequently.

To give clear instructions of how to complete a procedure or task, we use:

Time for action – heading

1. Action 1

2. Action 2

3. Action 3

Instructions often need some extra explanation so that they make sense, so they are followed with:

What just happened?

This heading explains the working of tasks or instructions that you have just completed.

You will also find some other learning aids in the book, including:

Pop quiz – heading

These are short multiple choice questions intended to help you test your own understanding.

Have a go hero – heading

These set practical challenges and give you ideas for experimenting with what you have learned.

You will also find a number of styles of text that distinguish between different kinds of information. Here are some examples of these styles, and an explanation of their meaning.

Code words in text are shown as follows: "For Windows XP, it is `C:\Documents and Settings\All Users\Documents\Reallusion\Custom\iClone 4 Custom\`".

New terms and **important words** are shown in bold. Words that you see on the screen, in menus or dialog boxes for example, appear in the text like this: "Click on the **OK** button to exit the **Preference** window".

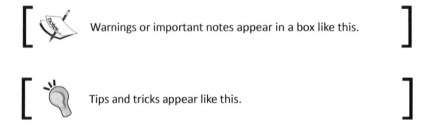

> Warnings or important notes appear in a box like this.

> Tips and tricks appear like this.

Reader feedback

Feedback from our readers is always welcome. Let us know what you think about this book—what you liked or may have disliked. Reader feedback is important for us to develop titles that you really get the most out of.

To send us general feedback, simply send an e-mail to feedback@packtpub.com, and mention the book title via the subject of your message.

If there is a book that you need and would like to see us publish, please send us a note in the **SUGGEST A TITLE** form on www.packtpub.com or e-mail suggest@packtpub.com.

If there is a topic that you have expertise in and you are interested in either writing or contributing to a book, see our author guide on www.packtpub.com/authors.

Customer support

Now that you are the proud owner of a Packt book, we have a number of things to help you to get the most from your purchase.

Downloading the example code

You can download the example code files for all Packt books you have purchased from your account at http://www.PacktPub.com. If you purchased this book elsewhere, you can visit http://www.PacktPub.com/support and register to have the files e-mailed directly to you.

Downloading the color images of this book

We also provide you a PDF file that has color images of the screenshots used in this book. The color images will help you better understand the changes in the output. You can download this file from https://www.packtpub.com/sites/default/files/1789EXP.pdf.

Errata

Although we have taken every care to ensure the accuracy of our content, mistakes do happen. If you find a mistake in one of our books—maybe a mistake in the text or the code—we would be grateful if you would report this to us. By doing so, you can save other readers from frustration and help us improve subsequent versions of this book. If you find any errata, please report them by visiting http://www.packtpub.com/support, selecting your book, clicking on the **errata submission form** link, and entering the details of your errata. Once your errata are verified, your submission will be accepted and the errata will be uploaded on our website, or added to any list of existing errata, under the Errata section of that title. Any existing errata can be viewed by selecting your title from http://www.packtpub.com/support.

Piracy

Piracy of copyright material on the Internet is an ongoing problem across all media. At Packt, we take the protection of our copyright and licenses very seriously. If you come across any illegal copies of our works, in any form, on the Internet, please provide us with the location address or website name immediately so that we can pursue a remedy.

Please contact us at copyright@packtpub.com with a link to the suspected pirated material.

We appreciate your help in protecting our authors, and our ability to bring you valuable content.

Questions

You can contact us at questions@packtpub.com if you are having a problem with any aspect of the book, and we will do our best to address it.

1
Installing and Configuring iClone

You always knew it and reading this somewhat proves it. You want to be an animator but have no experience with animating. Maybe like a lot of us you can't draw a straight line with a ruler or perhaps you have no clue what 3D animation is, but you know what you want to do. Maybe you are an experienced 3D artist wanting to get a quick grasp of the program. You are not only reading the right book, you are also among friends here. As long as you have the desire and know your mouse from a monitor, then you have as good a chance as anyone at creating fun animated videos of family, friends, stories, ideas, concepts, or whatever it is that you have a desire to share while having fun in the process.

The concept of this beginner's guide focuses on often used tools and features in an on-going project as well as several one-off projects for a hands-on learning experience with step-by-step instructions. Upon completion you will have animated an outdoor scene and space scene that covers the basics of the software. Plus you get to work with custom props including a "destructible" spaceship prop with built-in explosion animation. That's right... we're going to blow something up! With special effects too!

Before we can start creating any masterpieces or blowing anything up, we have to install the software and the extras that come with it.

In this chapter we shall do the following:

- ◆ Install the software and bonus pack
- ◆ Configure user preferences
- ◆ Locate the template and Custom Content folders
- ◆ Install new content

- ◆ Introduce you to the iClone community
- ◆ List free content websites
- ◆ Learn to use the Reallusion Marketplace and the Reallusion Content Store
- ◆ Explore the iClone Interface

So let's get on with it...

Installing the program

Installation of the software is a simple task as iClone is packaged in a professional installer.

Time for action – installing iClone 4 pro

Start the installation and follow the onscreen instructions:

1. Click through the opening screen and select the appropriate answer to the license screen. The following image shows a partial screenshot from the install routine:

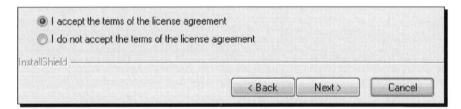

2. Enter **User Name**, **Company Name**, and your iClone **Serial Number** on the Customer Information Screen as shown in the following partial screenshot:

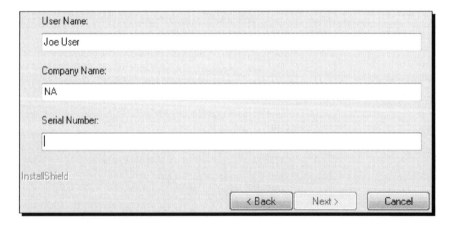

3. Choose the destination location for the install. It is recommended that you use the default location unless you have a specific reason to use another location. The partial screenshot in the following image shows the default location:

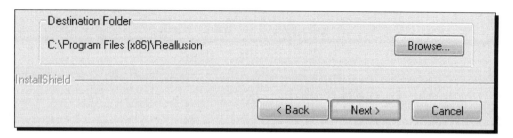

4. Specify a folder for iClone to hold your custom content. It's recommended you use the default location as it helps Reallusion to give you support if you have a problem. If, however, you want to use a different drive location or folder you will need to enter that location on this screen, as shown in the following screenshot:

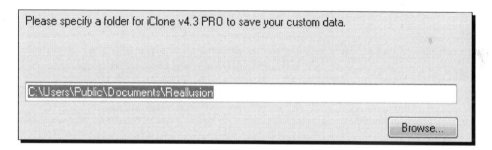

5. Choose the destination location where the stock iClone content is to be stored. This is referring to the content that is included in the iClone installation:

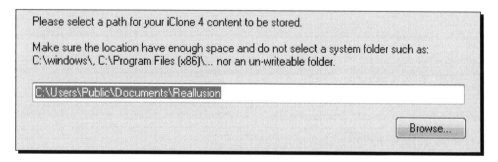

6. The program will install and configure itself for basic operations on the computer.

What just happened

We installed iClone and set the location for where the iClone content will be installed. Now we need to install the Bonus Resource pack.

Time for action – installing related iClone content

The bonus content is also packaged in a professional installer:

1. Sign in to your account at www.reallusion.com to access your Bonus Resource Pack and other related iClone content:

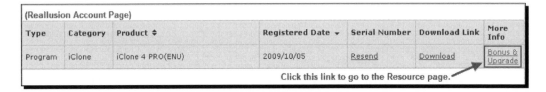

2. Follow the directions in steps 1 and 3 performed earlier to install the bonus content.

   When complete you should get the message shown in the following screenshot:

 Examine the resource page for other downloadable content that may be available.

What just happened?

We installed the extra bonus content that comes with iClone so we can have all the stock assets such as props, characters, and other items available for use.

Time for action – exploring iClone options

This section allows you to configure your working environment and preferred auxiliary tools. Setting the proper preferences will go a long way in helping you get the most out of iClone and your computer:

1. Click on the hammer icon in the upper-right corner of the interface to open the preference settings window.

2. Make the selections that are appropriate to your system. We will discuss the preferences next but you will have to experiment with the various settings to see what works best for your particular computer setup.

3. Click on the **OK** button to exit the **Preference** window.

    The following is a screenshot of the preferences as set up on the author's computer:

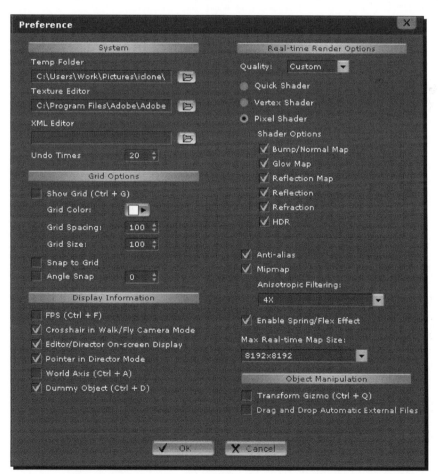

What just happened?

We opened the preferences window to configure iClone to work better with our system and select external editors. The following sections will cover the more pertinent features of the available settings.

Configuring work environment

◆ **System**: In this section, the editor you wish to use can be set by clicking on the folder icon then browsing to the application of your choice to select it. All of these slots will be empty upon initial installation of iClone as referenced by the XML slot in this example, for which no choice of editor has been selected.

◆ **Temp Folder**: This is the folder where iClone stores its temporary data including texture images.

◆ **Texture Editor**: This is an image editing program such as Photoshop, Paint Shop Pro, Gimp, or Paint.net that iClone opens to alter clothing and other image based assets.

◆ **XML Editor**: An XML editor is used to edit the Actionscript Markup Language (AML) that works with character and prop interaction. No selection has been made yet to choose an XML editor in this example. The XML Notepad from Microsoft is a very capable free XML editor.

Setting up the 3D grid

This section sets up the 3D grid for use in the viewport if so desired. The grid can help in getting acquainted with the 3D workspace in iClone and speed up scene building.

Show Grid, **Grid Color**, **Grid Spacing**, and **Grid size** are self-explanatory; they control the look, color, and spacing of the grid in the 3D workspace.

Snap to Grid is one of the most important features of the grid system when creating large scenes such as cities or villages. The props will snap to the grid allowing the easy creation of house and shop lined streets and complicated interior scenes.

Snap is something that most users either love or hate. If snap annoys you with its function then return to the preference panel and toggle it off until you need it again. Some users never turn the **Snap to Grid** off while others use it sparingly and some don't use it at all. Having the grid onscreen may help with your visualization of the workspace even if you never toggle on the **Snap to Grid** feature.

Grid shortcut
Use the *Ctrl + G* key combination to toggle the grid on and off.

Angle Snap is another great grid feature that can be set to numbers such as 45 or 90 degrees which will snap-turn the object selected by the set amount with each turn of the mouse. This is another feature that may need to be toggled on and off from the preference panel depending on how you use it.

Controlling display information

This section allows control over what information is displayed in the iClone workspace:

- **FPS (Ctrl + F)**: FPS stands for Frames Per Second, the speed at which iClone is working based on how many frames per second it can achieve during its realtime operation.

- **Editor/Director On-screen Display** – This toggles the Editor/Director icon on or off at the bottom-left of the iClone workspace. It shows the user which mode the software is operating in. It can be any one of the following:

    - **Editor mode** is the default mode of the iClone editor. It allows you to use point-and-click to move actors and work with interactive props (iProps). This is the mode in which you will build a scene. You can control actor and iProp movement with a point-and-click of the mouse to the location you want the actor or iProp to go to.

    - **Director mode** allows you to use keys on the keyboard to move the character or iProp (such as an iProp automobile) in certain directions. This type of movement is optional and moves the character/iProp as it would in a game. The following keys control the direction of movement for the actors and iProps: *W* (forward), *S* (backward), *A* (left), *D* (right), *E* (up), and *Q* (down).

- **Pointer in Director Mode**: This places a large point designator above the character that is being animated with director mode. It simplifies working with multiple characters to show which character in the scene is being manipulated by director mode.

◆ **World Axis (Ctrl + A):** This is a three dimensional icon that shows various axes of the 3D workspace. Traditionally, in 3D applications these axis are defined by red, green, and blue which represent the X, Y, and Z axis of 3D space, respectively.

◆ **Dummy Object (***Ctrl + D***):** A dummy is a primitive prop that can be used as a reference when other props or characters are linked to it. You set the prop as a dummy by checking the **Set as Dummy** checkbox under the Prop menu on upper-right side of the workspace.

Downloading the color images of this book

We also provide you a PDF file that has color images of the screenshots used in this book. The color images will help you better understand the changes in the output. You can download this file from `https://www.packtpub.com/sites/default/files/1789EXP.pdf`.

Exploring real-time render options

Quality: In most cases this is set to **Custom** due to the choices made within this section. The render options are some of the most confusing and technical parts a 3D animator has to deal with.

It's all about your video card and its capabilities. If your video card doesn't support shadows or pixel shading then you will not be able to use those features. Most users turn on what is available to see how that works with iClone . If the feature is not supported then it is not available for use in the user interface and its option will be greyed out.

Choosing the shader

Some shaders are better than others. The **Pixel Shader** gives the best overall result in terms of reproducing the lighting and other aspects of the scene. This is followed closely by the **Vertex Shader**, which does a good job but not up to the pixel shader standard. Lighting is weaker in the Vertex shader.

Finally, there is the **Quick Shader** which turns off a lot of bells and whistles in terms of render quality. The lighting is basic and shadows may be non-existent or very poor. It is usually desirable to do your final render in **Pixel Shader**, if available. There are two other shader modes available in the workspace: Smooth Shading and Wireframe. These are draft-only shaders and should be used when the workspace slows down due to the load on the 3D iClone engine.

The iClone workspace typically uses assets with 30,000 or less faces. This doesn't mean you can't use more complex assets with more faces but it will slow iClone down, sometimes to a crawl, and the render shader you have set while working can spell the difference between slogging along or working at a faster clip. When the workspace slows down, go to the QUICK SHADER or WIRE FRAME to reduce the load on the iClone engine and you will find the workspace responds much faster. Set the shader back to Pixel Render for your final render or to preview items that can only be seen with a higher level shader.

Anti-alias: While turned off in this image, anti-alias is a very important feature of iClone that eliminates those ragged edges or artifacts on characters or props. Artifacts appear when a higher resolution asset is used in lower resolution engines.

Mip Maps and **Anisotropic Filtering**: According to *Wikipedia*, Mip Maps are a group of images combined with the main texture that speed up rendering. Check this selection to take advantage of any content that uses Mip Mapping.

Anisotropic Filtering improves the quality of textures on surfaces that are at oblique viewing angles. This is a bandwidth intensive setting. While an 8X setting will make oblique surfaces render better there will a trade-off in system performance. I usually leave this setting at 4X.

Enable Spring/Flex Effect: Check this to turn on this feature as it allows for props built with spring technology to work properly. Content such as flags and capes use the flex feature to give those props an animated effect.

Max Real-time Map Size: This determines the maximum size of texture map iClone can use. It ranges from 256X256 to 8192X8192. The larger the map allowed, the better the texture will look, but it will also use more resources from the iClone engine. I keep my settings at the maximum range of 8192X8192.

Manipulating objects

Transform Gizmo: This handles manipulation of characters, props, and other 3D assets. You can drag or rotate assets without the transform gizmo but the gizmo will give greater control over precise movement of assets.

To use a gizmo, you set your mouse cursor on one of the colors, hold down the left button and move, scale, or rotate the object. This can also be done without gizmos via direct manipulation with the mouse and the proper menu choice.

 There are advantages to both direct and gizmo manipulation. Use *Ctrl + Q* to toggle back and forth between the modes.

Drag and Drop Automatic External Files: This is a real time saver. If you have iClone assets scattered around your computer you can open an explorer window showing those assets and simply drag-and-drop props and other assets into the iClone workspace with your mouse.

You can also drag-and-drop image textures and video! If you have a television in a scene that has a separate surface for the screen, then you can drag-and-drop a video onto that screen surface to emulate a broadcasting television.

Locating Custom Content folder

Content (props, accessories, scenes, and characters) that you create, download, or modify can be stored in the Custom Content folder, which makes the props available to the iClone content menu for viewing and selection.

In most cases, for Microsoft Windows® the default location of the custom folder is as follows:

- For Windows XP, it is `C:\Documents and Settings\All Users\Documents\Reallusion\Custom\iClone 4 Custom\`
- For Windows Vista/Windows 7, it is `C:\Users\Public\Documents\Reallusion\Custom\iClone 4 Custom`

 Since the custom content folder will hold a lot of custom made content that you can reuse in other productions and project files, it is suggested that you *routinely back up this folder* to a safe place.

Installing new content

New content comes in many sizes, shapes, and flavors. They can be in a self-extracting installer, zipped files, or native format, even drag-and-drop.

Let's take a look at the easiest method to get new content into iClone that is not packaged with an installer.

Using drag-and-drop

The following method is for general drag-and-drop usage of assets into the workspace:

1. Open iClone and open an Explorer window.

2. Navigate to the iClone content you wish to install in the Explorer window.

3. Choose the proper tab in iClone, that is, prop if it's a prop, accessory if it's an accessory, and so forth.

4. Grab the asset file with a left-click in the Explorer window and drag it over to the iClone workspace, then release your mouse button to "drop" the file into the workspace. For an accessory or motion you would drop it onto the character.

4. To store the asset for future usage, go to the **custom** tab on the left menu in the Content Manager of the appropriate type of assets (prop, accessory, and so on) then press the *Plus* button at the bottom of the Content Manager section to add the asset.

Asset management

The new folder option is located on the content management toolbar. You can create subfolders, if desired. After you use iClone for an extended time period, taking time to create a good file structure for your content will help to save time and frustration when looking for props and other assets. Use common sense folder names like transportation, weapons, aircraft, and so forth to define your file structure.

Importing new content

iClone provides an asset import feature for new content. This content must be in an acceptable iClone format before it can be imported. Click on the **Import** button under the **Modify** menu on the upper-right side of the screen for various tabs such as **Set**, **Actor**, or **Animation**.

The following table shows the asset type followed by the asset file extension:

Prop	iProp	Face	iFace
Accessory	iAcc	**Particle**	iParticle
Hand	iHand	**Scene**	iScene
Atmosphere	iAtm	**Camera**	iCam
Avatar	iAvatar	**Grass**	iGrass
Hair	iHair	**Animation**	iAnim
ImageLayer	iImgLayer	**Light**	iLight
Material	iMtl	**Motion**	iMotion
Path	iPath	**Teeth**	iOral
Shoe	iShoe	**Skin**	iSkin
Terrain	iTerrain	**Tree**	iTree
Water	iWater	**Upper**	iUpper
Lower	iLower	**Legacy**	vns

Working with zipped files

Most third-party assets, free and commercial, come in the form of a zip file. Double-click on the file to open the unzip dialog. Follow the steps for the pertinent zip application and save the contents to the custom content folder that was discussed earlier.

There are many zip file applications including the native Windows® zip file, WinZip, WinRAR, 7Zip, and others that share the same basic functionality. You can also unzip the file contents to a folder of your choice then copy and paste the files into the custom content folder.

Welcome to iClone

iClone is as simple or complicated as you want it to be and the interface design places lots of choices right in front of you where you won't miss anything or forget what features are available, and you don't have to use all of them either.

You add a character, a couple of props, apply drag-and-drop, or double-click on prepackaged animations for your character. What's this? There are dancing motions mixed in with other animations! You find your favorite song and add it to the project, apply the dance animations to the character, and sit back for a preview.

Your heart beats a little faster as you anticipate watching the scene you've just created. Having never animated anything in your life and having little to no idea what 3D real-time animation is, you now find yourself about to preview your first animation. You press the play button and can't help but smile as you watch your handiwork. Fifteen minutes ago you had no idea what real-time animation was and now you are grinning from ear to ear as you have crossed over the threshold to animator. Welcome to the world of iClone.

Interacting with the iClone community

The iClone community, as stated earlier, is a diverse group of users that are ready to help at places like the community forum over at the Reallusion website (`forum.reallusion.com`). Like any forum, it has a wide variety of iCloners with over a quarter of a million registered users as of this writing.

The forum is monitored by Reallusion employees and the company is very receptive to the feedback they receive from the community. Previous upgrades of iClone have brought many user requested features to fruition.

Reallusion City (`city.Reallusion.com`) was created with community spirit in mind, as a central location for all iClone users to post their work, chat with other citizens, and generally stake out their own place in the world of iClone.

You can claim your own portal in the city. Reallusion provides widgets and templates that you can tweak to make your city portal reflect your own taste.

You will find the top iClone developers here such as BigBoss, iCloneAlley, Shygirl, Wolf, and SquirrelyGirl. You'll certainly want to visit the marketplace superstores, where developers have teamed up to create a content paradise including BigBoss's Treasures, Content Wizards, The Forge (which carries some of my (WarLord) products), and FashionAlley.

The following image is from BigBoss's portal page in the Reallusion City:

"Reallusion City is a social network and digital content marketplace where people can meet, chat, and exchange their unique designs and content. You can customize your own web space with your own personalized look, develop content for the various Reallusion product platforms, and connect with new people from around the world. With a variety of active users globally, Reallusion City is the world's most unique online 3D user-to-user marketplace, where practically anyone can try other talented developers for FREE or buy it after you are satisfied." Reallusion Website

The homepage of the Reallusion City site is shown in the following image:

There are also many other places of interest in the world-wide community of iClone that deserve mention due to their passion for the product, development of content, or teaching users the tips and tricks that make it all fun.

One of the original user operated iClone communities is the Coolclones Forum, `www.coolclones.com`, which provides free iClone assets in addition to the forum. Though only a fraction of the size of the Reallusion forum, CoolClones is home to many of the original users dating back to version one of the software. iClone pioneers such as AnimaTechnica, Wolf, Rainman, Bigboss, and Stuckon3D can be found there. If you haven't heard of these names yet, then you soon will as they are some of the early adopters and masters of iClone.

CloneClips, (`www.cloneclips.com`) is the CoolClones affiliated site for iClone movies where iClone users can upload their animated films for other iCloners to view and comment on. The site is free and encourages any iClone user to make use of the streaming service.

Machinima communities such as TMUnderground (`www.tmunderground.com`) host movies made with iClone and other machinima films. TMOARadio (`www.tmoaradio.com`) produces the iClone based "Wolf and Dulci Hour", `wolfanddulcihour.blogspot.com`, that keeps users informed of the goings-on in the world of iClone. You can listen to podcasts of the show at the site if you can't listen to it live on Monday nights at 9:00 pm, central time. There is a chatroom that is monitored by the show hosts.

There is also myCLONE, `http://myclone.wordpress.com/`, one of the best user-based blogs for keeping up with the latest iClone happenings, free content, and animation tools. myCLONE provides links to a wide variety of iClone resources on the web. If it's happening in iClone, already happened, or about to happen, the myCLONE blog will tell you about it. It is recommended to visit this blog regularly.

CyberHermit, `cyberhermit.com`, is another great blog that has iClone information and general machinima/animation news and information. Premiers, film links, and a variety of iClone information sprinkled in with the general machinima happenings make this another valuable resource.

iClone certified training, `iclonecertifiedtraining.wordpress.com`, is a great site for iClone tips and tricks. The site's operator, James Martin, is a longtime iClone power user with close connections to Reallusion having worked for them in the past providing tutorials and other services. His brother John Martin is an officer of Reallusion and the chief evangelist for the company and software. You will find easy to follow, step-by-step instructions for some of the best tips and tricks in iClone.

AnimaTechnica's blog, `www.animatechnica.com`, covers a wide variety of iClone and machinima related topics from one of the true masters of iClone. He is also one of the most prolific animated filmmakers in machinima today. AnimaTechnica also maintains an invaluable production thread at the Reallusion forum explaining his animation techniques. This is another must see blog that informs, teaches, and inspires many other iClone filmmakers.

A French language blog is maintained by David-Josue, `http://www.iclone-fr.blogspot.com/`, that contains many quality freebies, tips, articles, and tutorials. This iCloner is also an earlier adopter and skilled iClone developer.

Last but certainly not least is the iClone Wiki: The Missing Link, `iclone-the-missing-link.wikispaces.com`, or simply The Wiki as it's known in user circles. Maintained by one of the most dedicated users in the community, Anim8torCathy, with help from the iClone community at large, this wiki provides tips, tutorials, and links to other helpful iClone learning sites and assets.

There is not enough room to mention all the iClone related blogs and sites that have popped up over the past few years. This in in itself is a testament to how popular iClone is among its users.

Free iClone assets

One of the best features of the community at large is how generous the users are who provide free assets to iCloners. I have compiled a partial listing of these sites:

- myclone.wordpress.com
- www.iclonerevolution.com
- www.icwarehouse.com
- www.coolclones.com
- www.machinimods.com
- myclonesforiclone.blogspot.com
- www.satscape.info
- www.iclonealley.com

Accessing Marketplace freebies

Don't forget the Marketplace as the stores also have vendors that furnish freebies too. The freebies have a zero price and can be placed into the cart for download. You will not be charged for these items.

There are several free content threads at the Reallusion forum with the monthly freebie listed in the Reallusion newsletter.

One of the absolute *must not miss freebies* at the Reallusion forum is Stuckon3d's free iClone tutorial thread listed under freebies. Stuckon3D offers commercial iClone training too.

Exploring the Reallusion Content Store

The Content Store is operated by Reallusion through a professionally built and reliable web-based sales and delivery platform.

The Reallusion content store is a separate store that has existed alongside iClone for many years. It sells Reallusion's professionally created assets, including packs. The content store has exacting standards for non-Reallusion produced products sold through it. This content is some of the highest quality content you can use with iClone.

The following image shows a listing of some of the content store items for sale:

Discovering the Reallusion Marketplace

Over the past few years, Reallusion has developed several different methods of making iClone content available and it became necessary to consolidate those platforms into the Reallusion Marketplace.

BackStage has its own location in the Marketplace alongside the other content vendors. This is the same content that is in Reallusion's Content Store, packaged in individual items for those who do not wish to purchase an entire pack. This is a very economical way to build up the assets you need for your iClone projects without busting your budget.

The following image shows the Backstage button next to the preferences icon:

The Backstage button is located in the iClone user interface upper-right corner. As of this writing the button pops up a web page that can take the user to the Reallusion Marketplace or the Content Store as shown in the following screenshot:

Backstage was originally integrated into the iClone interface as a convenient method to purchase and install individual items and packs. It also offered watermarked, free trials of content to try before you buy.

The following image shows the Marketplace homepage:

Only Reallusion produced content is sold under the iClone BackStage name. Very high standards have always been a hallmark of Reallusion produced 3D content.

Eventually, Reallusion's army of third-party developers wanted a convenient and quick method to sell their products other than the Content Store due to its high standards and review of every third-party product submitted. Each product was reviewed and tested by Reallusion, which was a lengthy process that could not be avoided and at times became a bottleneck in the process of getting more content on the market.

Forum discussions about developers wanting a method to sell their products individually instead of in packs with a segment of developers wanting to take advantage of the free trial feature, highlighted a need for such a platform. Reallusion was listening and developed the City Marketplace.

The City Marketplace is open to any iCloner that can develop content. Its quality is monitored by a rating and comment system that allows previous buyers to post their experience with the product. Marketplace vendors have the ability to offer their items for trial, as Reallusion has provided an upload utility and a quality web platform that is very reliable and convenient.

Eliminating the need to submit everything to the Content Store and wait on the approval process has led to an explosion of iClone third-party vendor content. Reallusion has always encouraged third-party development and over the years has amassed a large army of content developers, which has led to a massive amount of content available, such as the items shown in the following screenshot:

iClone Backstage is now the same as any other vendor in the Marketplace and utilizes the same functionality with selections for your trial downloads, wish list items, current purchase inventory, bookmarked items for future purchase, and your transaction history as shown in the following screenshot:

Backstage and Marketplace pages display a listing of all products you have purchased or downloaded as a trial. Within iClone you will easily be able to convert the trial for purchase by right-clicking on the item icon, which will be marked as **Trial**, and selecting to purchase the item. Digital rights to use the item without a watermark on the render will be transferred via the web.

The following image shows an inventory page from a Marketplace account:

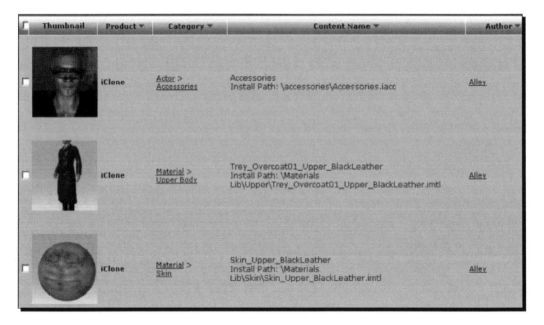

A thumbnail (shown in the following screenshot) of the trial product will display a trial maker in Content Manager until purchased:

Right-click on the trial thumbnail to buy the item:

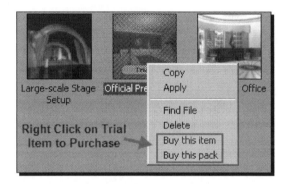

Items downloaded for trial will produce watermarks on the final iClone render until purchased or removed from the project. The watermark will be removed when the item is purchased.

The great feature of the trial item is that you can put them into your scene to see how they interact with the scene or if the items are what you thought they were. You can test built-in animations and motions to guarantee that it fits your project.

Not all items are available as trial downloads. It is up to the individual developer to enable this option.

Downloading your trial and purchased items

Reallusion is serious about making its products easy to use and this includes the downloading and installation process for content purchases. Downloading and installing content purchases from the Backstage or Marketplace has been simplified and automated for your convenience:

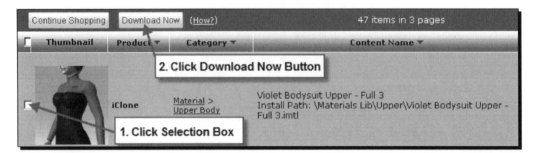

Time for action – download and installation steps

The downloader will open, starting the download process from the Marketplace:

1. Click on the **Trial** button for items you wish to try before you buy or place items for immediate purchase in the shopping cart.

2. In the popup download dialog, click on the **Start** button shown in the following image to begin the download:

3. A progress bar dialog will appear as shown in the following screenshot:

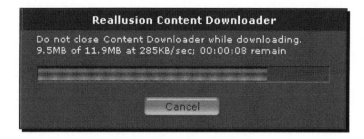

4. When you click on the **Complete** button, the download and installation process has ended. You will find the downloaded item in its pertinent section, such as props, the next time you open iClone.

The following image shows the **Complete** button, which finalizes the download and installation of the products:

What just happened?

We selected and downloaded our content by following the simple steps provided by Reallusion. That content was not only downloaded but it was also installed into its proper location and folder within iClone. This process is automated for ease and simplicity.

Reallusion has provided many methods for getting new content into iClone so the user can concentrate on creativity and using the product. As a company, Reallusion has demonstrated over the years that it does listen to its users and they try very hard to take the frustration out of using their products.

As soon as the download finishes we are ready to use those assets in a project!

Exploring the iClone user interface

The iClone interface is broken down into several sections, with each section having its own "focus dependent" context menu. If you click on a specific tab and button then the menu to manipulate that item will be displayed on the right menu panel. If a menu disappears on you it's because you don't have the same object selected as before when you were using the menu.

Reallusion supplies a great manual with more details on each area of the interface beyond what we are covering here, but we are going to discuss the basic layout of the interface which Reallusion took great pains to design to place as many tools as possible right in front of our eyes.

Exploring the workspace

Navigation pane: The navigation pane contains seven tabs and each tab has its own set of buttons located below it to access certain modes. For example, to load a terrain you would select the **Set** tab then click on the **Terrain** button to invoke the terrain editor in the right side menu or show available terrain assets in the left side menu.

The following image shows the first half of the navigation pane:

The following image shows the second half of the navigation pane:

Click through the various tabs and buttons to get an idea of where some things are located or what tab a certain button is under. It won't be long before you are navigating the various sections with ease. The interface really puts a lot of control and information into each tab. There is also the drop-down tools menu in the navigation pane for quick selection.

Content Manager: The Content Manager is located on the upper-left side of the interface. It provides a means to organize, load, and save 3D assets.

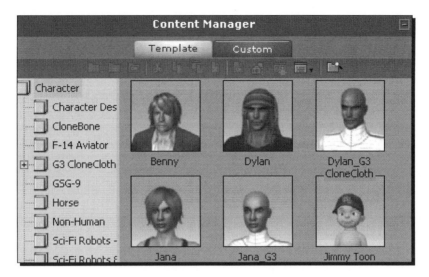

Double-click to load into the center of the workspace or drag-and-drop the asset over into the workspace from the Content Manager section.

Scene Manager: The Scene Manager is located on the lower-left side of the interface. It allows us to select objects, see the face count, and turn items visibility on and off among other features. The following image shows the Scene Manager with various columns displaying information about the project:

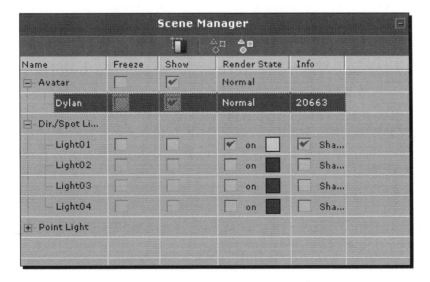

Control Bar: In the control bar, there are tools that manipulate the objects, cameras, and many other aspects of an iClone project as shown in the following image. If you select a character or an object and click on **Home,** the current camera view will center on that object.

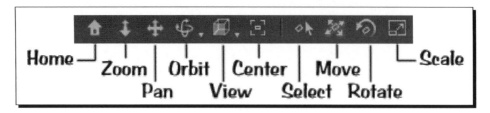

Modify: This is one of the single most important sections of the iClone interface. It's the area where most modifications take place involving scene assets such as props, characters, and particles.

This menu will vary in content depending on what item is selected in the 3D workspace. The following image shows a portion of the **Modify** section with a prop selected:

Timeline: This is really where everything that is animated or controlled happens. We will be discussing the timeline in more detail in *Chapter 4, Animating the Characters*.

This brief introduction to the interface is to help familiarize yourself with which side of the interface to use when doing certain tasks. Modifying will always be on the right side menu while the Scene Manager for asset selection will always be on the left side.

Selecting objects in the workspace

We can use either of the basic options to select a prop, character, or any asset in the 3D workspace to move, scale, animate, or otherwise manipulate.

Direct Selection: Left-click on the object in the 3D workspace. This is a simple task unless the object is obscured by another asset that prevents the object from being properly clicked with the cursor.

Scene Manager: Left-click on any item in the Scene Manager to select it. The standard Windows convention applies of holding down the *Shift* key for continuous selection or the *Ctrl* key for multiple individual selections.

Pop quiz

The following is a simple pop quiz to help you remember some of the highlights of the chapter:

1. The iClone installation file also installs all 3D resources available with the program.

    a. True

    b. False

2. All shaders are available on all computers running iClone.

    a. True

    b. False

3. The highest quality shader is:
   a. Quick Shader
   b. Wireframe Shader
   c. Vertex Shader
   d. Pixel Shader
   e. Smooth Shader

4. It is possible to install new content using:
   a. The Import button
   b. Drag-and-drop
   c. Double-clicking on the content item in the Content Manager
   d. All of the above
   e. None of the above

5. We can select assets and objects in the 3D workspace by:
   a. Left-clicking on the object
   b. Highlight the object in the Scene Manager
   c. All of the above
   d. None of the above

Summary

In this first chapter, we were introduced to iClone and we touched on many aspects of the iClone community and resources, as well as looking at the interface's basic layout.

Specifically, we covered the following:

- Installation of the program and additional resources
- Discussed options on configuring the preferences
- Added new content
- Discovered websites for free iClone content
- Found that we have a place waiting for us in the Reallusion City
- Went through the process of using the BackStage/Marketplace

Now that we've got the basic information out of the way, the *real hands on fun* starts in the next chapter, where we will begin building our first scene in iClone!

2

Creating Your First Scene

If you want to be an animator, director, storyteller, or 3D artist you must have a scene to get started. The scene can be as simple as an actor on a dark stage or a multi-ship science fiction space battle. Story is important but so are visuals!

In this chapter we shall:

- ◆ Explore the 3D workspace
- ◆ Create a scene with sky, terrain, water, props, and other assets
- ◆ Explore the concept of Live Plants and how to use them
- ◆ Introduce and work with standard and interactive props
- ◆ Use building blocks to create props
- ◆ Explain how to edit props by using diffuse, opacity, and other map channels
- ◆ Explore how to use lighting to set the mood or enhance the shot

So let's get on with it.

Let the animation begin!

This chapter will create a scene in a picturesque environment including grass, trees, flowers, flowing water, lighting, and a beautiful sky. You will be amazed at how fast you can create and light a scene in iClone.

Exploring your virtual studio

If you have never worked in a 3D workspace, you might be surprised at your results when trying to line up props or plant trees. The 3D workspace is 360 degrees in all directions You can view any object from any angle at any point within the workspace. Props, such as utility poles, may appear to be lined up in one axis or view, but may very well be out-of-line or completely off course when looked at from a different camera view or axis.

This just takes a little practice and getting used to the way the 3D workspace operates.

Exploring the 3D workspace

If you have never used a 3D program or worked in a 3D workspace, you may find it confusing at first, but the learning curve is very short. The 3D workspace is shown in the following image:

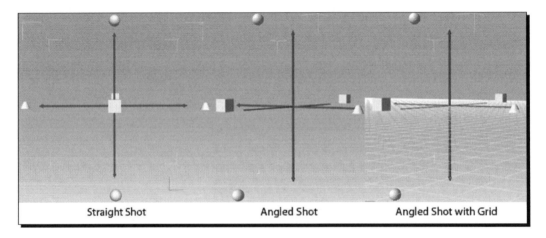

| Straight Shot | Angled Shot | Angled Shot with Grid |

By looking at the **Straight Shot** in the example image, we can see that the two spheres look to be lined up one above the other, but when you look at the **Angled Shot**, you will notice that the top sphere is behind the bottom sphere. The **Angled Shot with Grid** shows how the 3D space looks from side-to-side and front-to-back.

Traditional 3D applications work with multiple views of the workspace, usually in four parts—Top, Front, Side, and Perspective, but iClone works with one view and you need to rotate and move that view to see how items actually line up. The **Camera View** button will switch views.

The next image shows the tools on the camera manipulation toolbar:

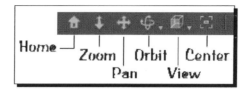

The camera manipulation toolbar has zoom, pan, and orbit to move the camera around inside the workspace. To move faster, hold down the left mouse button when selecting and move the mouse in the proper direction such as up, down, back, and forth, or side-to-side.

As you push an object into the background of the workspace, it will reduce in size as perspective is being maintained. This is the same as watching a train or car drive away from you. It will appear to shrink as it gets further and further away.

You can also use scaling to make an object appear to move away by reducing the scale of the object as it goes away from the camera as shown in the following screenshot, with the only difference in the left-to-right side props being scale. The left side objects are 100% scale while on the right, the front objects are 100% scale, and the back objects are 25% scale.

Time for action – creating the outdoors

We are going to create the outdoors for this scene, or at least a part of the outdoors by utilizing the stock iClone content.

 We are not using the grid in this scene so before we start going into the preference dialog (the hammer icon at the top-right of the screen) and deselect **Show Grid**, we make sure that **Snap To Grid** and **Angle Snap** are turned off as well. Alternatively you can use the *Ctrl+Q* key combination to toggle the grid on and off.

1. Select the **Set** tab, then click on the **Sky** button on the bar below the **SET** tab.

2. Double-click the **Clear Day 01** thumbnail in the **Content Manager** on the top-left side of the interface to load the sky into the workspace.

3. Click on the **Terrain** button from the top toolbar.

4. Double-click on **River Forde** from the **Content Manager** on the left.

5. Select the **Water** button from the top toolbar.

6. Double-click on **River Flow** in the **Content Manager** on the left.

7. Lower the height of the water by reducing the **Height** from 50 to 0 in the top-right side of the **Modify** panel. You can type the number directly in the input box or hold your left mouse button down on the down arrow to the side of the input box.

8. Set the water direction to 90, located just below the **Height** feature.

9. Pull the preview camera back by using the **Zoom** tool located on the left side of the top toolbar. With the **Zoom** tool selected, hold down your left mouse button and drag the mouse backwards, away from the screen, to get a feel for how the **ZOOM** tool works. Zoom back till you can see most of the terrain we loaded in step 3.

10. Press the play button on the bottom toolbar to preview in real-time the basic scene you have created so far. You should be able to see most of the terrain that you placed into the 3D workspace, as shown in the following screenshot:

What just happened?

You just created your first basic scene with flowing water! You have crossed that threshold to animator! It may be just that the water is moving with a built-in motion, but you are still an animator.

Now let's play with Mother Nature and create some greenery.

Working with Live Plants

Live Plant technology is based on the animated billboards that have a very small face count (low poly) so you can have hundreds or thousands of them in your scene. The plants will sway back and forth with the wind, which can be modified on the right panel.

 Live Plants work only with the Terrain assets when it comes to proper placement on the surface.

Time for action – creating virtual foliage

1. Click on the **Set** tab then select **Grass**.

2. Double-click **Grass** in the **Content Manager** on the left and then hit the clear button on the right menu under **Tool**. This will clear the grass that iClone places in the center of the screen so that you can place the grass where you want it to go. After all you are the director!

3. With the **Grass** still selected, your cursor will be a paint bucket. Set the **Size** to 1000 and set the **Density** to 59. If your computer struggles with this density, then reduce the density setting to improve performance. The following image shows an initial planting of grass with the bucket tool:

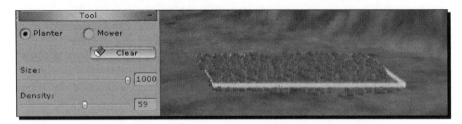

4. Use the **Grass** paint bucket to place grass anywhere on the terrain.

5. Select a flower from the left menu. This example uses Magnolia, but you can choose any Live Plant. Remember to **Clear** the flowers after selection and then start planting flowers around the scene with the bucket tool. Lower the density as grass is usually thicker than any other ground cover in its area and so the flower density needs to be reduced. Set the **Size** to 1000; lower the flower **Density** to 2. Set the **Height** and **Width** to 25. The following image is an example of plant density:

6. Now select the **Rice** and set the **Tool** and **Dimensions** to Size: 114, Density: 20, Height: 90, Width: 90.

7. Plant the rice along the water's edge by clicking on or near the waterline. If you make a mistake, use the **Undo** button or the **Mower** feature to remove the errant plantings. The next image is an example of planting rice along the sides of the river:

Right-click to toggle between planting and mowing mode.

8. What we need now are some trees to break up the ground and make the scene more interesting. Click on the **Tree** button under the **Set** tab and select the tree of your choice. This example uses the American Elm A and American Elm B. Scatter a few trees around until you are satisfied with the result. The default strength of 2 for the wind will provide a little sway in the breeze.

 Unlike the grass, the trees are not painted on the surface, but are placed one at a time like individual props. Double-click on the **Tree** thumbnail in the **Content Manager** and then select the **Tree** and use the manipulation tools (shown in the following image) on the top toolbar to move it to the desired location:

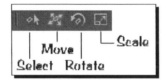

9. Save your file and preview your work by pressing the play button.

The following image shows an example of Live Plant coverage for the main scene:

What just happened?

We used the Live Plants feature to create a nice section of scenery by placing grass, flowers, and other Live Plant assets around the scene. In the process of placing these plants, we discovered that each plant may need a different density or other adjustment to look proper. These changes are made within the modification panel of each Live Plant species.

Live Plants take very little overhead to run in the iClone engine so we can place thousands of these plants in our scene to add visual appeal.

Start good animation habits now!

Now is the time to start developing good animation and work habits. Always reset the timeline scrubber back to frame 0 when finished previewing and before you add props or characters to the scene. You will quickly find that strange things can happen when you start adding other assets to the scene without the timeline being reset to zero.

Now that you have a good start on a nice scene, it's time to see what you can do on your own. Save the project first as we will continue to build this scene together after you flex your landscaping muscles a bit.

Have a go hero – clear the meadow

Save your project then clear the grass, flowers, trees, and experiment with Live Plants. Use different settings on the **Size** and **Density** so you can understand how each works. Try out different grasses and trees.

Paint the grass on the hills and the water's edge to see what happens. If you make a mistake, use the **Undo** key or the **Mower** located on the same right side menu panel as the Planter to cut out the area you wish to change. The **Mower** can also be used to create roads, pathways, building sites, and just about anything that needs to be cleared of vegetation.

Add to Terrain tip

If you experience trouble placing Live Plants or they are not going in the right place then right-click on the object you are painting with Live Plants and select **Add To Terrain**. If the prop is not built correctly for iClone then the Live Plants will not be placed in the proper locations even when the prop is added to the terrain.

The following image shows two primitive cones. The cone on the right shows the bounding box mesh that surrounds the cone. This was used as an early collision system in iClone. Some props have a bounding box that mimics the prop where others have primitives that can cause strange things to happen when using Live Plants.

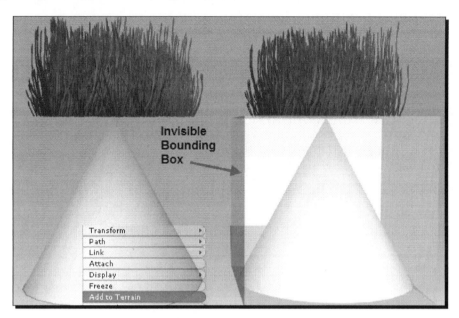

Adding props to the scene

Unless you are a minimalist, you are into props and I mean really into props, or at least you should be. Props are one of the most important aspects of scene building for the purpose of luring in or perhaps keeping an audience during the initial moments of a scene.

Attach, link, or duplicate props

Props are placed as individual items in the workspace, but can be grouped via the **LINK** or **ATTACH** button. Props can also be duplicated by selecting the prop and holding down the *Ctrl* key and then sliding the prop to one direction or another. Attaching props to each other also allows for the attached props to be merged into one prop.

You can also get props from a variety of sources. To use most of these props not made specifically for iClone, you will need a sister application to iClone—**3DXchange**, which converts props from 3DS, OBJ formats, and more importantly converts Sketchup props from the Google 3D Warehouse, which has thousands of free props from buildings to transportation, and so forth.

Free props are available as discussed in *Chapter 1, Installing and Configuring iClone* or there are websites like TurboSquid, `www.turbosquid.com`, that specialize in 3D props. Most 3D model websites have a selection of free props too.

So far you have discovered that props can be linked, attached, merged, and converted from certain 3D formats into an iClone compatible file. What we're going to focus on next is the face count of props selected for use in the iClone environment.

Reallusion recommends that as a general rule, props should have no more than 30,000 faces. Why? It is because of the load that a prop with a lot of faces places on the real-time engine. Does this mean that you can't use a prop over 30,000 faces? No it doesn't. In fact, it depends a lot on the computer that is running iClone. Older computers or computers with minimal RAM and lower performance graphics cards will not run without becoming sluggish as there are many assets in a scene, while newer computers with modern graphics cards running four gigabytes of RAM memory for 32-bit systems can use more props and props with larger face counts.

So what is a face anyway? A face is a flat triangle, but when grouped together forms a shape. This shape forms a polygon. Groups of polygons form the mesh. The iClone engine is a low-poly engine, meaning it works better with assets that have fewer faces. The more faces the more polygons, the more load on the 3D real time engine.

The maximum recommended face count is a rule of thumb to keep in mind. It's not set in stone. iClone won't shut down or crash just because you went over the minimum face count unless you got way over the recommended count. I have used multiple props in a scene with face counts into the hundreds of thousands without difficulty. It depends on the computer running the program. Also remember to reduce your render setting to **Quick** or **Wireframe** in the upper-right corner of the workspace to make the workspace more responsive under a heavy face count load.

Placing props

There are several methods place props in to the iClone workspace:

- Drag-and-drop from Content Manager
- Drag-and-drop from Explorer window
- Double-click on the prop in the Content Manager
- Import the prop from the Modify Panel

The simplest method of placing props in to the iClone workspace is to left-click and hold down the left mouse button on the thumbnail of the prop in the **Content Manager**. You can then release the mouse button anywhere in the iClone workspace to drop the prop into the scene. The following image shows dragging and dropping the **Robo Dog_A** prop into the workspace. The prop will appear in the location of the thumbnail image that was dropped into the workspace. This next image is an example of drag-and-drop from the **Content Manager** to the workspace:

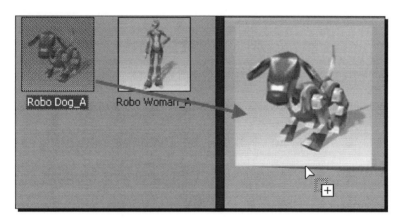

Be aware that due to the workspace being three-dimensional, you may not have dropped the prop exactly where you wanted it. You will need to rotate the view to see where the prop is actually located in the workspace.

Drag-and-drop from a Windows Explorer window works in the same manner as drag-and-drop from the **Content Manager**. Both are easy and fast methods to get the prop into the workspace near your intended target area. In single monitor configurations, you can open a smaller explorer window and use *Alt-Tab* to toggle back-and-forth between it and iClone. You can then drag-and-drop from the smaller explorer window directly into the workspace. Multiple monitor configurations make this even easier by placing the explorer window on another monitor.

Double clicking on the prop in the Content Manager will place the prop squarely into the middle of the 3D workspace, which can then be selected and moved by the proper tools in the top toolbar, or use the *Ctrl + Q* shortcut for toggling the Gizmo on-and-off.

Importing the prop into the workplace using the **Import** button in the **Modify** panel, works the same as double-clicking on the prop. The prop will be loaded into the center of the workspace.

After importing props with embedded animation, you may sometimes find that you need to right-click on the prop and select the **Remove All Animation** menu choice to set all animations back to their original state. Content purchased from Reallusion either in the **Content Store** or the **Marketplace** have their animations reset and must be triggered with the right-click on **Perform** menu choice.

Time for action – house building

We worked with the grass and discussed different methods of prop placement. So let's continue by adding the **Deckhouse** prop to the scene:

1. In the **Content Manager** under the **Scene** tab and **Prop** button, you will find the **Architecture** folder. Drag-and-drop the **Deckhouse A** prop from that folder.

2. Scale **Deckhouse A** to **50** percent in the **Transform | Scale** section of the **Modify** panel. For uniform scaling check the **LOCK XYZ** box. Enter 50 into the first input box. Place your scaled-down prop in the desired location while making sure that all the legs of the deck are on or in the terrain.

What just happened?

It's time to learn about scale as not all props and other content are scaled to the proper size. In this case, the island terrain is a little too small for what we are going to build. We could have increased the island terrain earlier but that would mean we have a larger area to plant the Live Plants so we reduced the overall scale of the scene.

You can scale terrain up to meet your needs or scale the rest of the scene down. It depends on the demands of the scene, such as planting Live Plants over a large area versus a smaller area when scaled down. It's really a matter of personal preference. We chose to scale down in this project so that we could work with and understand the concept of scaling in a 3D workspace.

The next image shows **Deckhouse** prop at 100 percent scale on the left and 50 percent scale on the right:

Reset button

The **Reset** button at the bottom of the transformation section can be used to reset the prop to its original size. We can be fearless when experimenting with the settings as we can always restore the prop to its original state with one click of a button.

Have a go hero – modifying the scene

Now would be a great time to make any modifications to the scene. Scene building is a constant placement and movement of props to fit your idea of what the scene should look like.

Save your scene before continuing. Place a couple of trees near the house (**Tree** button under the **Scene** tab), and move the house to fit the land while making sure the stairs sit properly on the terrain.

It's time to preview what you have accomplished. Pull the preview camera back to frame the scene to your liking and press the play button. You will have grass, flowers, and trees moving in the wind with flowing water. Adjust the wind settings on the Live Plants and trees to your liking.

The following image is an example of the scene to this point. The exact placement of props and Live Plants will vary depending on choices made while we built the scene:

Manipulating props

It is very difficult to utilize props in an effective manner if you don't know how to manipulate them. In our project, you were asked earlier to move the house to better fit the terrain. You have been briefly introduced to the gizmos and direct manipulation, but now that you have an idea of prop placement, we need to go into a little more detail about gizmo versus direct manipulation of a prop.

Selecting the tools

Select, **Move**, **Rotate**, and **Scale** are the main tools for manipulation props in the workspace and are shown in the following image:

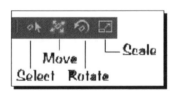

Select tool: You can directly click on the prop with the **Select** tool by double-clicking on the prop in the workspace. This also applies to actors and accessories. You can also select the prop by double-clicking on the props name in the **Scene Manager** (shown in the next image) on the lower part of the left menu:

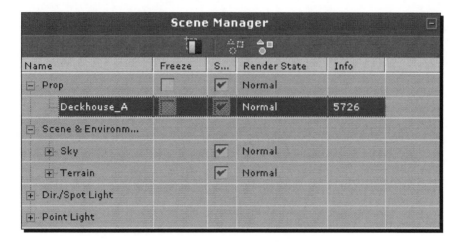

The **Scene Manager** is a very versatile part of the iClone user interface. To ensure that you don't accidently move a prop or other item in the workspace, you can lock that item in place by checking the **Freeze** box. Visibility is also toggled on and off via the **Show** checkbox so you can work on an object behind or otherwise blocked by a prop. **Render State** will allow you to set the real-time preview render of each prop to wireframe, smooth, or normal if you need to reduce the load on the real-time engine while you work. This affects individual props instead of the entire scene. It also displays the all-important face count of the prop under the **Info** column.

When a prop is selected, the body of the prop is surrounded by a bounding box with yellow corners. This makes for easy identification of the selected prop or other content.

Manipulating objects directly

For direct manipulation, left-click and move your mouse and selected props will move or rotate with the mouse. To increase the speed and distance, hold down the *Shift* key while moving the prop with the mouse. This is great for working in a large scene or when you first bring a prop into the scene. However, there will be a time when you will need more precise control.

Manipulating with precision using gizmos

As you may have already guessed, precise manipulation is done with the **Gizmo** tool. The following image shows different props with different gizmos—**Rotation**, **Move**, and **Scale**:

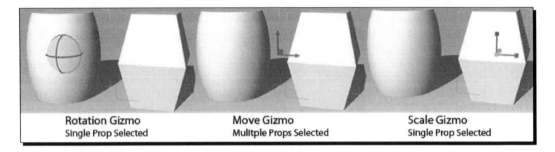

Rotation Gizmo	Move Gizmo	Scale Gizmo
Single Prop Selected	Mulitple Props Selected	Single Prop Selected

The **Gizmo** tool is color coded for each axis. If the gizmos are not visible, use *Ctrl - Q* to turn them on and place your cursor over the color section of the gizmo that matches the axis you wish to manipulate. To **Move** or **Scale** all of the axis at once, use the yellow center area of the gizmo. Any manipulation in the center of the gizmo will affect the entire prop.

Experimentation with the gizmos will quickly teach you how they work as they are very simple methods of precise manipulation.

Handling direct input

We can enter numbers directly into the prop's X,Y, and Z input boxes. We can use the up and down arrows for fine tuning. The following image shows the inputs used in this example:

Manipulating props

A combination of the manipulation methods can give you a lot of control and very quick placement of props and other content. Use drag-and-drop to place a prop into a scene. Use the object Gizmos (*Ctrl + Q*) to place the props more accurately based on rotation and movement along the axes. We can also use direct input into the X,Y, and Z Input Boxes for final tweaks to placement. This yields a very strong measure of control over speed and precision of prop manipulation.

Working with iProps (interactive props)

iProps are just what they sound like. They are props that interact with a character. Actual iProp usage with a character will be discussed in next chapter. So why am I bringing it up now? You need to know where to place those interactive props when the time comes for the character to actually use the prop.

Interactive props are driven by **Actionscript Markup Language**, known in the iClone world as **AML**. For those of you who have avoided any type of scripting in the past or freeze up at the sight of code, don't worry. You don't have to know AML to use it and AML will not be covered in depth in this book, but you do need to be aware of how it works with a prop.

iProps have the AML already coded in and while you can edit it with an XML editor or notepad, you do not have to do so. It is available as a more advanced option to those iClone animators who want to manipulate the code that drives the prop.

Time for action – placing the iProp

We will load a pre-animated iProp into the scene for our male character to pick up:

1. Locate the Beer iProp in the `iProps` folder on the left side menu within the **Content Manager**. Drag-and-drop the beer into the iClone workspace or double-click the beer if you prefer to load it into the center of the workspace. What? Where did it go?

2. Click on the **Pick Parent** button in the linkage section of the right side menu.

3. Use the **Eyedropper** tool to select a section of the handrail.

4. Click on the **Link To** button.

5. Correct the rotation and unlink the prop.

The following image shows the sequence of events:

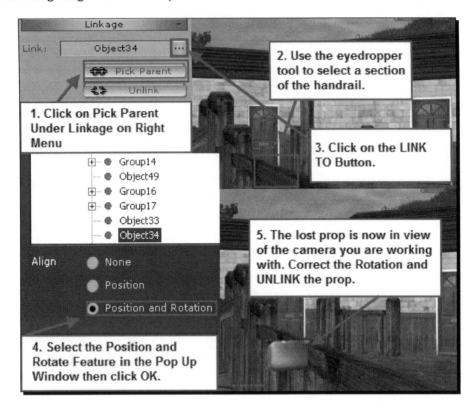

What just happened?

The beer iProp was actually placed at the right place but it may be hidden by the house or any other prop. We used the **Link** button to link it to the handrail of the porch then clicked on the **Link To** button next to the **Link** info box.

When the popup window appeared, we selected the **Position and Rotation** option and clicked **OK**. This placed the prop on the linked object. It may be rotated incorrectly but we can solve that. If the prop does not appear in the viewport, then **Unlink** the prop, select another section of the porch, and use the **Link To** button again. We can also select the prop and press **Camera View** button once to center the camera on the object.

Why not use the **Position** option instead of the **Position and Rotation** option that may rotate the object improperly? The **Position** option does not always place the prop where you want it, but the latter option will always properly place the prop in relation to the chosen object even if it is rotated incorrectly.

Remember to **Unlink** the prop once you can see it in the workspace. The **Link To** is used in this case as a shortcut to locate the prop that was hidden by other scene props.

Locating lost props by using the link feature

 Linking a prop to another prop that is visible in the workspace and using the **Link To** feature with **Position and Rotation** checked, will bring the unseen prop to the forefront of the camera that you are working with and will save a lot of time usually spent looking for the errant prop.

1. Import or drag-and-drop the Beer iProp into the scene. Locate the prop via the **Link To** method described previously. Then unlink the prop once it becomes visible.

2. Reduce the scale of the beer to 50% in the **Scale** input boxes on the right menu.

3. Rotate and move the beer to place it properly on the porch handrail.

What just happened?

In the next image, we have placed the Beer iProp on top of the rail, ready for interaction once we add the characters to the scene:

Scene viewing

We can view the scene from different angles by selecting a prop that is central to the scene and which can rotate the camera; it will rotate around the prop you have selected. You can also select any object in the scene and press the **Home** button or **Center** button located on the top toolbar to move the camera to that object.

Animated props

Animated props are not to be confused with iProps, which are scripted. Characters will not interact with animated props so we will have to manually key frame their interaction.

Time for action – importing animated props

Now that we've got the beer, we need the outdoor grill. There is no grill in the stock installation of iClone and so I will provide you with an animated grill that I've created just for this occasion! The grill is available in the code bundle of the book web page on the Packt Publishing website.

1. Download the grill and import or drag-and-drop the animated prop into the workspace.

2. If the grill disappeared like the beer prop, then follow the preceding linking instructions and link the grill to a section of the house porch by using the **Position and Rotation** option to put the grill where you can find it. Unlink the grill before using.

3. Reduce the scale of the grill to 50% in the **Scale** input boxes on the right menu.

4. Right-click on the grill and select the perform menu choice in the popup by right-clicking the menu.

5. Choose the `open lid` command.

 This grill is not interactive, but it is animated (the lid opens with built-in motion). This means the character will not automatically open the grill with their hand. We will do this in the animation chapter by placing the hand in the proper positions. We will also add smoke particles in the chapter explaining particles and their usage.

 Downloading the example code

You can download the example code files for all Packt books you have purchased from your account at `http://www.PacktPub.com`. If you purchased this book elsewhere, you can visit `http://www.PacktPub.com/support` and register to have the files e-mailed directly to you.

What just happened?

We have placed an animated prop into the scene and triggered one of the animations embedded into the prop to open the grill top. We will add Particle FX to the grill in the *Chapter 5, Enhancing Animation with Particles* and add glow to the charcoal Glow map when we cover the map channels later in this chapter.

The next image shows the right-click menu with the **Open Top** command under the **Perform** menu choice. This starts the animation at the point you click on the command and will run until the animation is complete or you press the stop button.

Creating props from building blocks

iClone building blocks are primitives that can be used to create a wide variety of props. Some of the building block types are as follows:

- Ball (sphere)
- Cone
- Cross
- Pyramid
- Box (cubes)
- Cylinder
- Torus and other primitives

By combining building blocks and changing the textures, you can build walls, buildings, and other assets for use in a scene. You are truly bounded only by your imagination as to what you can build with these primitive props.

What do you see in a primitive?

When you look at most of the objects, you can see the primitives that make up the object. A thin box can be a wall. A cylinder can be a round floor or column depending on the height.

For this example, we will create a gazebo for the yard. The roof could be a cone, long narrow boxes for columns, and a larger flat cylinder for the floor.

Time for action – building a gazebo without hand tools!

1. Save your project and open a new iClone blank project.

2. Double-click to load an iClone character/avatar for size reference. In this case, we used the Dylan character.

3. Double-click to load `Cylinder_001` from the top folder of the 3D blocks under the **Set** tab and **Prop** button. Set the x and y scales to 550 and the z scale to 5.

   The following image shows the flattened cylinder:

4. Load `Box_001` and set the scale to 15, 15, 246. This will be our post to hold the roof. Select the top view, as shown in the next image, in the top toolbar and hold *Ctrl* while dragging the mouse to a location for the second post:

5. With post selected, hold down the *Ctrl* key and drag the newly created post across the floor from the original post as demonstrated in the next image:

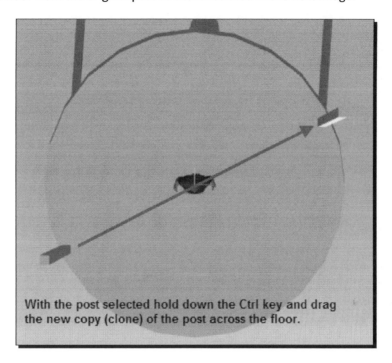

With the post selected hold down the Ctrl key and drag the new copy (clone) of the post across the floor.

Quick Copy for props and selecting multiple props

You can select any prop, press the *Ctrl* key, and then drag the prop over with either direct manipulation or the gizmos. A copy of the prop you are dragging will be automatically created when you move the prop.

To select multiple props, hold down the *Ctrl* key while selecting the props directly or clicking on the props in the **Scene Manager**. You can then duplicate this multiple selection of props by holding down the *Ctrl* key and dragging them as described previously. This is a real-time saver when creating props from the building blocks.

6. Select both posts and use the **rotate** tool as shown in the next image while holding down the *Ctrl* button to create more posts. Repeat this process until you are satisfied with the results.

The drag to copy with the *Ctrl* button feature will work with the **Move and Rotate** tools to quickly clone and move props within the workspace.

The next image shows the gazebo after the duplication and rotation of the posts:

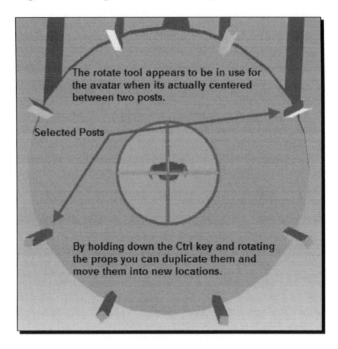

7. Select each post and click on the **Attach** button in the left panel for each post. Click on **Pick Parent** and select the cylinder as the prop that you want to attach to. Do this for each post till all posts are attached to the cylinder. When you select the cylinder, all of the attached posts will be selected along with it.

 Do not use Link, as that feature will not hold the links when the prop is saved. With Attach, the entire group of props will be saved when you save the main prop that the other props are attached to.

8. Change back to the front view in the same manner you changed to the top view.

9. Double-click on **Cone_006** to load it into the scene and set the scale to 670, 670, 100.

10. Move the roof (**Cone_006**) to sit on top of the posts. You can then adjust the roof match to your preferences.

11. Attach the roof to the cylinder using the **Pick Parent** button under Attach.

12. Save the newly created gazebo prop by selecting the **Custom** tab under **Props** and clicking the **Plus** button at the bottom of the **Content Manager** in the left menu.

The next image shows the newly created gazebo prop:

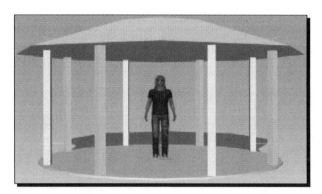

We will texture the prop with wood after we load the prop into the scene that we are building.

What just happened?

We created a gazebo by using the `Move`, `Rotate`, and `Clone` features to quickly and efficiently create parts of the prop. This prop is now available for texturing and can be used for future projects too.

> **Save the project file when creating a building block prop**
>
> When you spend time creating a prop from building blocks it would be a good idea to start with an empty project and save that project when completed for future use. This will allow us to save our work for future use should we need anything similar for a future project.

Diffusing opacity and other maps.

Texturing or coloring a prop gives more realism to the prop if done properly. It also makes a cartoon type prop fit into the scene better. This is all accomplished with channels and maps. To be more specific, it's accomplished with a map channel.

These map channels can hold color or an image. In most models, the image (texture) can be a very complex image that reflects what the model should look like such as wood, concrete, and cloth. It can be a combination of materials or a single material. A single map can also represent many different parts of the model such as skin tone for skin, cloth for clothing, concrete for sidewalks, and asphalt for streets. Simply stated, channels are placeholders for images. The next image demonstrates how using a good texture with a primitive can create a nice looking prop:

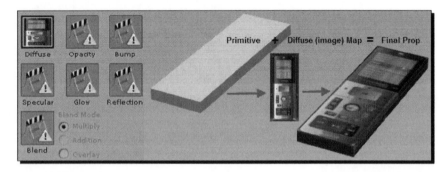

You can load an image into a map channel by double-clicking on the channel or you can drag-and-drop the diffuse maps onto objects with your left mouse button. The map channels work on clothing, props, terrains, skies, and other content.

Exploring the mapping channels

The following table shows the various types of channels available and an example map of each type:

Type of channel map	Example of channel map image
Diffuse: Maps a bitmap image to the prop. The diffuse map gives the prop its exterior look. (Works with pixel and smooth shader.)	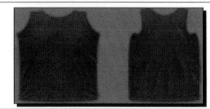

Type of channel map	Example of channel map image

Opacity: These maps are black and white. Areas in black are invisible while areas in white are visible. (Works with smooth, vertex, and pixel shader.)

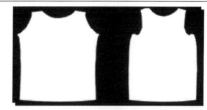

Bump: This map creates a sense of depth to the object. You will notice from the example that the t-shirt is not outlined on the map, and only the wrinkles in the cloth have been. This map makes those wrinkles stand out on the model. Bump maps are shades of grey and normal are shades of purple so be sure to check the normal box when using a normal map instead of a bump map. (Works with vertex and pixel shader.) *Be sure to check the box in the file dialog window to import as a normal map if you are using the purple normal maps instead of grey scale bump maps.*

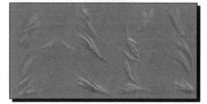

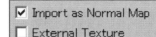

Specular: This map adds shininess to a model. One example being a sidewalk wet from rain. The sidewalk will look wet, puddle, or both depending on how the specular map is constructed. (Works with vertex and pixel shader.)

Glow: This channel is self-explanatory as it adds a glow to the object that it is mapped to. This can make a light glow on a passing ship or airplane.

Reflection: This channel like the glow channel does just what the name says. It adds a reflection (mimics a reflection) on the object.

Type of channel map	Example of channel map image
Blend: This is the grunge channel—the channel that adds dirt, wear and tear, and other similar effects to the object it's applied to or decals can be added here.	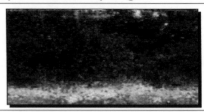

Time for action – painting the gazebo

We built a nice gazebo, but it's definitely missing something. Therefore, let's fix it up with a texturing or if you prefer, you could paint it a solid color:

1. After saving the gazebo project file, open the file that we have been working on.

2. Navigate to the Gazebo prop that we just built and double-click or drag-and-drop to place it in the scene. It's your choice where to place it.

3. Is it too big? Remember we are working at 50% scale on this project so reduce the scale to around 50% of the current values for all three axis of the gazebo.

4. Click on **Set**, **Grass**, and select the **Grass** from the **Scene Manager**. On the right-side menu, select the **Mower** and size it to whatever size you are comfortable using. If you make a mistake with the mower, you can use the undo feature to go back to before the mistake. Clear the grass growing through the floor. Repeat the process to clear the flowers or any other Live Plant that may be showing through the floor.

5. Highlight the cylinder we used for the floor. You can do that by either clicking directly on the screen or by selecting it in the **Scene Manager**.

6. Click on the **Load Material** button in the Material & Texture settings section of the right-side menu and choose **Wood 005**.

 Don't see the iMaterial files? In Windows 7 and Vista, the iMaterial files are located at:

`C:\Users\Public\Documents\Reallusion\Template\`
`iClone 4 Template\iClone Template\Materials Lib`

If you have not used any of the channel buttons before, then the iMaterials should be visible immediately after clicking on the **Load Material** button.

7. Select Cone_006 from the **Scene Manager** and press the **Load Material** button again to load the same wooden material as you loaded in previous step or click on the Paint Bucket icon in the right side panel then click on the roof of the gazebo to apply the same texture to cone as the cylinder has. The only problem with this is the material may not be properly applied to every prop with this method, as shown in the next image with the wavy wood texture on the roof:

What just happened?

We mowed the grass and picked the flowers of any plants that were growing through the gazebo floor. If you have a clear area large enough for the gazebo, you can skip this step.

Time for action – correcting the texture mapping

You have now discovered your first mapping problem as the roof will be mapped erratically. We will correct that problem in the following section:

1. Click on each of the boxes one at a time and detach each building block prop from the cylinder.

2. After detaching the props, select the cone (roof) again.

3. With the cone selected, click on the **Box** under **UV Type** in the **UV Settings** section of the right – side menu.

4. Click on the **Z**-axis under **Align**. The mapping of the roof changes to reflect your choices. Type 6 into the **Tiling** box under the **U** section. Click on the **Apply** button. The next image shows the proper settings:

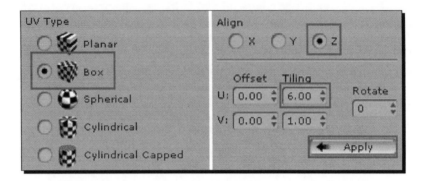

5. With your mouse click on one of the support beams (box) or choose one of the Box_001 building blocks in the **Scene Manager**.

6. Click on the **Load Material** button or use the **Paint Bucket** as described earlier to apply the texture to the posts.

7. Select the box under **UV Type** and B or Z under **Align**. Click on the **APPLY** button. This will change the mapping on the posts.

8. In order to save time, click on the **Paint Bucket** tool, and then click on each of the posts that have no texture until all are textured, as shown in the following screenshot:

What just happened?

We now have a custom made gazebo prop! We had to detach the parts to texture it as this will allow us to assign different UV Mapping to each Building Block. When attached to the floor cylinder, the child Building Blocks inherit the mapping from the parent Building Block. Detached Building Blocks are covered by one UV map for each Building Block.

Painting option

If you want your gazebo to be a solid color instead of a texture, then use the color selection boxes instead of the texture maps. There is no need for remapping when using a solid color. You paint one and then use the Paint Bucket tool to apply that color to the rest of the gazebo by clicking on each Building Block until your prop is completely painted, as shown in the next image:

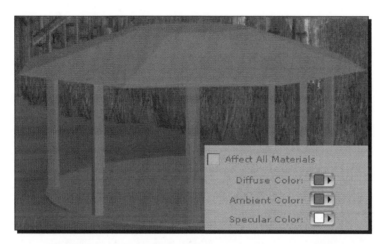

Time for action – adding fire effects to the grill

The outdoor grill that we placed on the deck earlier has a fiery charcoal texture already added to the inside of the grill, but to make it look better, we need those charcoals to glow. The built glow channel will take care of that for us. We just need the right glow map and one is provided with iClone.

1. Select the grill in the **Scene Manager** or select it with your mouse and then press the home button in the upper toolbar to bring the grill into view.

Focusing the camera on an object

The **Home** key is a very important tool that focuses your camera around a particular prop, character, or other object in the scene. With the object that you want to focus on being selected, press the **Home** key to move the camera to that object. You can then adjust the camera angle to your preference. The following image shows the camera controls:

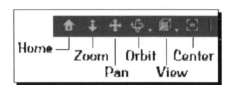

2. With the **grill** selected, click on the right mouse button to invoke the prop's right-click menu. Choose **Remove All Animation**. If the grill is open in the first frame then you can go to the next step. However, if the grill is closed, we need to make sure we are both working on the same animation state and that is why we are removing the animation. This does not strip the animation out of the prop as it only removes any active animation currently triggered in the prop.

3. With the timeline scrubber at the beginning of the timeline, right-click on the **Animation**, go to **Perform**, and select **Open Grill**.

4. Right-click again on the **grill** and once again select **Remove All Animation**.

5. Move the timeline scrubber back to frame 1 before continuing to the next step.

6. Select the grill directly with the mouse or in the **Scene Manager**.

7. In the drop-down box located within the **Material** and **Texturing** settings section of the right menu, select **Charcoals**. You should now see the charcoal texture in the Diffuse channel.

8. Double-click on the **Glow** channel and select **Desert-Sun** as the glow map.

You should now have glowing charcoals. You can set the intensity of the glow by adjusting the slider bar under the **Strength** setting.

Adjust this setting to your preference.

What just happened?

As mentioned in step 5, we need to make sure we are both working at frame 1 on the timeline with a grill that is already open instead of waiting several frames for it to open. This allows us to see the charcoals in the grill. Had we gone down the timeline to when the grill opened to apply the glow, then the glow would not have been triggered until that frame. This would leave the coals without a glow until the timeline reached the frame in which we applied the glow.

The next image shows the **Charcoals** material selected in the drop-down box and the **Glow** channel that was used to add an orange glow to the charcoals material:

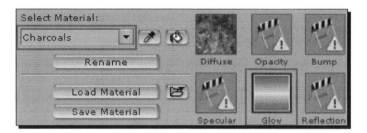

Remembering our place on the timeline

When adding glow or textures to a prop or arranging a scene such as placing props and characters, always remember where you are on the timeline. If you are not in the proper location to add a prop, texture, or movement to the timeline then that prop, texture, or movement will not be visible until the timeline reaches that point. For example, let's say we intended for a change to happen at frame 1 but we applied it at frame 124 because we forgot to reset the time scrubber to frame 1, so the change we made will not appear until frame 124.

In some 3D applications changes are not recorded until a mode or button is pressed but in iClone, the timeline is always active, therefore, any changes made are reflected at that point in the timeline.

The left grill has no glow map applied while the right grill has a glow map set at 100%.

Creating see through material

As stated earlier in this chapter, opacity maps are black-and-white, with the white areas being visible and the black areas invisible. Shades of grey also control the amount of visibility in the same manner as black, but grey will show depending on the color of grey used. This can be used to create see through material.

In the case of the grill shelf, the diffuse map and the opacity map are the same image, but in most cases, you will have a colored diffuse map with a black-and-white opacity map.

A chain fence texture map (as shown in the following image) was used to simulate the expanded metal grilling shelf above the charcoals:

The diffuse and opacity channels when used together create the grill shelf, with the black areas of the diffuse map being canceled out by the black areas of opacity map and thus leaving a shelf that can be seen through. The following image reflects the difference which the opacity map makes:

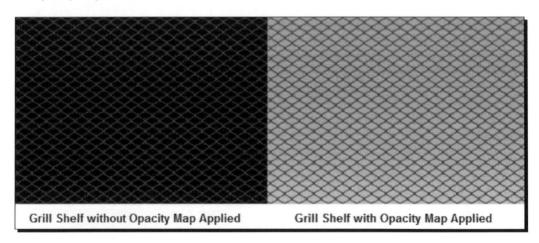

Grill Shelf without Opacity Map Applied   Grill Shelf with Opacity Map Applied

Turning nothing into something

Opacity maps are also used with billboards and flat planes or even Live Plants to represent 2D content in a scene. A billboard will always face the camera whereas a 2D plane will maintain its original position.

Opacity is a powerful tool that turns nothing into something.

The character in the foreground of the following image was made with a billboard using diffuse and opacity maps. The group located behind the 2D character is a Live Plant Grass planting made with the same diffuse and opacity maps. They even cast shadows.

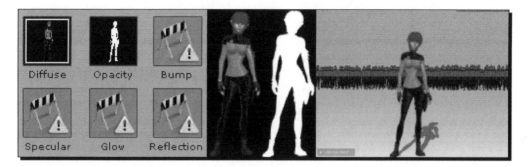

Live Plants are basically hybrid billboards with a plant diffuse image and an opacity image.

A meadow full of flowers or an entire army of characters can be placed on-screen with little or no overhead from the 3D engine by using billboards. The opacity map makes this possible.

The cast of thousands Live Plant trick

If you need an army but don't have the army or the computing power to display a 3D army, then use Live Plants and change out the plant diffuse and opacity image with that of a posed soldier. Since Live Plants move in the breeze, you use that movement to simulate an army standing in a loose formation or milling about waiting for something to happen.

The following scene was created by planting Live Plant grass and changing out the grass image for the soldier image:

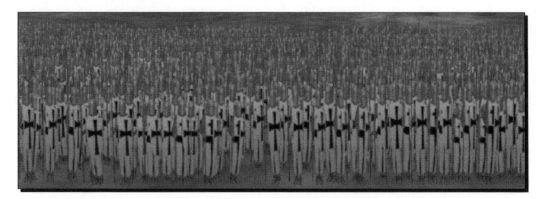

The following image shows the diffuse and opacity maps that are used to create the standing army:

 Never underestimate the power of opacity maps when combined with billboards, planes, and Live Plants.

Lighting in 3D animation

In 3D animation, lighting is a very important aspect of selling a scene to a viewer. It is often overlooked as the single most important aspect of what the scene is trying to portray. You can build a great scene with wonderful props, plants, and fantastic vistas but if the lighting is done poorly, all that work will be a waste of time. Viewers have grown very sophisticated and have been indoctrinated by the wizards of animation like Pixar, for which lighting is a big part.

Lighting is not just a means to make the scene visible, but rather it creates mood, which is very important in any animation or movie. Just as in live action photography and videography lighting takes time, effort, and forethought.

When lighting a scene there are several things that you need to keep in mind and these are just the basics:

- The mood of the scene. Scary? Sunny? Stormy?
- Interior or Exterior.
- Colors of the scene: Warm, cold, or indifferent to either.
- Location of the lights.
- Type of lights used.
- Animated, fixed lighting, or both?

A hospital room would be lit differently from a sunny meadow or snow covered field. A darkened children's playroom might infer something sinister whereas a brightly lit playroom would invite fun.

Bluish lighting in a snow scene could infer more cold than pure white lighting or adding a touch of red to a scene involving fire can add an element of dread and help sell that scene.

Selling a scene is very important because after all is said and done, if we did a poor job of selling the scene, then we will get a poor return on our effort.

Light types and shadows

iClone has one ambient, four directional and/or spotlights, four point lights, and atmospheric lighting effects. The following chart is taken from the `Reallusion Help` file:

	Ambient Light	Point Light	Directional Light	Spotlight
On/Off	Always On	Adjustable	Adjustable	Adjustable
Type Switching	Not Applicable	Not Applicable	Switch to Spotlight	Switch to Directional Light
Shadow	No Shadow	No Shadow	Drop Shadow, Self-Cast, Wall	Drop Shadow, Self-Cast, Wall
Shadow Range	No Shadow	No Shadow	Available	Available
Setting keys	Not Available	Available	Available	Available
Picking	Color Changing	Available	Available	Available
Intensity	Not Available	Available	Not Available	Available
Beam and Falloff	Not Available	Not Available	Not Available	Available
Look At Feature	Not Available	Not Available	Not Available	Available
Link To Feature	Not Available	Not Available	Not Available	Available

There are four spotlight/directional lights available. The limited number is due to the amount of resources required for lights and its load on the engine.

Directional lights

- Have a color picker available to change color
- Rotate globally within the 3D workspace
- Animated by the timeline
- Turned on and off by the timeline
- Cast shadows

Spotlights

◆ Have a color picker available to change color

◆ Can be moved or rotated to any location within the 3D workspace

◆ Animated by the timeline

◆ Turned on and off by the timeline

◆ Can be linked to objects

◆ Cast shadows

◆ Can set range, decay, and falloff

Point lights

◆ Have a color picker available to change color

◆ Can be moved or rotated to any location within the 3D workspace

◆ Animated by the timeline

◆ Turned on and off by the timeline

◆ Can be linked to objects

◆ Cannot cast shadows

◆ Can set range and decay

Experiment with the lights

Don't be afraid to experiment with the Spotlight by modifying the range and decay while rotating the light around to see how it affects the scene.

The next image shows the lighting control section in which we can select and manipulate individual lights:

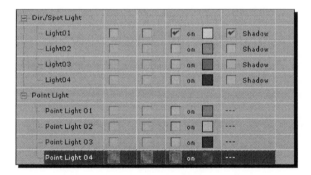

Understanding ambient light

Think of ambient light as sunlight or moonlight. The scene's natural light is ambient light.

- ◆ Ambient light is always on. To darken it for night, select a dark gray, black, or whatever dark color you desire in the pop-up color window.

- ◆ Ambient light affects objects in the scene and casts shadows from those objects. You cannot animate the ambient light with keyframes.

- ◆ Ambient light helps to set the mood for the scene.

Due to the limited number of lights, it is critical that you take care in the planning and placement of these precious resources. Lighting used wisely can make for an unforgettable scene. Some animators start with black ambient light with judicious use of the spotlight and point lights to achieve certain moods. A brighter ambient light can also keep outdoor scene from appearing dull.

Manipulating the lights in the 3D workspace

The lights are controlled within the **Scene Manager** located in the left-side menu and the right side **Modify** menu. You can also freeze the light or turn on an icon to represent the light source to locate it in the 3D workspace.

The lights that can be manipulated within the 3D workspace share the same gizmo or direct manipulation as the props.

Remembering where we are on the timeline

When we move and rotate lights, we are creating key frames on the timeline. Hence be sure to start from frame 1 or on the area on the timeline where the light will first appear.

Setting the mood with lighting and atmosphere

Just because this is a daylight scene doesn't mean we don't have some lighting work to do. Lighting any scene is important whether it's in total daylight or darkness.

Volumes have been and will continue to be written about lighting and its impact on the visualization of the scene. Even if you are only rendering out a single image, the lighting is just as important to that single image as it is to a 10 minute scene.

There is much that can be discussed about lighting, but this guide concentrates on beginner-level skills to get you going instead of bogging you down in the minutiae of the process. With that in mind we are going to tackle lighting our outdoor scene in this next section.

Time for action – setting the ambient light

Ambient light has a tremendous effect on the mood and the interaction of other lights in the scene. We will set up a darker ambient light than the default setting:

1. You must select a light (**Directional/Spotlight** or **Point**) to access the ambient light setting color box that is located at the bottom of the light setting section on the right side menu.

2. Click on the Ambient light color square in the right side menu.

3. Set the RGB input boxes to 45, 45, 45. This darkens the ambient light to let more mood come through as it could be morning or evening instead of midday or afternoon.

What just happened?

We added and adjusted the ambient light for a morning or evening shot.

Adjustments to ambient light may be necessary as work on any scene progresses through this. You cannot always think of all the variables when setting up your ambient light so doing adjustments as you work is just part of the process. This **Ambient light** setting will give us a good starting point.

Time for action – working with shadows

In order to keep things simple, we are only going to work with shadows on light number 1. Trying to keep up with the direction of multiple light source shadows can be a chore when we begin to learn lighting. Hence, all subsequent lights will have the **shadow box** unchecked.

1. Click on the **Shadow** input box for **Directional/Spotlight 1** to turn it on if it's not already.

2. Set the shadow to **Self-Casting** in the **Shadow Settings** section of the right menu.

 If the **Self-Casting** shadow option is not available due your hardware configuration, then select **Drop Shadow** or whatever shadow available setting you may have. If you can't see a shadow at all, no matter what options you try then skip this section. Shadows are hardware dependent. Your video card is an important part of this dependency.

3. Set the **Opacity** to 80%.

4. Set the **Blur level** to 3.

    Now we have a shadow casting light that will cast a dark, blurred shadow for scene objects.

5. Click the checkbox of Light 2 in the **Scene Manager** to turn it on.

6. Click on the color square for Light 2 in the **Scene Manager** or click on the arrow next to the colored square in the **Light Setting** section of the right menu. Either of these will pop up a color window.

7. Choose one of the orange colors in the **Basic** section of the color popup and notice the difference this has made in the scene.

8. This could be too much orange so let's click on the color square in the **Scene Manager** again and move the right-side slider up about 1/4 of the distance towards the top of the color window. This will decrease the amount of orange that the light casts.

What just happened?

White light can be rather flat when it interacts with props and other scene objects, even for a daytime outdoor scene. We wanted to add a touch of warmth to the scene and that can be done by adding a warm color to a light. You'll notice that we didn't change the white color of Light 1 because that will cast a heavy shade of the selected color over everything in the scene. We just want highlights of a warm color. For this we will use Directional/Spotlight 2.

If you don't think this light is affecting the scene then turn it off to notice the difference. Experiment with the orange color to achieve the lighting you desire. Watch out how the orange lighting interacts with the leaves on the tree and also with the other objects. As you adjust the intensity of the orange color, you will notice that moving the slider to a darker color of orange adds more color and less light to the scene.

We will not be changing the direction of the lighting, which is done by selecting the light and using the **Rotate** tool. Check the light's **Show** checkbox in the **Scene Manager** and you will see a colored line on the screen that displays the direction of the light to help in adjusting the light's affect.

Time for action – manipulating the atmosphere

While atmosphere isn't technically a light it does affect the mood of the scene so we will incorporate its use in this scene. There are also atmospheric presets available.

1. Click the **Stage** tab and then click the **Atmosphere** button to give us access to the **Atmosphere** menu.

2. Click or turn on the **HDR Effect** and then do the same with the **Tone Map**.

3. Increase the **Exposure** under **Tone Map** to **40** to increase brightness.

4. Set the **Glare** to **Cheap Lens** and the **Scale** to **1**.

5. Click or turn on **IBL on** in the **Image Based Lighting** section of the right side menu to further lighten the scene.

What just happened?

We turned on the **HDR** and **Tone Map** atmospherics. You will notice that the scene darkened significantly with the **Tone Map** checked. The glare was then scaled back to one and set on the **Cheap Lens** tool.

> The tone map can have radical effects on lighting at different camera angles so extreme settings can cause lighting blow-outs overpowering the scene. Adjustment must be made as the scene and camera shots are developed. This can be controlled with the atmospheric timeline.

We are going to leave the rest of the settings at default as this is another area that may require some adjustment as we make progress on our scene. The **Tone Map** is affected by object and camera movement. It can brighten or darken the scene when these items are animated to move across the workspace.

Time for action – lighting up the grill

To add light to the outdoor grill, we will use a point light:

1. Click or turn on **Point Light 1**.

2. Select the grill in the **Scene Navigator** or click on the grill prop.

The following screenshot shows the grill pop:

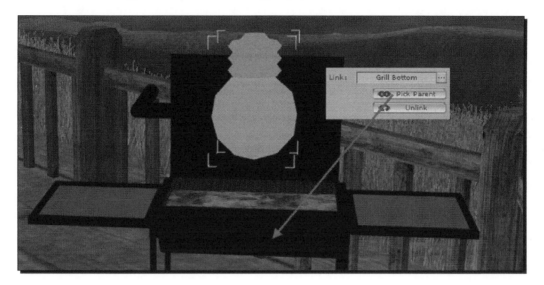

3. Press the **Home** button on the top toolbar to move our camera focus to the grill.

4. With **Point Light 1** selected, use the **Link To** feature in the right menu to link the light to the grill.

5. Click the **Link To** button and select the **Grill Bottom** and also select **Position and Rotation**. Click on **OK**.

6. Select the **Rotate** tool from the top menu and rotate the light into its upright position.

7. Change the color to orange, set the range to 150, and click the **Decay** box.

8. Use the gizmos or direct manipulation to place the light within the grill prop.

What just happened?

We added a nice warm orange glow to the area around the grill by placing and linking an orange light, to the grill. The following image shows before and after placing the point light near the grill:

The distance the camera is away from the house prop will determine how your scene atmospherics look. Too close and the scene will wash out with too much bright light. Pull the camera back and you should have a nicely lit scene with shadows and sunlight, bathing sections of the house, and other parts of the scene.

Bravo! You have taken a plain, daylight scene, and added character and mood with lighting and atmospherics. Just imagine what you can do in a dark scene with spotlights and point lights if you can improve a daylight scene this much! The next image shows the project to this point:

Summary

This was a monumental chapter in terms of what we've learned.

Specifically, we covered:

- Creating a new scene with Terrain, Sky, and Live Plants and how to manipulate them
- Adding props to a scene while being introduced to the idea of interactive and animated props
- How to manipulate props in the workspace and working in scale
- The importance of lighting and atmosphere even in a daytime outdoor scene

Basically you have built the scene from the ground up, literally, to a scene that is ready to be expanded upon.

Now that we've created the scene, we're ready to add the avatar/characters in the next chapter.

Pop quiz – face-off

1. What is meant by the term low poly?
   a. Low face count
   b. Low polygon count
   c. Both of the above
   d. None of the above

2. What is the recommended maximum face count for props and other assets used in iClone?
   a. 15,000 faces
   b. 150,000 faces
   c. 30,000 faces
   d. 300,000 faces
   e. There is no limit on faces

3
Adding and Customizing Characters

Now we get to have a lot of fun by adding one of the strongest components of any story—the characters.

In the world of iClone, **actors, avatars, and characters** *are the same thing. They are pre-rigged functional 3D characters than can be animated and have a built-in automatic lip-sync feature. Characters can use pre-made motions or animations and can be keyframed manually with the timeline.*

Clothing can be modified to suit the needs of the scene. Facial features and other aspects of the character can be changed with the click of a button or the move of a slider control. Body parts can be changed and even hair and shoes can be modified.

In this chapter we shall:

- Add characters to a scene, change their features, and learn to manipulate them
- Use characters with accessories and animated props as well as interactive props (iProps)
- Change or modify the character's looks and clothing
- Get a handle on basic dialog and how to get audio dialog into iClone and the right character

Save your project and save often!

Reallusion is attempting to put very powerful 3D tools into anyone's hands that will run on a wide variety of computers and crashes will happen to varying degrees. Always save your projects many times while working.

Time spent saving your project will be much easier to handle than losing a few hours of work or worse yet... that perfect tweak that you may never reproduce!

When in doubt... SAVE!

So let's get to the task at hand—adding and manipulating characters!

Developing unique characters

A dull character won't win any reviews whereas a well tweaked character can stand out and draw a viewer into the story. Actors change their physical appearance as much as possible to meet the demands and requirements of the role they are playing.

Stock iClone characters are a great asset but they are really just a starting point for the above average iClone animator and great care needs to be taken during the character modification process to ensure your characters look as good as they possibly can.

The following image shows the library of stock iClone characters:

We must always strive to make our characters unique and iClone gives us the tools to do just that.

Time for action – loading characters

Just like props, characters can be loaded into the workspace by several methods:

- Drag-and-drop from the **Avatar** panel in the **Content Manager**.
- Drag-and-drop from a Windows Explorer window.
- Double-click on a character or use the **Apply** button in the **Content Manager**. The character will be loaded into the center of the workspace with their feet on the ground.
- Import a character using the **Import** button in the **Modify** section.

It's time for us to import and scale our first character:

1. Click on the **Avatar** tab on top and double-click on **Dylan** from the left side panel or drag-and-drop the character to the porch. If you can't see the character, then link it to something visible like the grill and with the **Link To** button use the **Position** option to position the character in your view.

     Remember to unlink your character after using this method.

2. We are working at 50% scale so click on the **LOCK XYZ** box and move one of the sliders all the way to the left, reducing the character by 50%.

Your character should now be in scale for the scene:

What just happened?

We loaded our first character into the scene. We then made sure the X,Y,Z scale box was checked and scaled the character down by 50% to fit our scene scale.

It's not critical to keep objects in exact scale unless they are at the forefront of a scene. A few percent variance in scale may not be noticed, depending on the object's importance to the scene, but scale is a very important aspect of any scene and an improperly scaled prop or character will destroy the continuity of a scene.

Customizing character features

There are several options to customize existing characters—clothes, face, body shape, eyes, teeth, and mouth. One of the greatest features of iClone is its photo facial mapping feature.

Time for action – loading a face image

Our next task is to load a custom face on the character with an image. This can be a photo or a computer generated image with a forward looking facial shot including friends and family!

With the Dylan character selected:

1. Click on the **Head** tab.

2. Click on **Load Image** and load the **Fighter** image or browse to a face image of your choice. The **Fighter** facial image is in the `FaceFront` sub folder of the template folder if you have previously navigated away from this default location:

Resizing trick for your character

While iClone limits what you can do to change the scale of a character in one session, there is a trick that will allow us to shrink or enlarge our character to suit our needs. Reduce or enlarge your character to the maximum amount allowed by the sliders then save that character. Reload the character and the sliders will be reset and you can again modify the character to the maximum allowed by the sliders. Repeat this process as many times as necessary to achieve the proper size character:

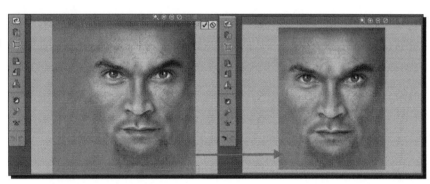

3. Click on the **Next** button.

4. Scale the facial fitting outline to the photo:

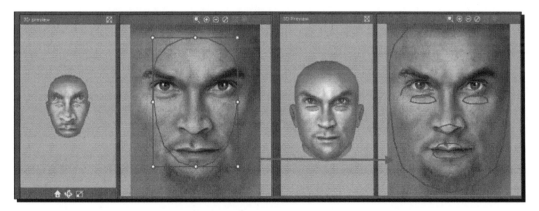

After scaling and moving the facial mask we will continue with lining up the mask.

5. Line up the mouth and nose as best you can. Don't worry about the eyes yet. The eyes will be adjusted on the next step of the process. When you move or scale the face fitting outline pay attention to what is happening on the left-side pane. The left pane will show you how the image is fitting to the head. Move the facial fitting outline until you are satisfied with the mouth and nose fitting:

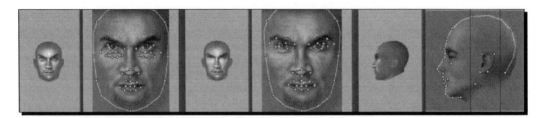

6. Click on the **Next** button.

7. Move the eyes up to where they cover the eyes of the image.

8. Move the nose to fit while watching the results on the left side.

9. Move and resize the mouth for fitting to the mouth area.

 Make note of the **Mirror** checkbox. When you are moving the eyes, initially you may want to keep the MIRROR box checked, then uncheck the box to move individual parts of the outline.

10. Click on **Edit Side** on the top and make any adjustment to the side of the face while keeping track of the changes in the left pane.

11. When you are satisfied with the results click on **OK**.

12. You will then be presented with a save file dialog window. Browse to the location you wish to save the face with your preferred name and click on the **SAVE** button.

 If you don't like the results of your initial face fitting then it is recommended that you try again. Once you have fit a few faces you will start to develop your own style for this feature. Perseverance pays off with facial fitting.

13. Click on the **Actor** tab and the **Hair** button.

14. Adjust the scale and positioning of the hair to fit the new head properly.

The position of the hair to the head pivot point is saved as part of the head attribute. The **Reset** button will restore the hair to its default position in most cases, depending on how the hair was constructed.

What just happened?

We have just loaded and fit a customized face which will change the overall shape of the head to match the face features we used during the fitting process. Even though we may change out the hair, we adjusted the existing hair to fit the face.

Not all photos will face fit in the same manner. You may have to go back a step or two and modify the placement or you may have to fit the eyes first then fit the nose and mouth in the next step. While this is indeed a powerful face fitting tool it will take some trial and error experimentation to get used to how it operates. You will develop your own style of facial fitting as you use iClone.

Time for action – correct the lighting

You'll notice the face seems washed out with the lighting after we added the character. This is due to the settings we used when we created the orange point light for the grill. The light is too intense for a character to be this close. You can either move the character or correct the light. It might make more sense to correct the light as you really don't want any limits on where your characters can be placed in a scene.

1. Click on **Point Light 01** in the Scene Manager on the left menu.

2. Reduce the **Range** setting to 75 in the **Light Setting** section of the right menu.

Too bright or too dark in the 3D workspace

If the atmospheric effects are affecting your workspace, turning it too dark or too bright while you work because of the changing camera angles, you can go to the **Stage** and **Atmosphere** button then turn off the **HDR Effect** and the **Tone Map** until you are ready to render the final movie or image. Just remember to turn them on before rendering or you won't have the lighting and atmospheric look we achieved earlier!

Another option would be to reduce our render to smooth shader or less. If we have the **Final Render** box checked on the **Render** menu it will be rendered with the highest quality render setting available regardless of the render setting we are working in.

What just happened

We didn't really turn out the lights but we did turn them down. We used the light modification settings to lower the intensity of the light. This reduced the harsh glare on the character's face.

We have limited the glare from grille's point light on the character and surrounding area. This is an example of what we discussed earlier with adjusting your lights and atmospherics as you work on your scene.

Time for action – customizing our character

This is where we start to customize a character we can call our own. Reallusion has given us many tools to change our character and they can be used subtly or at full capacity. These body styles are quick and easy for a starting point. It also depends on what generation of character you are using as to how these different styles will affect them.

1. Click on the **Actor** tab.

2. Click on the **Avatar** button.

3. Under the **Body Style** section of the right menu click on **Slim**.

The following image highlights the slim body style option we are using in this project:

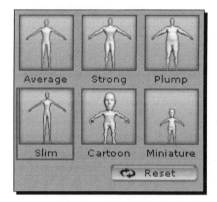

Most of these **Body Style** modifications in the right side menu under the **Avatar** section work better on older generation characters than they do on the latest generation but they do work with G3 characters. Experimentation to familiarise yourself with the options is encouraged.

What just happened?

A **Slim** button? Oh yeah. I could use one of those in the real world! We just slimmed our character down with the click of a button. This morphed the overall shape of the character instantly.

Not all of the body styles will work as expected with the different generations of characters. These body style options were originally designed for the G1 character when iClone was introduced and the significance is waning in some respect as some body styles can have downright comical results on newer characters.

On the other hand, these exaggerated body styles can be used for projects that call for comical characters. In particular, the cartoon and miniature styles still have many uses.

Time for action – customizing the head of the avatar

1. Select the character.

2. Click on the **Head** tab then **Faces** button.

3. Click on the **Head** button in the **Facial Features** section of the right menu.

4. Click on the **Slim** button under the **Head** section located lower in the right menu.

The following image highlights the choices made to load the slim head morph:

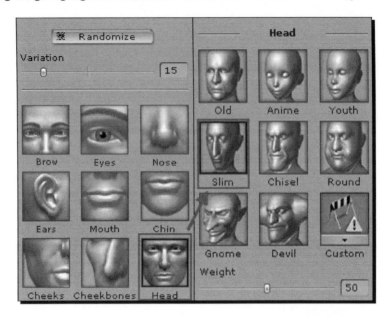

 The **Head modification** button is only available on G3 characters with G4 heads such as Dylan and Jana. Other G3 characters and below will not have this option available.

What just happened?

We slimmed down the facial structure to match the slim body we loaded earlier. The regular size face was out of proportion for the body.

Have a go hero – customizing the avatar's face

Save your project. Instead of specific instructions, it's time to experiment with the face features.

Go through the various sections like brow, eyes, nose, and see what is available. Experiment with the sliders and if you don't like what you've done you can use the **Reset** button to reset that particular section.

The following image shows some of the sections devoted to facial modification:

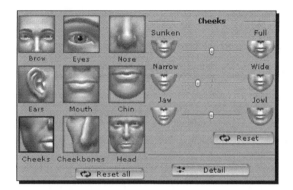

Use these buttons along with the sliders available in each section to make unique changes to the facial structure of the character. In this case, we narrowed the **Cheeks** using the slider. Though it's not shown the chin was made longer under the **Chin** section. This is where iClone flexes some of its muscle. Time spent here will pay dividends later if you are looking to create a unique or different character from stock. We are not going to spend any more time modifying the face but you can come back anytime during your work on this project or others to further tweak the facial features. When you are finished with your experimentation, either reopen the project you saved before experimenting or if you like your results then save the project again to save the changes.

Experimenting with model detail

The detail panel triggered by clicking on the **Detail** button is a very powerful feature, in that you can push and pull the various points shown to further customize the face. In this case, the chin was pushed up a little but you are encouraged again to experiment here. Use the **Reset** button if you don't like the results:

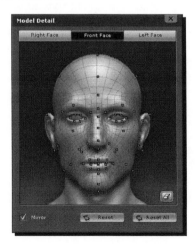

Views include front, left, and right. There is a **Mirror** checkbox to speed up facial sculpting by mirroring what you are doing to both sides of the head. It cannot be stressed enough how powerful and important this detail panel is to custom facial sculpting. To create pointed ears or a blunt nose or sharpen the eye sockets you can simply sculpt them by moving the points in the detail window. Select multiple points while holding the *Ctrl* key. Click on the eraser icon to release selected control points. Click on the left or right button to change face views.

This is another area of iClone that Reallusion has worked hard at to give us a lot of control and power over the final look of our characters.

Time for action – giving your character a new do!

Hair is another critical feature of modifying the look of characters. Reallusion has a variety of stock hairstyles and there are additional hair packs on the Reallusion website in the **Content Store**:

1. With the character selected, click on the **Hair** button on the top toolbar.

2. Double-click on the **Short** hairstyle:

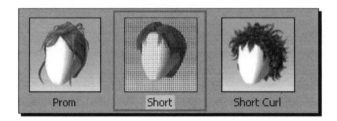

3. Click on the **Lock XYZ** check box under **Adjust** on the right panel.

4. Set the scale to 115 for X,Y, and Z, or adjust to your liking:

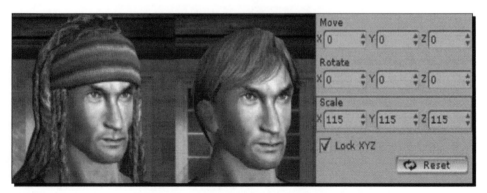

What just happened?

Indeed our male character got a haircut. Those dreads were high maintenance. A more conservative hair style was in order for this particular scene. We replaced the hair and scaled it to fit.

Now if it was just that easy in real life some of us would still have hair!

Time for action – customizing the eyes and mouth

These features are easy to use and customize. You can have cat's eyes and fangs for teeth along with several more typical eye and mouth options:

1. With the character selected click on the **Head** tab.

2. Click on the **Eyes** button.

3. In the left menu of the Content Manager select **09_Brown_A**, or whichever eyes you want to use.

4. Under **Adjust Size** in the right panel change the **Narrow/Wide** to **-21**.

5. The mouth covers the teeth, tongue, and the inside color of the mouth. For Oral (Teeth) select **Normal B** in the **Content Manager** left panel or whichever teeth suit your purpose.

 Clicking on the **Mouth** tab will force open the mouth for a better view. The mouth will remain open until you select the eyes or face tab to exit the mouth mode.

This is another great area to explore and discover what options are available before moving on.

What just happened?

There are numerous modifications available for each eye too. Each eye has its own set of channel maps along with many other sliders that control brightness to glossiness. You can scale the eyes or move them.

Skin

The skin color of a character will change to match the face color of any imported face or it can be changed with its own set of sliders and controls. You can also export and digitally paint directly on the skin maps. For example, you could paint a T-shirt on the skin of an upper.

The top-left 10X10 pixels of the face texture are used by the iClone engine to determine the skin color of the character.

iClone provides a set of skin tones in the **Content Manager** and all of these skins can be modified. They are good starting points. This is yet another example of the control Reallusion provides us over the character.

For this project, we will not be altering the skin.

Have a go hero – loading and customizing a female character

Loading characters is no more difficult than loading props and other objects. In this section, we'll load another character and then turn you loose to customise the character. It doesn't matter how your character looks to continue with this project but polishing those new found skills will help you remember them for future use.

Select the Jana character to load and place it near the original character. Customize the character using the features we've just covered to customize the second character to your liking.

Specifically, you can experiment with any or all of the features in the following list:

- Facial features
- Body proportion
- New face
- Eyes, mouth, and hair

Positioning the characters

The positioning of characters works in the same manner as positioning props and other objects in the 3D workspace. The same methods are available to place and fine tune your character's position. Use a combination of:

- Direct movement using the mouse
- *Ctrl + Q* to invoke the Gizmos for more precise placement
- Direct input in the value input boxes of the character for fine tuning

Place the characters close to the grill as demonstrated in the following image:

Using character accessories and attaching props

Using accessories and props as accessories is a simple process in iClone. Accessories attach to certain areas of a character and props can be attached to characters too.

Props and accessories differ. Props are independent objects whereas accessories are dependent on the character they are attached to. A hat as an accessory will fit on the head of the character it's attached to and move with that character. The same hat as a prop (detached from a character) can sit on the floor, a hat rack, or on a table.

Any prop can be attached to a character. After attachment, the prop then becomes an accessory. Its corresponding pivot points and 3D placement will change to that of an attachment and the prop will function as an attachment until detached from the character. After detachment, the prop will function as a prop again. You will notice that the units in the input boxes for the prop will change when the prop is attached as an accessory.

 Any prop attached to a character will function and can be saved as an accessory. Items that are attached as accessories are saved with the character. Items linked as props are not saved with the character.

Time for action – can't be cool without shades!

Time to get these characters some sunshades:

1. Click on the Dylan character or select **Dylan** in the **Content Manager** in the left panel.

2. Click on the **Accessories** button under the main tabs at the top.

3. In the left panel of **Content Manager**, double-click or drag-and-drop **Glasses 01** onto Dylan.

4. Using the up and down arrows adjust the Y and Z axis. Set the X scale to 120:

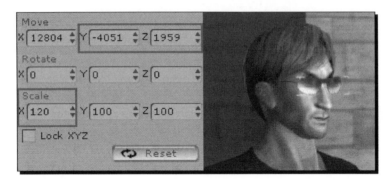

5. Repeat the previous steps for the female character.

What just happened?

We loaded the glasses onto the first character by selecting the character and then adding the accessory which automatically loaded into place for us. We then used the available controls to adjust how the glasses fit on the character's face. The prop was scaled up to 120 on the X axis to make the glasses wider.

Center that prop pivot before attachment

For a prop as an accessory to rotate properly around its center pivot, the prop will need to be centered using the **Center** button in the **Pivot** section before being attached as an accessory. This will make the pivot point closer to the center of the accessory and provide easier rotation and alignment of some accessories.

The following image shows the **Pivot** options in the **Modify** panel when a prop is selected:

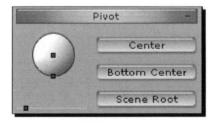

Time for action – shading the glasses

To further create the look of sunshades versus glasses we can take the following steps:

1. Select one of the eyeglasses in the **Content Manager** or by direct selection.

2. Select **glass** under **Select Material** in the right side panel.

3. Change the three colors to black in the **Material & Texture Settings** section of the right menu.

4. Use the Paint Bucket tool to paint the black color onto the lens of the other characters glasses:

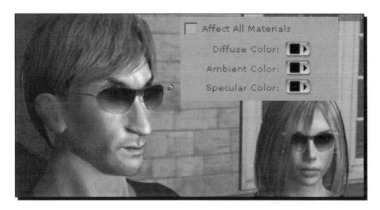

What just happened?

We used the color selectors for the diffuse and ambient channels to change the glasses into sunshades for our characters. These can also be tinted to different colors.

Time for action – attaching the fork prop

1. Import the grill fork that is located in the Code Bundle on the book page if you haven't downloaded it already.

2. Attach the grill fork to the left hand of the male character.

3. Scale the fork to 125% or whatever size you desire.

4. Select the male character. Right-click on the character and in the right-click menu choose **Motion Menu**, then **Hands** on the submenu.

5. Select the left hand from the right side menu and double-click on **Hold Stick** from the left side **Content Manager** menu.

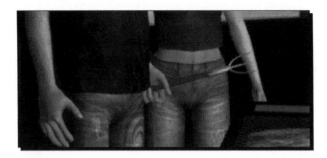

What just happened?

Our character needed a fork so we imported a custom fork, which is included in the code bundle located on the book page at the Packt Publishing website. We then used a premade **Hand Motion**, **Hold Stick**, to appear to grasp the stick.

We will go further into animations and motions in the next chapter. Now that we've properly attached and modified the glasses and the grilling fork our characters are starting to look more like a couple enjoying the outdoors.

Interacting with the iProps

We are going to have our male character pick up the beer to demonstrate how interactive (iProps) work.

In order for the character to interact with the prop the character needs to:

◆ Be at terrain height

◆ Or the character must be standing on an object that has been *added to the terrain*

This is important. Otherwise, the character will jump down to terrain level to grasp the beer can and will seem to disappear, when in fact it's dropped down below the porch or part way through the porch.

With **Deckhouse A** selected, right-click and choose **Add to Terrain** from the popup menu.

We have now let the iClone engine know that the floor level of the house is now a part of the terrain.

Time for action – grabbing a beer

The iProps operate on a built-in XML file that can be modified or used as is and can be imported into similar props. It is beyond the scope of this beginner's guide to modify the underlying code so we will instead adjust the iProp and character as necessary:

1. Select the **Deckhouse A** prop. Right-click on the prop and select **Add to Terrain**.

2. Click on the male character.

3. Click on or select the beer can iProp.

4. Right-click on the beer can iProp and select **Take** from the menu.

 If the male character is hovering in the air above the deck after you have implemented the take action, move the time scrubber back to the beginning and use the Move tool to move the character back down to the floor.

5. Move the time scrubber back to the beginning and select the female character.

6. With the female character selected, click on **Pick Target** under the **Look At** section in the right menu. Make sure **Head** is selected. Click on the **Look At** button, if necessary, and set the **Look At Subnode** to **Head**.

What just happened?

We used the built-in scripting of iClone to sit the prop down on the rail. Don't be surprised if the can doesn't exactly go where you want it to. We can do some adjusting with the Move tool when necessary. iProps are still in their infancy and can have a few hiccups here and there.

We used the **Look At** command to direct our female character to watch continually at the male, which will add some movement to her character as well as improve the scene.

Altering the characters' clothing

This is another area that allows us to modify the characters' looks or in this case their clothing. As stated earlier, diffuse maps with bump maps and opacity maps can make new clothing or give existing clothing a new look.

If you will remember in *Chapter 2, Creating Your First Scene,* when using opacity maps anything that covers black will not show, such as their outer clothing. Anything covered in white will be visible so you can make a long sleeve shirt into a short sleeve shirt.

Let's alter the shirt that Jana is wearing.

Time for action – altering female avatar clothing

In *Chapter 1, Installing and Configuring iClone* , we discussed how to select our image editing program via the **Preference** button (hammer icon) in the upper-right corner of the iClone interface. If you haven't set up your image editor, then you need to do so now. We'll be using Photoshop but the same principles apply to any image editor, including open source (free) editors like Gimp or Paint.net:

1. Select **Jana**.

2. Under **Actor** select **Upper Body**.

3. Click on the **Diffuse** channel then click on the **Launch** button to launch your favorite image editing software.

4. In your image editor, create a new layer above the existing layer.

5. Fill that layer with red or whatever color you prefer.

6. Set the blending mode for the red (top) layer to **Color**.

7. Save the diffuse map image then go back to iClone.

8. Click on **Update** in the **Material & Texture Settings** section of the right menu.

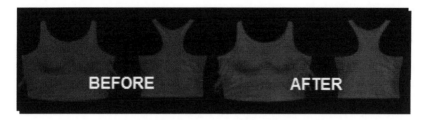

We will now lengthen her shirt to meet the top of her jeans. We will use the diffuse image to accomplish this:

1. Click on the **Opacity Map** for Jana's upper body.

2. Click on the **Launch** button to open the opacity image in your photo editor.

3. Add a new layer or draw a rectangle over the existing area in with white to expand lengthen the T-shirt Jana is wearing. Don't worry about side-to-side.

 There is an upper and lower for each of the characters in the Code Bundle on the book page at the Packt Publishing website that reflect the changes made in this chapter.

Added White Area to Opacity Image to Make Shirt Longer

4. Save the image in the photo editor and return to iClone.

5. Click the **Update** button in iClone to get the final result of the opacity change.

6. Click on the **Diffuse** channel again and launch the image editor.

7. Use the clone tools in your image editor to clone the fabric to the bottom or resize the image of the T-shirt to stretch down to the bottom.

8. Save the image with your external editor.

9. Switch to iClone and click on the **Update** button in the **Material & Texture Settings** section of the right panel.

What just happened?

We increased the length of the shirt by increasing the white area at the bottom of the shirt in the opacity map of the character's upper section. This is another area where experimentation with the opacity map will demonstrate its utility and power.

Altering clothing using color

Just like with the gazebo earlier, we can also use colors to change the diffuse map to alter the shirt. Even though we used the diffuse method in our project the alternative method can be very effective.

With the **Upper Body** selected, click on the **Diffuse** channel. Turn the diffuse slider all the way to zero to turn off the image so the black won't bleed through our new color. Set the three color choices to dark red or a color of your choice:

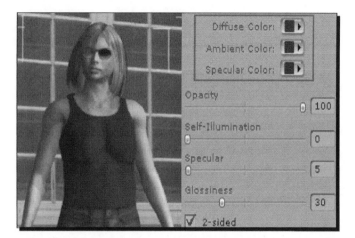

Time for action – altering the male avatar's clothing

We need to alter the male character's clothing to get a unique look from a stock character.

1. Select the male character in the Content Manager or by direct-click.

2. Select the **Upper Body** button under the **Actor** tab.

3. Click on the **Diffuse** channel.

4. Click on the **Launch** button to launch the diffuse map in your image editor.

   We are going to add a design to his T-shirt. For this example we are using the Reallusion logo, which can be downloaded with the code bundle located on the book's web page:

Shirt with Reallusion logo placed over the top in image editor.

You can use any logo of your choice but the Reallusion logo has transparency, it is a great image for this example, and will make a nice looking T-shirt too! Remember that opacity maps make decals and logos work.

[The basic opacity map rule: Black hides and white shows.]

5. Place the Reallusion logo image over the top of the front of the T-shirt in your image editor. You may have to resize the logo in your editor.

6. Save the diffuse map image.

7. In iClone, click on the **Update** button to display the change.

[Now is the time to tweak your work or make any changes. If you don't like where the logo is or need to make it larger or smaller, then go back to your image editor and make those changes. Don't close your image editor file until you are sure you are finished. Leave it open to make changes then save the diffuse image and use the **Update** button in iClone to show the changes. Do this as many times as necessary to get the results you want.]

8. Remove any image that may be in the Blend channel by highlighting that channel and pressing the trash can icon at the bottom of the right side panel in the **Material & Texturing Settings** section.

9. Change the **Diffuse**, **Ambient** and **Specular** colors to white:

What just happened?

We now have custom shirts on both characters. We could have changed the color of the black shirt in our image editor with overlays or color substitution but in this example we left it black because the logo looks very good on that color of shirt. You can also download the uppers (shirts) in the Code Bundle located on the book page at the Packt Publishing website.

Time for action – modifying the avatar's pants

We are now going to change out the lower, or pants, on the male character:

1. With the male character selected, click on the **Lower Body** button under the **Actor** tab.

2. Select the **Diffuse** channel.

3. Load the **Tartan** diffuse map located in the Code Bundle of the book page on the Packt Publishing website.

4. Set the tiles to 6 and 6.

We now have a leisurely attired male character. So let's do something for the female next:

1. Click on or select the female character. Click on the **Lower Body** button under the **Actor** tab.

2. Select the **Diffuse** channel.

3. Click on the **Launch** button to load the image into your editor.

4. Cover the bottom two-thirds of the image in black.

5. Cover the upper one-third of the image in white.

6. Save the image as male_lower_opacity, as shown on the right side of the following image:

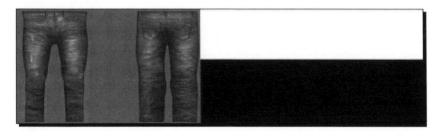

7. Double-click on the lower Opacity channel and browse to the newly created opacity map (male_lower_opacity) and load it.

What just happened?

We changed the texture on the male and created shorts for the female. The female jeans had no opacity map so we launched the diffuse map to save as an opacity map, and to use it as a guide to how long or short we will cut off the pants. Remember, black hides and white shows. We are using the black to cut off some of the pant's leg to create shorts out of the pants, as shown in the following image:

Now our characters look more like they are relaxing at a home cookout with casual clothes.

[Working with perfect RGB black 0,0,0 or perfect RGB white 255,255,255 will eliminate artifacts. Use a gray opacity color for semi-transparent clothing.]

Basics of character dialog

Once again Reallusion has minimized a tedious, labor-intensive process and somewhere along the way made dialog fun to add and work with iClone. Dialog can consist of multiple characters and can be as complicated or as simple as the scene or mood calls for.

Reallusion has taken most of the work out of this part of the production process (pipeline) and turned a difficult animated process into more of a timing exercise, which we will learn more about in the animation chapter. iClone takes the work off of you so you can concentrate more on the timing of your dialog to get those "just right" sequences.

Lip-sync

Lip-synching in iClone is as basic as typing in dialog or loading an audio file. iClone takes care of the mundane but important lip sync work as it analyses and applies the basic phonemes after loading the audio file.

That's it. No weeping or gnashing of teeth as iClone does a very respectable job of it. The lip-sync can be further tweaked using Reallusion's Crazy Talk to export, analyse, and tweak in minute detail the facial expressions and lip-sync then reimport.

It is not always necessary to use Crazy Talk, as iClone will do an excellent lip-sync job by itself and you can add more spice to the dialog with the facial puppeteering feature.

Recorded audio will need to be in as good quality as possible and the voice must be audible. The better the recording the better iClone can analyse and implement the lip-sync.

A lot of users prefer MP3 audio format as it is very compact, but many use high quality wav files too. It really doesn't matter which format so much as it matters about the quality of the recording.

USB headphones and mics are great and can record nice dialog but if it's within your budget to get a quality USB microphone like a Blue Snowball then do so, as the clearness of the spoken lines helps in the lip-sync process.

Adding dialog

There are three basic types of dialog input in iClone:

- ◆ Text-to-speech: Typed directly from the iClone interface
- ◆ Direct Record: Record the dialog directly into iClone via a microphone
- ◆ Audio Files: Imported into the selected actor

Creating dialog using the interface

Text-to-speech has been around a long time. In fact, it has been under development for so long it is now taken for granted. iClone has a built-in text-to-speech converter.

The text-to-speech feature is a very simple and straightforward tool. You will find the feature under the **Animation** tab, **Facial Animation** button, then over to right menu for the **Text-to-Speech** section under the **Import Voice/Add Emotion** section.

Select the proper character and type in the dialog and you have instant voices for your characters. To have a conversation between two characters you must highlight each character while typing in that character's dialog:

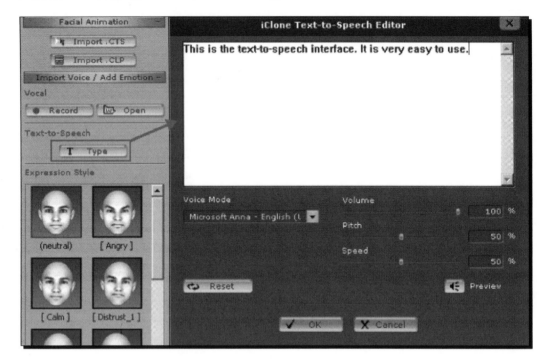

Text-to-speech options include:

- ◆ Volume
- ◆ Pitch
- ◆ Speed
- ◆ Voice Selection (Microsoft Anna is the default voice)

There are many voices available out there but Microsoft Anna was the only voice that was installed on my system. AT&T and other vendors have commercial voices available too. Just search the Internet for AT&T Labs and Cepstral online demos. There are male and female voices as well as accented voices.

While text-to-speech voices are nice they are not capable of producing a decent dialog and will detract from any animation work no matter how good it may be. In fact, in The Movies Underground community it is one of the most common complaints and almost no movie made with text-to-speech voice gets out unscathed.

The argument against using text-to-speech is that it always takes away from good work created by the filmmaker, as some viewers are so opposed to hearing it they cannot get into the storyline. No matter how good the voice synthesis may be, the majority of viewers do not like mechanical voices unless the characters are robots.

None the less the feature is available and has its place and its uses but don't expect mainstream media viewers to be impressed with the faulty diction and sometimes horrid delivery.

Recording dialog using a microphone

If your voice actors are available or if you do some of your own voice overs, Reallusion has included a direct recording option. This option works with the system sound card and microphone. If the computer system recognizes the microphone then iClone should recognize it too.

To record directly into iClone your computer system must have a properly functioning microphone and sound system. Headset microphones can work and produce good quality recordings but if you wish to get a superior recording then good microphones can make a big difference in quality.

The popup **Record wave** dialog is simple and efficient, providing an easy interface to control the recording. Included is a play feature to replay what you just recorded before continuing:

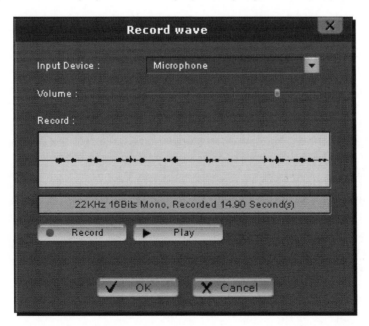

Direct recording might not be feasible for all projects or all aspects of a project but it can produce great results in terms of sound quality, dependent on your sound components.

Inserting audio files

Audio files are the most common method of importing dialog into iClone. The method is straightforward .

Only WAV and MP3 formats are compatible at this time.

We will be using dialog in the next chapter so to be prepared for this let's go over the basics of importing or loading dialog into a character.

The basic steps are as follows:

1. Click on the actor.

2. Go to the **Animation** tab, then **Facial Animation**.

3. Click on the **Open** button:

4. Import a voice file in either MP3 or WAV format.

5. iClone will load the file then analyse it for lip-syncing.

It cannot be stressed enough that dialog recordings need to be in the highest quality possible when the actor is recording the dialog. Quality microphones make a huge difference in lip-sync and other aspects of dialog.

There several great open source and inexpensive audio editing software applications available to fit our needs. My personal favorite low-cost audio editor is Goldwave (www. goldwave.com), and the open source Audacity (audacity.sourceforge.net) is priced even better, it's free!

Some of the more compelling features of Goldwave are the Copy and Paste New buttons that with two mouse clicks can copy and then paste that copy into a newly opened file. This is handy when an actor sends in their lines in one or several large files that require the lines to be edited out into individual files. Goldwave also has good noise filtering, hum/buzz removal, and other features like volume control that can increase or decrease volume. It also has pop and click removal which is present in a lot of PC recordings. A pop screen for your microphone can help to reduce or eliminate that problem too.

Finding voice actors

There are voice actors available and many are willing to work on good projects for nothing more than proper credit. Getting voice actors is never easy but one way to get a head start on this important task is to join a community like The Movies Underground (www.tmunderground.com).

You will find a forum that welcomes casting call threads and an active voice actor community as TMUnderground is a common area for voice actors to find roles and directors to find the actors. Unless otherwise noted these are non-paid roles and some are animated by top tier directors, animators, and storytellers.

The best way to get started is to join the community websites and watch, rate, and comment on the movies at TMUnderground. Get known around the community and post some demo reels of your work, if possible. Let people know that you are looking for voice actors and let them get to know you by posting comments on their movies.

Summary

We covered a lot of features in this chapter to prepare us for what lies ahead.

More to the point, we covered:

♦ Loading and placement of characters

♦ Triggering interaction between a character and an iProp

♦ Modifying the character's physical and facial features including eyes, hair, and teeth

♦ Change character clothing using the map channels and an image editor

♦ Using accessories and props with characters

♦ Basic concept of importing dialog

We now have a scene, some props, and a couple of characters but something is still missing. What could that be?

Animation you say?

Well, why didn't you say so sooner? That's exactly what we are going to do in the next chapter. Animate!

4

Animating the Characters

We are about to embark on one of the most fulfilling adventures of this book. This chapter will begin the process of animating parts of an outdoor scene. This is an exciting part of the learning process, the actual animation of characters and props. If you are new to this type of animation it is quite possible that the processes and habits you form in this chapter will shape the way in which you view animation and go about achieving animation tasks within iClone and possibly other 3D applications.

In this chapter we shall discover:

- ◆ Motion versus animation
- ◆ The timeline, it's importance, and how to use it with key frames
- ◆ Animating characters, hands, and props
- ◆ Character dialog and timing
- ◆ Movement through Point and Click, Director Mode, and Path
- ◆ Blending and editing motions on the timeline

So let's get on with it...

Using motions versus animations

It's very easy to confuse these terms when you begin using iClone. At first glance they seem to be one and the same, but in actuality they are two different concepts that concern characters.

Motions are prerecorded animations that are packaged into drag and drop files that can be used with a character. For example, a talk motion would have the character act out part of a conversation as though they are talking. Hands and body movement along with head movement will all be parts of the motion.

Motions have certain features that can be modified:

- ◆ Speed – Faster or slower
- ◆ Reverse (when available) runs the motion backwards
- ◆ Timing – The motion's place on the timeline
- ◆ Lead In Or Mixing for multiple motions

Motions start as animations. Motions are created through key frame manually, by motion capture (mocap), or by other animation programs, or by a combination of these methods. Being prepackaged has its advantages, but also has its drawbacks.

 While the packaged motions are much easier to use they are limited to what animations they contain until you learn to cut and edit motions on the timeline, and even then there is only so much you can do to alter a motion.

Animations are what we create with the timeline and key frames which can be saved as motions. Props with built-in actions such as a door that opens are animations created in other programs.

Introducing the timeline

The timeline is one of the most powerful and important features and its basic usage must be understood to really enjoy and get the most out of the program.

We can show the timeline for any character or prop by:

1. Selecting that object.
2. *Right-clicking* and selecting **Timeline** from the menu.

You can also view it by:

1. Clicking on the **Show Timeline** button on the bottom toolbar.
2. Then clicking the **Object-related track** button to show the timeline for the selected object.

Or you can view it by:

1. Using the *F3* keyboard shortcut key.

The next image shows the timeline with its buttons and controls:

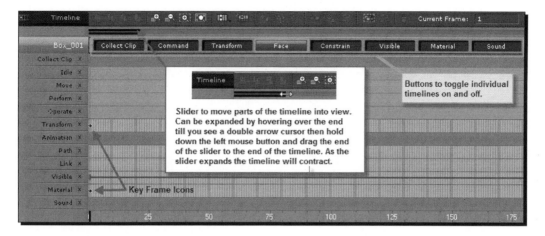

- The zoom feature (slider) as explained in the preceding image can also be moved up and down the timeline to show parts of the timeline that are hidden when the timeline is expanded.

- **Collect Clip**: When this button is pressed this opens up the **Collect Clip** timeline where an area can be highlighted by dragging out a marquee over the various timelines, then right-clicking to save.

- **Command**: Controls right click initiated perform motions.

- **Transform**: Controls scale, movement, rotation, and other physical aspects of movement.

- **Face**: Controls facial movement, emotion, and dialog.

- **Constrain**: Controls the link to feature such as on and off.

- **Visible**: Controls visibility for objects and characters.

- **Material**: Controls changes to the textures or colors of an object or character.

- **Sound**: Controls sound effects and other sounds.

Controlling action on the timeline

Key frames are a means of controlling action on the timeline. If you want a car to move from point A to point B in 100 frames then a key frame will be created in frame 100 reflecting the change.

At maximum level each grid rectangle represents a **frame**. **Key frames** are represented by dark dots in the grid rectangle of a frame. Any action that happens since the last key frame will create another key frame icon at that frame grid. When you select a key frame for editing it will turn blue.

Key frames can be selected by:

- Clicking on the key frame icon on the timeline.

- Highlighting a group of key frames on a single line by dragging a rectangle over them while holding the left mouse button, then releasing the button.

- Clicking on individual or groups of key frames while holding the *Ctrl* key down to select only the key frames necessary.

Any action that changes since the last key frame will generate a new key frame icon on the timeline. We can control animations with these key frames. It is a good idea to keep your eye on the timeline to see where key frames are being inserted as you place or move objects.

Time for action – the timeline concept ... A mini-tutorial

The best way to grasp the timeline is to work with it, so we won't be distracted by all of the props, trees, and terrain. We will work on a new blank project with a simple prop to demonstrate exactly what features of that prop are controlled by the timeline, then we will close that project and use what we've learned in the main project.

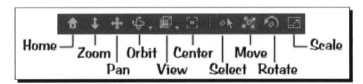

1. Save your project if you haven't already and open a new blank project.

2. Click on the **Set** tab then click on the **Props** button.

3. *Double-click* on the **Box_001 Building Block** under **3D Props** in the **Content Manager**.

4. Click the **Home** key in the top toolbar.

5. Zoom out a comfortable distance.

6. The following image shows the **Box_001** in the 3D workspace after zooming out:

7. If the **Timeline** isn't visible then *right-click* on the **Box_001** prop and select **Timeline**.

8. Select the **Box_001** prop and click on the **Move** button. If the Translation Gizmos are not visible then press *Ctrl + Q* to toggle them on or turn them on in **Preferences**.

9. In the Timeline's **Current Frame** box, type in **1000** to go to frame 1000:

10. Move the box to the left side of the workspace with the red axis gizmo. This will create a key frame at frame 1000.

 Return the time scrubber to the first frame and press play to see the box move across the workspace to the location you chose when you moved it.

11. Move the time scrubber to frame **2000** or type **2000** into the **Current Frame** box.

12. Use the Gizmo to move the box up towards the top of the workspace.

13. Timeline controlled movement is shown in the following image:

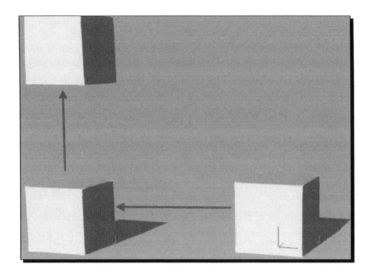

14. Return the time scrubber to frame one and press the play button to review our work so far.

15. Select **Box_001** from the **Content Manager** or click on it with the time scrubber at frame one.

16. Go to the Color Selection boxes on the right menu under the **Material & Texture Settings**. Making sure you are on frame 1, select blue color from the **Color** dialog and click on **OK**.

17. Set the color to the same blue used in the previous step for the **Ambient Color** selector. Leave the **Specular Color** set to white.

18. You should now have a blue box in the center of the screen.

19. Move to frame 1000 either by typing it in or *double-clicking* the key frame at 1000.

20. The following image shows a key frame created at frame 1000:

If the **Transform** line is not visible in the **Timeline** then click on the **Transform** button to open the line.

21. On frame 1000, with the key frame highlighted, click on the **Diffuse Color** under the **Material & Texture Settings** section of the right menu.

22. Set the color to yellow.

23. Now move to frame 2000 either by typing it in or clicking on the key frame at 2000.

24. Set the color to red.

What just happened?

We have animated movement and color change. Save your project and press the **play** button to see the results. The box should move across the screen and up.

Saving motions

To save a simple motion such as we just created you can select the object that was animated (in this case the box) and press the + key at the bottom of the Content Manager on the left side of the workspace when in the **Motion** section of the **Animation** tab.

Time for action – adding basic camera movement

Now let's do some basic camera movement. The camera will be covered in more detail in a future chapter, but this will give you a basic idea of creation and operation:

1. Click on the **Stage** tab, then the **Camera** button.

2. Click on the **Add** button in the **Camera** section on the right side menu panel.

3. You now have **Camera01** created and selected as evidenced by the camera controls on the right menu panel.

4. Click on the key frame at frame **1000** or type **1000** into the **Current Frame** box.

5. Click on the **Box** prop so the camera will use it as a pivot point.

6. Click on the **Orbit/Roll** tool on the top toolbar and rotate the camera to the left, right, or whatever direction you desire.

7. Now go to frame 2000 with **Camera01** selected and move the camera again such as using the pan tool to place the camera in the approximate center of the screen.

What just happened?

We have now animated a camera! Save your project and press play to review what we have accomplished.

Time for action – changing the speed of the animation

While the movement we have created is smooth it's a bit slow for our purposes. The only way to change the speed of timeline animated objects is to shorten or lengthen the number of key frames between the beginning and end of an animation. This is done by moving the key frame.

Right now we have key frames at frame 1 (created when we opened a new project), at frame 1000 and at frame 2000. We need to speed up the movement so we will move the key frames closer to each other. Key frames can be selected individually or in groups.

1. Select the key frame at frame **1000**.

2. With the key frame selected and holding your left mouse button down move the key frame back to the approximate area of frame **500**.

3. Select the key frame at frame **2000**.

4. Move that key frame to **1000** in the same manner in which you moved the previous key frame to **500**:

What just happened?

We moved the key frames down the timeline towards the start frame. These new key frame locations cut our time in half between them so the animation should play almost twice as fast as before. We could also change the speed of the camera movement with the same method. Save your project and press the **play** button to see this for yourself.

You now have a basic understanding of how the timeline operates. Over the course of this book you will find out what can be animated in this manner.

We are now ready to save and close this project and open our main project so we can apply some of these features to our scene.

Adding motions to characters

As we discussed earlier, motions are prepackaged animations that you apply to characters either by drag and drop or highlighting the character and double clicking on the motion clip. In this section we will briefly cover the types of motion and take a look at their editors then get into the actual use of the editors in the project.

Applying motion clips

Motion clips affect the body parts of the actor except for face and hands. From idle to walk motions these animations can be used in complete form or edited within the timeline for that motion. The available attributes for editing include length, lead in, lead out, blending, and splicing.

Adjusting the motion

Length allows you to adjust the action by looping the motion as many times as needed or by speeding up and slowing down the motion. This is accomplished by shortening or lengthening the motion with the loop button turned off.

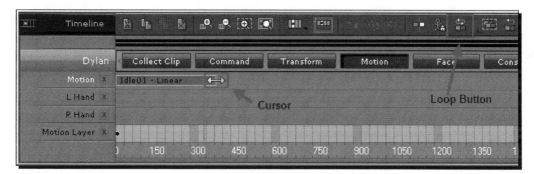

The motion clip is represented by the grey rectangle, which turns blue when selected. This rectangle may be long or short depending on the length of the animation stored within it.

To slow down a motion move the cursor over the end of the selected clip. Hold down the left mouse button and pull the end of the clip to the right side of the timeline. This lengthens the motion which slows it down.

To speed up a motion move the end of the clip to the left, shortening the motion clip and speeding it up.

If you cannot stretch or expand the motion then make sure you have the **Loop** button toggled on at the top of the timeline toolbar.

The following image compares the same clip with different lengths on the timeline:

 To loop a motion make sure the **Loop/Speed** button is activated, place your cursor over the end of the clip, and pull to the desired length on the timeline. The animation will then loop to that point.

Controlling facial expressions

Expressions and facial puppeteering are two exciting features for facial control in iClone. With the **Puppeteering** panel in iClone you control the facial bones by selecting which area you want to control.

You can preview your actions for practice then press record and move the face around with the mouse. These actions are recorded along the timeline for you. This takes a little practice.

This is considered an advanced skill outside the scope of this book and will not be covered in detail, nor is it a part of our on-going project. This is a powerful tool we need to be aware of and practice with after we master the basics and move on to more advanced features as our skills grow.

The facial **Puppeteering** panel is displayed in the following image as this feature is used to select and move various parts of the face:

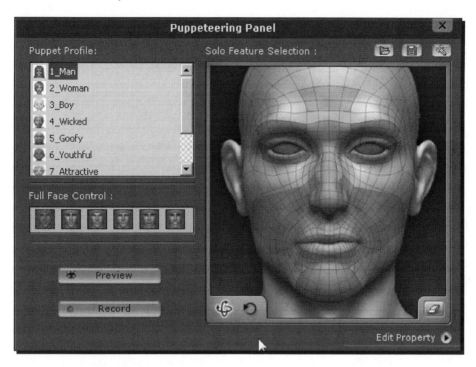

Invoking hand motions

iClone hands is a very powerful feature that is often overlooked by most users. The hands can be controlled as one unit through motions or individual finger control with key framing can be used for more complicated animations or tweaks to the hand motions.

Like any motion, hand motions can be edited through the timeline. If a motion doesn't do exactly what you want, you have the option of using the Motion Editor to modify the existing motion to better fit your needs.

To invoke the Hand motions select the **Animation** tab, then click on the **Hands** button or with the character selected *right-click* on the characters, move your cursor over **Motion Menu** then Hands.

The next image shows the right-click popup menu with the **Hands** selection located in the sub-menu. Use this menu as a shortcut not only to the **Motion Menu**, but to the other menu features as well:

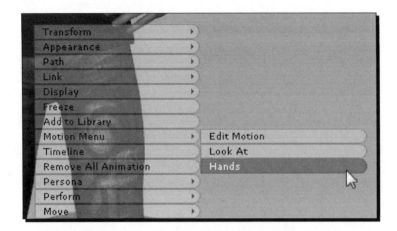

You can also control the finger and hand movement through the main motion editor, the **Edit Motion Layer** dialog. The dialog allows you pick the bone or finger you wish to manipulate.

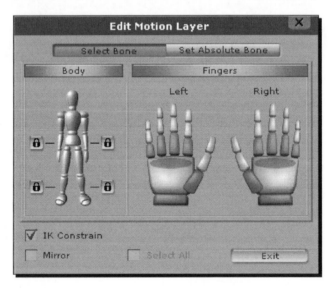

Manipulating character's fingers

The iClone motion editor is a sleekly designed pop-up that allows you to select which bone or finger you want to manipulate.

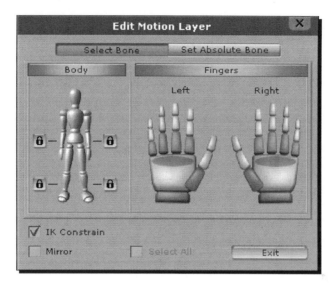

On the **Body** side of the editor you can select individual bones for movement. On the bottom left you will find the **Mirror** checkbox that mirrors movement to the opposing limb. The bones can be manipulated along their axis by the **Move** and **Rotate** tools in the top toolbar.

There is also an **IK Constrain** option. IK (Inverse Kinematics) sets up the bones as a chain where movement on one bone effects the movement of the attached bones. This is another area you are highly encouraged to experiment with.

The fingers work the same as the bones. Select the fingers you want to move and use the appropriate tool to move or rotate them.

Creating custom animation

Custom animation is created with the Motion Editor in combination with the timeline. The Motion Editor manipulates the limbs and the timeline controls when this movement will happen and how long it will take. You can invoke the Motion Editor to alter animations within premade motions too. Now factor in the fact that you can also control an object's movement via the timeline and you can begin to understand how many tools combined together create custom animation.

Using paths to move objects

Paths are another 3D tool with a long history. Paths can be projected to the ground, which is very handy for vehicles.

Paths apply movement to an object such as a car moving along a street, an airplane moving across the sky, in a dogfight or an air race, cars on a racetrack, and small crowds. A character using a path combined with a looped walk motion can be a very convincing background asset.

The physical paths are never visible in the final render even if they are visible in the viewport.

The simplest method of using a path is as follows:

1. Click on the object that is to move along the path.
2. Go to frame 1 or whatever frame you need the action to start in.
3. Use the **Select Path** tool to click the first waypoint in the path.
4. Move time scrubber to the end or to the last frame of the action.
5. Use the **Select Path** tool to click on the last waypoint in the path.
6. Click follow path and orient the object in the right direction.

Boom! Instant object movement.

The following image demonstrates using a path to land an aircraft in a smooth movement:

Paths can twist, curve, and go in any direction.

 In fact you may experience some trouble in orienting your paths when you first start drawing them on screen. Use the grid when possible and the snap to grid when practical.

Use the path edit tools to move and/or rotate the path to match your needs. You will eventually adapt your own methods of creating paths in the 3D workspace.

 For the movement to be smooth use a path. For terrestrial vehicles use the **Project to Terrain** checkbox option to force the path to glue to the terrain.

Now that the overview is out of the way let's have some fun.

Time for action – adjusting the starting frame

Before we get started with animating we need to adjust the starting frame to where the action we want to film will take place. This will help us in maintaining timeline discipline by not allowing us to start any action or prop movement before the specified start frame. We can use the **Range** feature of the **Video Export** panel to accomplish this:

1. Click on **Export**.

2. Click on **Video**.

3. Set the **Range From** frame to **320** in the Output Range section of the right menu panel:

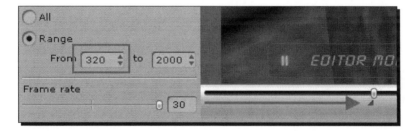

What just happened?

We moved the start frame to a frame that is after the grill lid is open and the male character is holding his beer.

This will keep us in the proper area of interest within the video to start animating. You will notice that the time scrubber has moved forward in the timeline, as has the start video marker below it.

This will place us at a moment on the timeline when the grill is open, and the man has the beer in his hand and is turned toward the rail while the woman is looking at him. It doesn't matter if you are not at exactly frame 320 on your project as long as you have the same conditions when the start frame is set.

Time for action – animating the hands

Let's start with the hands. As mentioned earlier it's an often overlooked feature of iClone. Many a character has been animated only to have its lustre tarnished by stiff hands.

1. Select the male character.

2. *Right-click* on the male character to invoke the right click menu.

3. Choose **Motion Editor | Hands** to invoke the **Hands** menus.

4. On the right side menu, click on **Left** under **Apply Gesture** to apply to the left hand.

5. On the left menu, choose **Hold Stick** from the **Content Manager**.

6. Depress the **Loop/Speed** button on the top of the **Timeline**.

7. Hover your cursor over the end of the motion clip until the cursor changes to a double arrow then move the clip towards the end of the **Timeline**. In this case all the way to the end.

8. Check to make sure the male character is still selected.

9. *Right-click* to invoke the menu.

10. Choose **Motion Menu | Edit Motion**

11. Select the fingers of the left hand and close them down onto the fork handle with the **Rotate and Move** keys from the top menu bar.

What just happened?

We closed the left hand with a **Hold Stick** motion, but we needed to let iClone know to hold that hand motion for the duration of the clip. To accomplish this task we depressed the **Loop** button in the **Timeline** and expanded the end of the Hold Stick clip to the end of the timeline.

We then went into the **Motion Editor** for the Hands and manipulated the fingers until they fit the current prop.

When we initially load a Hand motion there will be no looping so the motion is lost very quickly. To make sure that the motion plays long enough we add the looping by depressing the **Loop** button on the timeline and dragging out the end of the clip to whatever length we need before we change the hand pose again. In this case we need to extend it to the end of the clip. For animated gestures you may want to stretch the motion out to slow it down to a more realistic speed.

The following image shows the before and after results of adding the Hold Stick motion and adjusting the hand and fork position:

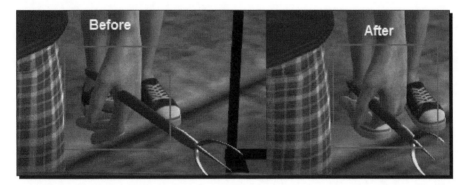

Customizing animation using the motion editor

Perhaps the most difficult aspect of any animation project, character animation has been steadily evolving into a skill that almost anyone can learn. Gone are the days of taking months to years to acquire animation skills and thanks to real time animation programs such as iClone we can all be animators to various degrees.

Even with all the tools we have available to us, character animation still takes the most time and skill to achieve. We are not going to become top animators overnight nor is this book going to teach you advanced techniques, but we are going to learn how to do the basics of interaction and movement.

As always timing is very important in character animation and as such the timeline will become an indispensable tool. We will work with key frames and the Motion Editor to customize or create animation for our project.

The immediate goal is to have the male character set down the beer then turn to the grill. After checking the fire in the grill he will close the lid and the female character will watch.

Time for action – animating the male character

The sequence of events will start with setting the beer down.

1. Select the male character.

2. Select the Beer in the character's hand.

3. *Right-click* on Beer iProp and choose **Operate | Put** to place the beer back on the handrail of the porch.

What just happened?

We used the Beer iProp right click menu to trigger the built-in character motion to put down the beer. The Beer iProp goes back to the original place it was located before we had the character pick it up in an earlier chapter. This is how the script driven action knew where to place the beer.

 You must always click on the character first then the iProp when triggering the perform function from the iProp's right click menu.

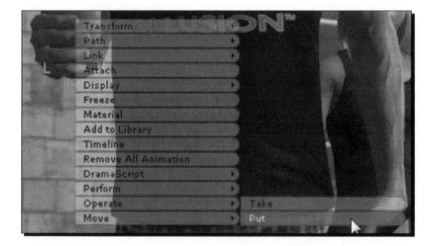

Turn the character

We now need to turn the character towards the grill. In many cases some would actually animate the turn with a full screenshot showing the character twisting at the hips, but we are going to use a half screenshot that shows only the actors upper torso. In the next action section we will then rotate the character, which is a much easier task. This is using the camera to mask the lack of some difficult animation.

How far do we go in animating a sequence of events?

In animation it's not so much mimicking or reproducing a sequence of events as it is giving the viewers the impression that action or movement happened. Judicious use of camera angles and key framed movement can go a long way towards selling the audience on an event without actually animating the entire event.

Keep it simple when possible.

While we know that the body twists and other motions will be made when a person turns towards an object do we necessarily have to animate all that? Why not frame the camera angle tightly and key frame a simple turn using the **Rotation** tool instead of getting bogged down in the tedious work of key framing individual limbs which could take hours?

If that is what it takes to sell that scene then by all means animate the entire movement with full body camera angles, but in our case we just need a simple movement to accomplish our task. Never sell your screenshot by taking the easy way out that would hurt quality, but also look for ways to accomplish your task without getting bogged down in too much work. Creativity can plummet when animating too many details becomes a tedious chore.

Time for action – animating the turn

We are not going to worry about the camera angle at this point. We are just going to rotate our character. We will fine tune the rotation when we get to the camera chapter because the final adjustments will be camera angle dependent.

1. Select the character.

2. Select the **Rotation** tool from the top toolbar.

3. Rotate the character towards the grill.

4. Open the **Timeline** for the character by *right-clicking* on character and selecting **Timeline** or clicking the **Timeline** button on the bottom control panel.

5. Click on the **Object-related track** button on the **Timeline** top toolbar.

6. Using the **Object-related track** button on the timeline as shown in the next screenshot ensures that we will see the timeline for the selected object instead of another scene object:

7. Hold the *Shift* key down and left-click or drag a box around both key frames. We want to select both of the key frames to move at one time.

8. The next image shows the two keyframes highlighted together to be moved down the timeline:

9. Move both key frames by sliding them down the **Timeline** to around frame **500**. Just make sure you have slid them past the time the male character is setting down the beer.

10. The following image shows the same keyframes after being moved down the timeline so the turn will start at the proper time:

What just happened?

First we selected and rotated the male character towards the grill. Then we adjusted the timing of the turn to start after the Beer iProp is set down on the porch rail.

In this case the turning action starts at frame 319 and ends at frame 459. We highlighted both key frames and moved them down the timeline to span from frame **511** to frame **651**.

At this point the male character should set the beer down on the handrail and turn towards the grill. Don't worry about any rough transitions or problems with the beer can action script. The can may jump from the hand to the rail. This will be masked out by our camera angle later.

The AML markup language in iClone is in its infancy and has some drawbacks to its use, but it is a great starter motion at any rate. We can smooth the motion with manual animation or we can mask it with camera angles as we will in this case.

Selecting multiple frames

Key frames can be selected individually, grouped with the *Ctrl* key, or selected as a group of key frames by holding the left mouse button down and dragging a box around the multiple keys on the timeline then releasing the left mouse button.

The next image shows the male character after setting down the beer on the deck railing and turning towards the grill:

Time for action – closing the grill cover

Now we need to close the grill cover, which will require the character reaching towards the cover, appearing to grasp the handle and closing the cover. We will accomplish this by triggering the Close Top animation on the grill and then matching the character's movements to that action:

1. Select the male character.

2. *Right-click* on the male character and choose **Motion Menu | Edit Motion.**

3. The following image displays the character right-click menu and the **Edit Motion Layer** popup:

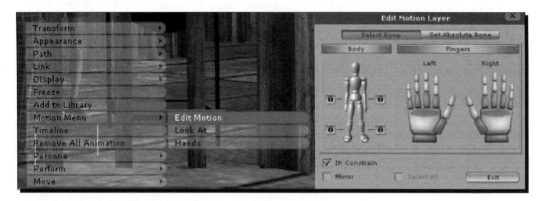

4. In the **Edit Motion Layer** window select the upper body by clicking on it.

5. Next select the **Rotate** tool in the upper toolbar.

6. The **Move** and **Rotate** tools are highlighted in the following image:

What just happened?

We selected our male character, invoked the right-click menu, then selected the **Edit Motion** option from the **Motion** menu to invoke the **Edit Motion Layer** popup. We are ready to proceed with direct limb manipulation, but first we will discuss some movement basics.

Animating the limbs

The Motion Editor (**Edit Motion Layer** window) is a far more powerful tool than it first appears to be. We will use this tool to move different axes of the limbs and in the 3D space that means it covers a lot of movement.

> The **Rotate** tool works on all three axes. With the character's limb selected, *right-click* to change between the three axes. Each axis will have its own color coded rotation gizmo; however, this gizmo only works on one axis at a time.

You move the axis by selecting the gizmo while holding down your left mouse button and then moving your mouse or using the wheel on your mouse if so equipped.

Invoking the Rotate Tool Axis

If a rotate tool axis does not appear when the **Motion Editor** is invoked, **Rotate** will need to be selected from the top toolbar. In some cases you may have to click on the body part to see the axis if the **Rotate** tool is already selected.

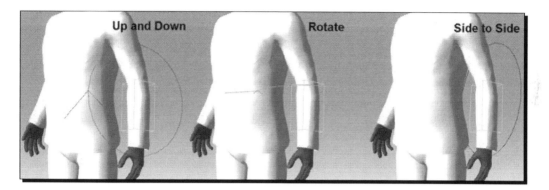

Working with the limbs of characters will take some thought as to how to get the character into a pose. You must keep an open mind and focus on the fact that you are working in three dimensional space. You may need to move an arm up to reach a certain point, but in mimicking human movement you may need to bend the forearm at the elbow and swivel it in or out and then up or down to reach your target.

It depends on the motion being used and if there will be any collisions between the body part and the prop. If at all possible we do not want the elbow or arm going through (colliding with) any part of the grill.

Setting the starting point key frame

Before we move the arm we need to set a new key frame 50 to 100 frames in front of the frame that starts the arm movement. Otherwise the character will start moving his arm too soon and the timing will be off.

Pick a key frame *after* the character sits down the beer and finishes his turn towards the grill. Make sure that he has completed all the previous animations so the new movement will not interfere with them. There will be times when we will want to trigger animations while another animation is already playing, but in this case we are keeping it simple to learn the concept.

Every animation you create has a starting point and an ending point. We always designate our ending point when we animate the movement. That automatically creates a key frame, but we do not have to set our starting point; this can lead to trouble and unexpected results if you do not get into the habit of setting a starting point key frame.

A starting point key frame is essentially a snapshot of what is taking place at that moment on the timeline. Only action after that starting point will change.

- *Double-click* on a blank key frame to generate a new key frame (starting point). In this example it is around frame **650**.

- The double-click places a key frame marker which stops any movement after that key frame from affecting movement before that key frame, and vice-versa.

- The red boxed key frame shown in the following image is the key frame we created with the double-click:

- With the male character selected, click on the upper torso and swivel it slightly down towards the grill. Nothing drastic. Try to keep it looking natural:

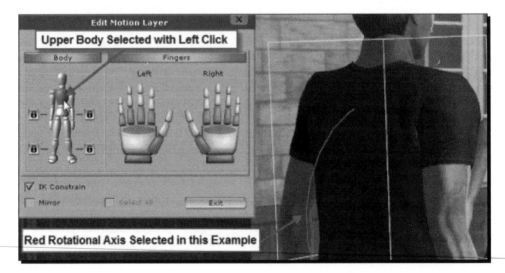

What just happened?

We first created a starting point for the torso to swivel down. Then we actually swivelled the upper torso down towards the grill.

As soon as we swivelled the torso a new key frame was created on the timeline, just as happens with all movements. This movement initiates the entire sequence of closing the grill.

Time for action – animating the arm movement

We have our starting key frame set so we need to move down the timeline and manipulate the arm:

1. Move **50** to **100** frames down the **Timeline** with the scrubber to a blank frame. We will execute the arm movement from this point. This key frame can be adjusted later if necessary.

     Whatever you have to do, DO NOT MOVE THE ACTOR FROM ITS PHYSICAL LOCATION. We don't want to move the actor because that would cause the actor to slide around on playback. You can use *Ctrl + Z* to undo if you accidentally move the actor.

2. Select the upper right arm. We will be using the rotate tool move it towards the grill handle. Don't worry about getting the hand on the grill handle at this point, just move it to its approximate position near the handle without modifying or moving the grill.

3. With the Red axis selected (right-click to change axis) move the arm up.

4. Right-click twice for the Blue axis then rotate the arm away from the character body.

5. Right-click twice to get to the Green axis and roll the arm down to get the hand into the proper position.

6. The following image shows the red key frame we created with the double-click and the blue key frame we created manually:

What just happened?

Moving the upper body down and the arm up has given us some closure on the grill handle. Don't rotate the body too low or you will be short of your target. Rotate the upper arm too high and we will lose the natural look.

It's time to make more adjustments to the position of our props. We want to move the grill closer and scale it down. We will move the grill into place at our current position on the timeline so we can see where it needs to go.

Time for action – scaling and moving the grill

We want to make sure we are past all the previous animations and motions. In our example frame 700 was chosen as it is several frames after we animated the male character's arm:

1. Move the grill closer to the male character using the **Move** tool.

2. Scale the grill down for a better fit with the **Scale** tool or use direct entry with the input boxes under the **Scale** section of the right menu. Use your best judgement.

What just happened?

By moving and scaling the grill we can get it into a position with the handle of the grill just below the male character's hand, as referenced in the following image:

Time for action – copying and pasting the key frame

We will now copy this key frame and paste it to frame 1 on the grill timeline so the grill will be in the proper position when the scene starts:

1. With grill selected click on the key frame we just created when we moved and scaled the grill.

2. Click on the **Copy** button on the timeline.

3. Click on the key frame at frame 1 (it will turn blue when selected) and click on the **Paste** button on the timeline to paste the copied key frame over the first key frame.

4. Click on the key frame we created when we moved and scaled the grill (in this case frame **700**) and press the *Delete* key to delete that key frame, as it is no longer needed after we pasted a copy of it to frame 1.

What just happened?

Had we gone back to frame 1 to move and scale the grill, the character would have been out of place as it was facing the other direction at that time. As we do not want the grill to move and scale down while the animation is playing, we must paste a copy of the frame we just created to frame 1 on the grill's timeline.

In this project our rendered animation will not start at frame one, but will start at frame 320 when the male character sets the beer down and turns toward the grill. Props and characters may be out of place on any frame before this starting point, but it doesn't matter as we are only going to render from frame 320 forward.

Now we are ready to close the grill with its built in animation and animate the character's hand to mimic the closing.

Time for action – closing the grill

We need to move down the timeline to select a spot to close our grill. Choose a frame that after all the animations to this point, has played to completion. In our example that was frame 700:

1. Move the timeline scrubber to frame **700** or the frame you chose to start closing the grill cover.

2. Select the grill and *right click* on it to invoke the menu.

3. Select **Close Top** from the **perform** section.

> Do not advance any further down the timeline to start this motion or the timing will be off.

4. Select the male character.

5. *Right click* on the male character to invoke the right click menu and select **Motion Menu | Edit Motion**.

6. Make sure the **IK Constraint** is checked as we will be using this constraint with our move tool when we push and pull on a limb.

7. Select the male character's arm, forearm, or hand in the **Edit Motion Layer** window.

8. With the male selected, click on the **Move** tool in the upper toolbar.

Most of the time we will use the **Rotate** tool with the **Motion Editor**, but there is also the **Move** tool which when combined with the **IK Constraint**, will allow you to select the hand and move the entire arm into position. Or you can select the upper arm to pull back or push forward with the Move tool. Working with the **Motion Editor** will require time, practice, and patience.

In the case of closing the grill due to the proximity of the body to the prop, we will have to use BOTH the **Move** and **Rotate** tools to get the hand and arm into place as the top of the grill closes. As the lid arcs down, stop the timeline where the hand first penetrates (collides) with the top near its deepest penetration. Pull, push, and rotate the hand into a proper position. This can be done with the upper arm, lower arm, and Hand, but you could also twist or rotate the upper torso if needed:

1. Move the arm down to the handle in its closed position.

2. Move the time scrubber down the timeline until the deep penetration of the hand colliding with (going through) the grill.

3. Again adjust the arm and hand to the proper position on the grill handle.

4. Repeat this process every time the hand collides with or penetrates the grill or its handle. Just adjust the hand to a better position each time.

5. Move the arm to a more relaxed state after the grill is closed. In this case it was moved out and back a little to move it away from the body.

6. Move the time scrubber back and forth to identify collision points and correct them until you are satisfied.

What just happened?

As the grill was closing we moved the arm and hand to the approximate areas that would match the grill handle location. We are not trying to make a perfect animation here. We are just trying to learn the fundamentals so don't worry about getting it perfect and concentrate on understanding the concepts being discussed.

You can always delete the key frame that you just created if you don't like the outcome and want to try again. Select the key frame and press the *Delete* key then have another go at it.

Remember to always save your project before attempting anything difficult so you can start over by reloading the file without losing all your previous work should you find yourself past a point of no return, which happens to most of us eventually. Use as many key frames as necessary, but try to limit them to as few as possible to simply any final modifications to the animation.

The following image shows the stages of correcting the arm/hand position as the top closes:

 Create the first and last key frames. Then fill in the middle as you find collisions and/or penetrations. Make as many adjustments as necessary to the key frames you created to keep the hand in the proper position.

Time for action – finishing out the movement

1. With the male character selected right click and open the **Motion Editor** if it's not already open.

2. Select the upper body of the character and swivel it up to a straighter posture as shown in the following image:

What just happened?

We added one final touch to the male character's movement by straightening the character from the forward leaning position we placed him in earlier.

Save your project and pat yourself on the back. You've earned it as you just completed some difficult concepts to grasp in 3D animation and working with iClone in particular.

Blending motions

Blending motions is just as the term describes. Mixing together multiple motions or parts of multiple motions to create a single motion is what blending is all about.

So far we have discovered that motions can be:

◆ Shortened or lengthened to speed them up or slow them down.

◆ Looped for longer playing animation.

In addition to these actions motions can also be:

◆ Edited to use only a part of the motion. This uses the *Break* button.

◆ Reset the pivot point of the motion.

◆ Aligned and reversed.

Time for action – animating the female avatar

The female character is as exciting as a lump of coal so we need to animate her and give her some action so she won't be standing there like a statute:

1. Select the male character.

2. In the **Scene Manager** section of the left panel uncheck the box in the third column named **Show** to hide the male character.

3. Move the time scrubber to the beginning frame which in this example is frame **320**.

4. Select the female.

5. Click on the **Animation** tab.

6. Click on the **Motion** button on the row below the **Animation** tab.

7. Click on the **Female Motions** folder.

8. Click on the **Mode_01** folder.

9. Click on **Idle_00** and let it play till it stops.

10. Click on **Idle_01** and let it play till it stops.

11. Click on **Idle_02** and let it play till it stops.

12. Click on **Idle_00** again to load it one more time.

What just happened?

First we needed to hide the male character to get him out of the way so we can have an unobstructed view of the female character and to familiarize you with the **Scene Manager** options of **Freeze** and **Show**. We could have used **Freeze** to lock the character, but it would still be in our way so opting to not *Show* it was a better choice.

To finish off this particular movement we also needed to put the male character in a more natural pose after closing the grill top so we moved the arm manually to a more natural location.

We have just used blending in its simplest form. These motions were made to work with each other so all we had to do was load one right after the other to get a smooth string of continuous motions.

You will not always be using motions that were created to work together. In fact and in most cases you will be using widely disparate motions that have different pivots or root. Some will have different tempos or speeds. When you string two or more of these clips together there will be some editing that needs to be done to smooth the motion out and refine the animation.

iClone gives us a great feature to blend two motions with a transition handle at the beginning of each motion clip. This handle can be lengthened or shortened as it coincides with the clip preceding it.

We can grab the handle by selecting the start of the clip and holding down our left mouse button to capture the blend handle as shown in the following image:

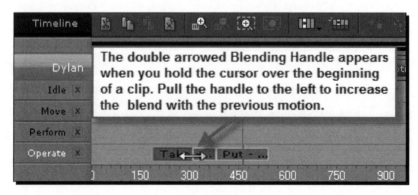

Time for action – add more time to the animation

Before we go any further we need to add more frames to our overall animation length, which can be done anytime. It becomes necessary if we have up to 18,000 frames:

1. Click on the **Clock** icon on the bottom toolbar to invoke the **Time Setting** popup dialog.

2. Change **2000** frames to **4000** frames:

What just happened?

We invoked the **Time Setting** popup window to increase the number of frames in the scene, making it longer to suit our needs. This should give us plenty of frames for what we have left to animate, and if not we can always add more and we can always reduce it later.

Adding more motion to the female avatar

We need to have the female do something besides just stand there so let's look through the female perform motions to see what is available. We'll have to stick to the Mode_01 folder of animations as the other modes are different postures.

Within the **Mode_01** folder of **Female | Female Motion**:

1. Select the grill in the **Scene Manager** and hide it by unchecking the **Show** box to get the prop out of our way for a clear view of our female character.

2. Select the female character. If the **Timeline** isn't open then right click and choose **Timeline** from the female character's right-click menu.

3. Place the time scrubber at the end of the Idle motions. **Idle00** should be the last motion; place the time scrubber at the end of this motion.

4. The next image demonstrates placing the time scrubber at the end of the last motion:

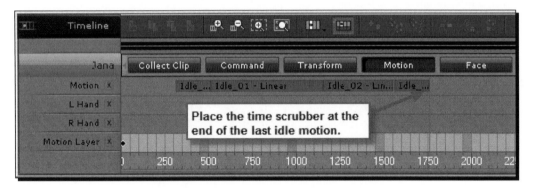

5. With the female character selected, click on the **Animation** tab.

6. Click on the **Motions** button.

7. Click through the Male motion folder and subsequent folders until you get to the **Perform** folder in motions.

8. Double-click on the *Waiting* motion to load that motion next. Even though this is a Male motion it can still be used. You will see the posture change when the clip is applied to the character.

Each clip has a **Blending Handle** at the start of the clip. Hover your cursor over the beginning of the clip until it changes to a double arrow then hold down your left mouse button and drag the handle to blend the clip into the previous clip:

Not all motions will blend together as smoothly as the motions that come with iClone and may require more adjustments in terms of clip speed and blending length of the clips. To illustrate this point we will now need to use the custom motion, Packt Female Idle Motion, which is included in the code bundle available on the book page at www.packtpub.com.

This motion was created with ipiSoft motion capture software and a gaming motion sensor. This will give us a motion clip to blend with the stock clips.

9. Move the time scrubber to the end of the Waiting motion.

10. With the female character selected, import the **Idle Packt Custom** motion clip from the code bundle or drag and drop the custom clip onto the character.

11. Pull the blending handle over part of the previous clip to smooth out the transition:

12. Click on **Idle_00** to highlight it at the beginning of the motion clips and press *Ctrl + C* to copy it.

13. Move to the end of the Waiting clip and press *Ctrl + V* to paste the clip at the end of a row of motion clips.

14. Move the **Blending Handle** on the **Idle_00** clip forward to blend the motion.

15. Press the **Loop** button on the **Timeline** toolbar.

16. Hold the cursor over the end of the **Idle_00** clip and drag it out looping it to the end of the animation.

17. Save your project.

18. The results of our blended animations are shown in the following image:

What just happened?

Pulling the blending handle over the previous motion blends the separate motions together. This is another area where experimentation is encouraged. Save your project and try different blending lengths to get an idea of what can be done.

The custom idle motion was not created to loop. It has a slight jump if you use the loop feature, but we can still use it over and over with copy and paste and the blending handles. If we need three loops we copy and paste the motion two more times using the blending handles till we smooth the motions out. This is being shown as an alternative method of using non-looping motions.

To finish up the female motion we copied and pasted **Idle_00** to the end, blended it and then looped it to the end of the animation. We could also load the clip in the usual manner of highlighting the character and double clicking the motion, but this demonstrates copy and paste as a quick method to create a looping motion.

We created a running string of continuous motion for the female to help alleviate the mannequin look of a non-animated character. Even at idle we still move around and this type of mundane, everyday movement is what adds strength to the overall animation project. These small bits of movement here and there add some much needed action and a little bit of realism to the scene.

Time for action – creating new motions

 There are two distinct methods for removing unwanted animation from a motion. The first method we will cover will be breaking, deleting, and blending motions to create a new motion. Save our working file now under a different name to be reopened when we cover the Absolute Bone method later.

Another great tool that iClone provides is the ability to break motions apart anywhere and string them together to make new motions. The break feature is more than just a place to cut off an animation or to start one. If the tool is used properly, it can combine two or more parts of existing motions to create an entirely new motion or to just trim some unwanted motion from the original clip.

To demonstrate this procedure we will tune-up the female movement a little more. When we added the Wait motion there was a moment when the character glanced at her watch towards the end of the clip. We need to correct that for continuity. That's not a good looping motion.

For one thing she isn't wearing a watch to look at. Sure we could add a watch at this point, but what if you had already animated hours of footage before you noticed this? We plan ahead to avoid these problems if at all possible but sometimes we just don't see far enough ahead or have no way to plan for everything that could happen.

In this case we will edit and remove the piece of animation that has her looking at the watch. This will keep the project moving forward.

Select the female character and in the timeline locate the *Waiting* clip:

1. Move the time scrubber down the timeline until right before she starts to look at her watch.

2. Right-click on the motion clip and press Break to slice the animation at that point.

3. Move the time scrubber down the timeline until she completes her movement and returns her hand to a normal position.

4. Right-click on the motion clip and select **Break** to slice the animation again.

5. Highlight the animation between the breaks (the part we cut out) and delete it.

6. Select the rest of the clips (hold *9* while selecting to group them) and move them forward on the timeline using the blending handle to blend the front of the group of clips to smooth out the transition.

7. Save the project file with a unique name.

8. The following image demonstrates the steps taken above:

What just happened?

We created a custom motion clip by cutting out part of the clip we didn't want to use. We then relied on the blending handles to blend the clips together to create a different motion. Now we need to collect and save these motions for future use.

Building our custom motion library

When you have imported or created a new custom animation it would be wise to collect and save that animation. Reuse of 3D assets is common, particularly in animation. Why re-invent the wheel every project? Build that library of custom motions from the first day you start creating them.

There has generally been a good market for selling custom motions as it is an underserved area of iClone assets. If you are good enough at creating motions you might find a nice little bonus in selling them through the Reallusion Marketplace.

> You need to be careful how those motions were created before you sell them. If they are derived from existing motions then you must make sure that you have the license grants for redistribution of derivative works from existing works. Even free assets can have restrictions on redistribution and commercial sales.

If you key framed or motion-captured the motion then it's up to you to decide what to do with it. Reallusion has gone out of their way to make selling custom made iClone assets an easy option.

You do not have to complete the steps in the methods shown in the next section to progress in the project, but it is recommended that you go through the collecting of multiple clips and saving steps to familiarize yourself with the process.

Saving custom animations as motions

iClone provides us with easy methods for collecting and/or saving our animation work as clips. These methods include single and multiple clip actions.

Time for action – saving single clips

When you have cut out part of one clip and have no need to save other clips then:

1. Select the clip on the **Timeline** (the clip will turn blue when selected).

2. At the bottom of the **Content Manager** are icons for managing custom content. We are interested in the PLUS sign icon (**Add**). Click on it to save your selected motion.

3. Name the motion appropriately.

What just happened?

We selected the clip on the timeline then used the add icon in the **Content Manager** on the left menu panel to add the motion to the iClone custom library and named the motion. This makes our new motion available to us for future use.

When naming motions, use practical terms that are descriptive as you can't always count on the thumbnail to jog your memory about the entire clip. It is also recommended that you create a descriptive folder system to hold the motions such as Walks & Runs, Idles, Driving, or whatever makes sense to you.

Time for action – collecting and saving multiple clips

Collecting involves highlighting and saving a group of merged and blended clips (key framed animations can be collected too). We will collect our new motion and save it. While you could save the entire string of motions we only want to collect the two parts of the Waiting clip that we edited.

1. Click on the **Collect Clip** button on the top of the timeline.

2. In the **Collect Clip** line of the timeline hold down your left mouse button and drag a box across the two parts of the Waiting clip to select them for saving (if you want to save the entire string of motions then drag a box around all the motions).

 The motions you have selected will NOT turn blue, but will be covered in a dark shade of grey defining the area you drew out with your mouse.

3. Right-click within the selected area of the **Collect Clip** timeline to invoke the popup save menu.

4. Select **Add Motion to Library**.

5. The following image shows the popup add menu for saving motions:

5. Browse to the location of your choice and save.

What just happened?

We highlighted and saved a group of motions for future use. This was saved as a single motion. The saved clip is now available as a standalone motion clip. We can select any group of contiguous motions for saving as a single motion.

Time for action – using the Absolute Bone method

 [Open the file we saved under a different name to continue with this alternative method.]

We can remove unwanted motion in a clip by using the **Absolute Bone** button on the motion editor to remove the movement without blending. We could have used this method by itself to accomplish our earlier action section, but we would not have discovered breaking and blending to create unique motions:

1. Right-click on the character and open the **Motion Editor**.

2. At the top of the **Motion Editor,** click on the **Absolute Bone** button to change the mode to absolute.

3. Move the time scrubber down the timeline of the waiting clip and stop when the female character begins to move her left arm up to check her watch.

4. In the **Absolute Bone** section of the **Motion Editor** click on the left shoulder, left upper arm, left lower arm, and left hand to stop the motion of these bones, as shown in the following image:

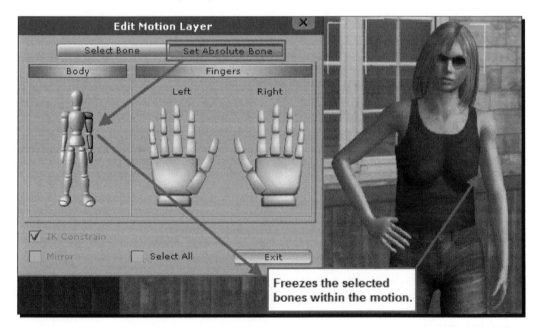

Freezes the selected bones within the motion.

What just happened?

We removed the unwanted watch motion by freezing the bones with the **Absolute Bone** function of the **Motion Editor**.

This may make for a stiff arm, but we can work that out anytime by refining the movement with key frame animation as our skills improve.

Manipulating transitions

Transitions or curves (as they are known in the 3D industry) are a perplexing feature to a lot of new animators until they actually use them, then it becomes quite clear what purpose they serve. The curve itself refers to the method of manipulating a transition between certain events. The events could be key frames as a camera moves from one point to another or they could be prop movement. Reallusion refers to curves as transitions in their documentation.

iClone has taken the mystery out of curves by providing them as a tool, but not requiring us to adjust them as they have provided pre-set curves that we will apply to event key frames. All that is required of us is to decide what curve, if any, to use.

The different types of curves available are:

- Linear (Default)
- Ease Out
- Ease In
- Ease In/Ease Out
- Ease Out/Ease In
- Step

These curves are self-explanatory in their naming. Think of a camera shot that moves between two points in a straight line. Instead of having the default linear curve just blow right on through the timeline, we may want to have it slowly take off, generate some speed, then slowly stop at the second point instead of abrupt movement from point A to B. This is what curves help us with.

We can think of the Linear curve as having little or no effect on the transition, hence it being the default curve.

An Ease Out curve makes a transition between key frames, do just that. Ease out of one key frame before moving on. The combo curves call on an Ease at the beginning and end of the transition to the next key frame. To some users the Ease curves are very intuitive and to others they seem to do just the opposite of what the name implies. With iClone all we have to do is adapt to its style of curves.

Experimentation is encouraged. Use all of the transitional curves until you understand what they are doing so you can apply the proper curve. You can ruin a scene with a poorly used curve.

By now you know we wouldn't be discussing this if we weren't going to need it so let's put these curves to use in our project by smoothing out some previous animation work.

Time for action – polishing character moves

We are going to go back to our male character and add a couple of curves to smooth out some of his initial movement. Please keep in mind that the goal of this book is to acquaint you with iClone, not to make you a super animator, but we will go over the tools that with usage and time will make you a better animator.

Using curves can be dramatic or it can be subtle. Either way it is an added touch of detail that helps to sell your scene to the audience. We are going to smooth out the character's initial motion when he sets down the beer iProp and turns towards the grill to close the grill top:

1.   Select the male character.

2.   Right-click on the male character and select **Timeline**, if it is not already open.

3.   Turn off any buttons that may be on across the top except for **Motion**. Click on **Motion** to open its timeline if it is closed.

> Your timeline will not look exactly like the one used in this example as we all animate a little differently. Even following directions so the key frames will be in different locations and there could be more or less of them than used in the example.

4.   Select the first two or three key frames. In this case the first two were selected.

> **Multiple Key Frame Selection and Editing**
>
> You can select key frames as a group to apply a curve. Hold down the control key and left mouse button while selecting individual key frames. After selecting the individual key frames right click to trigger a menu that will affect all the selected key frames instead of one key frame at a time..

5.   Right-click to invoke the menu and mouse over **Transition Curve** to pop up the curve menu to select **Ease Out & In**.

6. The following image shows the **Transition Curve** menus:

What just happened?

We used curves to smooth out the transitions between key frames. These movements may be very subtle at times or quite pronounced. This is another area where experimentation will pay off.

The common uses of transitional curves are:

- **Key Frames:** In a particular camera movement as the camera moves from key frame to key frame the proper curves will improve the shot and at times may become necessary to produce the desired camera effect such as slowing down and speeding up in between camera waypoints.

- **Motion Clips:** Not only do you have your other tools available such as blending and editing you also have the curves available to further smooth out motion between clips. Curves are very subtle when used with clips.

Have a go hero – experimenting with curves

It's time to strike out on your own again and experiment with transitional curves. Save your project then apply all of the available curves to some of the various character movements we have already created in this project.

Identify the places the curves are used and use each available curve to see what difference it makes so you will have a visual grasp of what each curve actually does.

Animating paths for smooth movement

Whether you call them animated paths or just paths, they are cool and easy to use tools for smooth movement with cameras, characters, and props. Better yet, paths make us all look like professional animators as it does most of the work for us!

We don't animate the path, but rather the path animates whatever is attached to it by moving that object along the path. Add motions to this and you have a lot of possibilities for smooth movement. There are paths provided by iClone or you can create your own path and edit it as necessary.

Drawing a path in 3D space can be frustrating when it's not oriented on some props or the terrain, but as in anything that is three dimensional it can be mastered with practice. Using a path on the terrain is much easier and is another great feature of iClone, as it has a **Project Path to Terrain** feature that does a lot of the heavy lifting for us by mapping the path to the terrain height.

Let's say hi to Benny so we can create a path for him and send him along its way.

Time for action – using a path to animate Benny's walk

First we need to load Benny and place him over towards the right. Then we will create a path for him to use:

1. Click on the **Actor** tab, then the **Avatar** button.

2. Drag and drop the **Benny** character from the **Content Manager** to the upper-right of the screen. Refer to the next image located at the end of this section for placement.

3. Pull your camera back enough to see most of the scene so we can see where to place Benny.

4. Move the time scrubber back to the beginning of our animation, in this case it was frame 320, before the male character sets down his beer.

5. Select the **Animation** tab and click on the **Path** button.

6. Click on the **Create Path** button in the **Path** section of the right menu.

7. Multiple left-click to draw a path to a spot near the gazebo where Benny will stop.

Use plenty of path markers when creating paths

Click as many times as needed to make a smooth path. You can also click on the Edit Path button and use the Move and Rotate tools to edit the path markers. The path animation is usually smoother when we use many path markers to create the path. A corner can be rounded in six or more markers much smoother than it can be rounded with three or four markers. It just depends on what the situation calls for as to how many markers you can use. Don't use a ridiculous amount but don't be stingy with them.

8. Click the **Project to Terrain** checkbox and notice how the markers move to fit.

9. Make sure once again the time scrubber is at the beginning of our animation and select the Benny character.

10. Click on the **Pick Path** button in the **Path** section of the right menu panel.

11. Select the first path marker. It will be a different color (light blue) than the other markers.

12. Click the **Follow Path** checkbox and select the direction if he is facing the wrong way. Try all the directions if you want to see how it works before proceeding.

13. Move the time scrubber all the way to the end of the timeline.

We must be at the end frame for this to work properly and have enough time to execute the walk without being too fast or too slow.

14. With the time scrubber at the end frame and with Benny selected use the **Pick Path** button to choose the last waypoint on the path near the gazebo.

15. Click on the **Animation** tab if not already active with the Benny character selected double-click on the **Cat_Walk** motion in the top motion folder of the **Content Manager** on the left side menu.

16. Right-click the Benny character and select **Timeline** to make sure the timeline is open and focused on Benny.

17. Depress the **Loop** button on the top of the **Timeline** toolbar to activate it.

18. Depress the **Motion** button to open the motion timeline.

19. Hover your mouse over the end of the Cat_Walk motion clip then drag the end of the clip all the way to the end of the timeline to loop the walk all the way to the end.

20. Move the time scrubber till Benny is near the halfway point of the path.

21. With Benny selected (we may have to click the **Actor** tab and **Avatar** button to get the proper right side menu) click on the **Choose Target** button in the **Look At** section of the right side menu.

22. Select the female character for Benny to look at. In the **Look at Weight** section move the **Eye Head Convergence** slider towards the middle otherwise Benny will have a severe angle to his head when he reaches the end of the path.

23. In the following image you can see how our scene looks at this point, with Benny located in the upper-right corner of the screen on the first path waypoint:

What just happened?

We created a path for the Benny character to follow, after which we chose which path waypoint marker he was to be at in the beginning and end of his walk. At first he would just slide along the path. Then we added a walking motion, looped it as needed, and he appeared to be walking along the path.

As he neared halfway down the path we use the **Look At** feature to have Benny turn his head to look at the other two characters.

The path hugging the terrain created a smooth walk for Benny as he strolls by and stops at the Gazebo which where this scene will end.

Pat yourself on the back again as you have just animated a walking character that hugs the terrain. Well done!

Using alternative methods of character movement

The following alternative methods will be discussed, but will not be used in our ongoing project. It is important to know these alternative methods exist so you can choose the method that suits your needs for a project.

Let's use a new project so we can discuss the alternative methods without affecting our ongoing project.

Time for action – point and click movement

Point and click movement is just as it sounds and very easy to use, but like any generic system for doing a complex task it may not do exactly what you want or as smoothly as you want. Invoking and using the point and click movement system is simple:

1. Save the on-going project if you haven't already done so.

2. Create a new blank project.

3. Load the Violet character.

4. Pull the camera back with the zoom tool to get more space between the camera and the Violet character.

5. Right-click on the selected character.

6. Choose **Move**.

7. Choose **Walk_Forward**.

8. Click on a spot on the terrain you want the character to go to, either in front, to the side, or to the back of her present location.

You are now at the mercy of the iClone engine as to how the character will get to point B. You may want to use several of these movements to get to a location, such as moving once to get to the apex of turn and moving again to complete the turn to continue walking to the next waypoint.

9. To mute the footstep sound select the character and go to the bottom of the right side menu panel to the **Sound Track** section and check the **Mute** button.

10. The **Walk_Forward** choice of the right-click menu is shown in the following image:

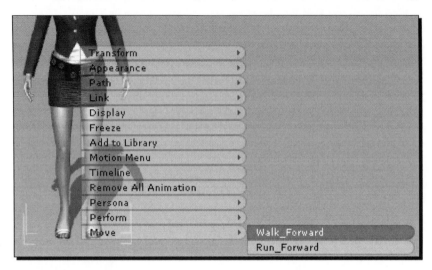

What just happened?

Using point and click we can walk a character over to a specific point. We may find out that we have to move the character through several waypoint choices instead of a direct route to get to the desired location. There is very little collision detection in iClone at the moment, but it is there. You can check the Collision box in the Prop section of the right menu panel, which will force the props to use its collision mesh. If the prop doesn't have a built in collision mesh then iClone assigns a very basic primitive box shape collision mesh.

We are again at the mercy of generic systems, including the collision system so it may take some time and experimentation to use this method, unless it's a simple move across a room a short distance or to take a few steps of movement.

The point and click movement system works great with simple actions and short distances and does work at greater distances, but the results can get unpredictable when complicated moves and long distances are involved.

If you need a character to walk to the front door and open it then point and click is great, but if you need a character to navigate a cluttered living room, office, or take a long walk down the street, then a path can do it for us and in some cases do it easier and simpler than point and click.

Time for action – using director mode

To try this mode you should:

1. Select the character and click on the **Director Mode** button on the bottom toolbar. You will then be presented with a popup dialog window that gives you a choice of starting to record immediately or set your camera angle first.

2. The following image highlights the button on the toolbar that invokes **Director Mode**:

3. Set your camera angle and then start recording by clicking on the **Record** button (red circle) on the bottom toolbar.

4. Use the *W* , *S, A, D,* or the arrow keys (up, back, left, right) to move the character. The *W* key or up arrow will move the character forward, the *S* key or down arrow will move it backwards, and so forth.

What just happened?

Control of the character's direction of travel is with the conventional *W,S,A,D,* or the arrow keys (up, back, left, right). To turn while traveling press and hold the forward key, then tap the left or right arrow (or *S* or *D*) key to turn in that direction. Enough practice with this method and you find yourself able to make many variations of the character turning while walking.

Director mode was introduced to customer demand for those users who wanted to be able to control their characters on screen like a game, with the thinking being that those accustomed to this type of movement would prefer it. It is quite possibly a very underrated and under used feature for producing smooth walks.

Director mode is very simple. After you invoke the mode you use your keyboard to direct the movement of the actor. Like learning a game you do have to practice with the movement keys before you get the movements down smooth, but it's certainly not rocket science.

After you familiarize yourself with the nuances of the key controlled movement you may find yourself using it more often than you'd think.

Have a go hero – using the alternatives

We have just discussed alternatives to using an animated path for character movement. While the path was the best solution for our project you need to be aware of the alternative methods and experiment with.

Save your project and remove the path then use point and click as explained above to move the character to the same area of the scene.

Select Benny and right click to invoke the menu, then select **Remove Animation** to remove the animation you just created. Now go into director mode as described above and use the keyboard to move Benny to the appropriate location.

This will give you a good idea as to how each method works.

Animating character dialog

Character dialog. Two words that are used to bring frustration and dread to an animation project, but it's progressed from being a chore to being a pleasure with iClone's lip sync capability and timeline dialog control.

In *Chapter 3*, we discussed the basics of dialog and getting the dialog into iClone. For our purposes we will be focusing on using imported files, which need to be either WAV or MP3 files.

It should be noted that some wave file formats such as IEEE can have problems with iClone whereas PCM formatted files work great. Some iClone experts such as BigBoss recommend 16 bit Wav files at 48K bps for high quality when available.

Time for action – using dialog with characters

You will find audio files in the code bundle on the book page to use in this example. There will be male, female, and Benny character dialog files in mp3 format. These files are numbered sequentially:

1. Move the time scrubber to the start of the animation. In this case it was frame 320.

2. Select the female character.

3. Click on the **Animation** tab.

4. Click on the **Facial Animation** button.

5. Press the **play** button and let it play for a second or two and press the **stop** button.

6. Click on the **Open** button in the **Import Voice/Add Emotions** section of the right panel.

7. Browse to the location of the dialog files and select **female1**.

8. If you still have your time scrubber where it was located after the import continue on to the next step. If, like a lot of us, you previewed your work and the time scrubber has been moved, then open the **Face** button on the timeline and place the time scrubber at the end of the clip:

9. Select the male character and click on the **Open** button and select the **male1** dialog file.

10. At the end of the clip just loaded, select the female.

11. Click the **Open** button and select **female2**.

12. At the end of that import select the male character.

13. Click the **Open** button and select male2.

14. Place the time scrubber at the end of the male2 clip.

15. Select the female and click on the **Open** button and select **female3** from the audio files.

16. At the end of **female3** motion select the male.

17. Click the **Open** button and select **male3** from the audio files.

18. Select the female and click on the **Open** button and select **female4** from the audio files.

19. At the end of **female4** motion select the male.

20. Click the **Open** button and select **male4** from the audio files.

21. Select the female and click on the **Open** button and select **female5** from the audio files.

22. Select the male and click the **Open** button and select **male5** from the audio files.

23. Click on the female and click on the **Open** button and select **female6** from the audio files.

24. Select the Benny character and load his one line from the audio files.

Tip – Viewing the actors in a conversation

Click off the **Object-related track** button on the timeline and manually select both characters to see the relationship between clips on the timeline as shown in the next image. You can do this with as many characters as you can see on your screen.

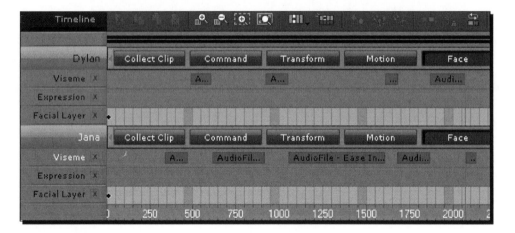

What just happened?

We alternated between characters loading each audio clip in sequence to produce the conversation as it goes down the timeline.

The time scrubber does not always have to be at the end of the previous clip before you can import the clip for another character. This can happen while another character is talking. In fact this is one way to produce tension in a conversation by having one character step on the end of another character's line.

Audio tip – Short Lead ins are problematic

There can be problems with very short phrases or one word pieces of dialog if they do not contain a short lead-in of a few seconds before the words are spoken. Some clips will already have this built-in buffer, but some will be trimmed very short, leaving little time between the start of the clip and the first sound processed. You might even get a click or a pop on these extremely short pieces of dialog that a lead in should solve. In extreme cases put the dialog file into your favorite sound editor and add a few seconds of silence to the front of the clip.

Have a go hero – adjusting the conversation timing

Time to test your understanding of the dialog placement on the timeline. Move the various clips back and forth till the timing of the conversation is consistent with the flow of natural speech.

And as you have guessed by now, this is another great opportunity to experiment.

It's also time for another round of congratulations as you have now animated a conversation between three people!

Summary

Wow! What have we not learned in this chapter? We have covered a lot of ground and this chapter alone should give you a very good handle on what iClone is capable of in terms of basic animation.

By now you should be starting to get a good understanding of the timeline and what it's all about.

If it's animated through key frame in iClone then the timeline is involved.

If you want a light to dim or brighten, a camera lens change from 50 mm to 35 mm or various depths of field, this can all be animated on the timeline. We learned early on that the timeline is always active, recording every move we make whether we want it to or not.

A general rule of thumb in scene building: *ALWAYS* make sure you go back to the first frame the animation begins with before you add, modify, or move items in your scenes. Strange things happen when we forget to move back to the beginning to change something in our scene and you will experience this sooner or later. At least I've yet to talk to anyone that hasn't done this more than once!

Another highly recommendable practice is to preview our animation constantly. In fact most great iClone animators like BigBoss, Wolf, and AnimaTechnica have at one time or another stressed the importance of previewing our work often. If you are like most of us then you will preview your work so often that its lustre will start to wear off, but don't let your guard down. Continue to preview every change or addition just as you would when the project was fresh.

Specifically, we covered:

- The timeline and how important it is to any animation in iClone
- Linear editing which is how the timeline works
- Editing the hands
- Manipulating motion clips with **Break**, **Loop**, **Collect Clip,** and **Add to library**
- Manual key frame animation (closing the grill top)
- Curves to smooth things out
- Paths for smoother movement
- Director Mode for easy movement
- Dialog and timing

We also discussed the concept of key frames and how important they are to our animations, as well as animating a character interacting with an animated prop and an interactive iProp.

So now that we have enhanced our skills with one of the most comprehensive chapters in the book we can move on to refining our scene. Specifically we are going to dive right into iClone's Particles, which will cover Special Effects. You know FX, the cool stuff!

5

Enhancing Animation with Particles

Fire, smoke, rain, dust, and fog are just a few of the available particles in the iClone particle system. Each particle adds an element of eye candy and depth when used properly.

In this chapter we will discover:

- ◆ What particles are
- ◆ How to use particles
- ◆ Attaching the particles to props
- ◆ Adjusting the particle attributes

What are we waiting for? Let's go have some special effects fun!

 Experimentation is encouraged and vital to understanding particles, how they work, and how to use them. When attempting to do anything for the first time that might be difficult and in particular using particles, always save your project first so you can reload if necessary. This will allow us to be fearless when experimenting with these fascinating effects.

Using special effects (FX) wisely

One of the absolute sins of special effects is overshadowing the story or the message, which cannot be delivered to the audience if focus on the purpose of the scene is lost. The job of the special effects artist is to complement the scene, not to take it over.

 You need to realize the difference of wanting to accurately complete a shot versus showing off what you can do.

Always strive to complement the scene and occasionally when the scene calls for it knock their socks off with your skills, but keep the focus on moving the story forward.

Exploring iClone particles

Particles in general, from Wikipedia:

> The term particle system refers to a computer graphics technique to simulate certain fuzzy phenomena, which are otherwise very hard to reproduce with conventional rendering techniques. Examples of such phenomena which are commonly replicated using particle systems include fire, explosions, smoke, moving water, sparks, falling leaves, clouds, fog, snow, dust, meteor tails, hair, fur, grass, or abstract visual effects like glowing trails, magic spells, etc.

Breaking down an iClone particle

An iClone particle consists of several components:

- Particle: This is the type of particle itself. Smoke, fire, rain, or whatever. Diffuse and opacity maps are once again called on to create the particle. These maps can be modified with your favorite image editor just like we did with the clothes. Photoshop, Gimp, or Paint Shop Pro are popular editors.

- Emitters: This is an invisible box of particles but you can't see the box! There is a bounding box for reference that will not render. We can scale this box to change the emitter or we can change the volume and other features of the box.

- Gizmo: This is the physical location of the particle group within the 3D workspace. This Gizmo is different from the other Gizmo we use, in that it has no handles but represents the location or seed of the particles in use.

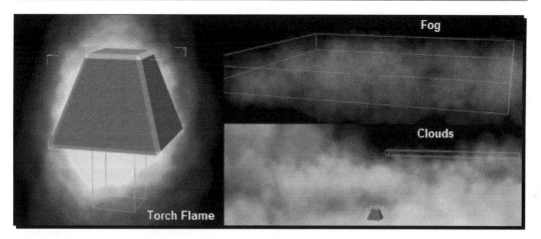

Particles can:

♦ Be linked or attached to other scene objects

♦ Have visibility toggled on and off

♦ Move around in the 3D workspace

♦ Have attributes of the particle adjusted

Extending particle usage

In addition to the usual rain, fog, and sandstorm we can also attach particles to objects like the fire and/or smoke to a missile or rocket. We can attach more than one particle to an object. In fact, we can attach as many particles as necessary, in which case you may want to use a primitive building block object as a dummy to attach particles to then attach the dummy to the prop.

Multiple particle effects container/visual cue tip

Use a box primitive as the container/visual marker to attach multiple particles to. Then we only have to attach and align the box to whatever object the particles are for, such as fire and smoke for a campfire or the flame of a torch. Remember to either check the **Dummy** checkbox on the primitive or set the opacity of the primitive to zero before rendering the video. The visibility attribute is part of the project and turning it off will turn off the visibility of the attached particles too.

Using iClone particles

We have an outdoor scene. The grill is going, the conversation is flowing, and the wind is blowing. What are we missing? Wait! The wind is blowing as evidenced by the trees and live plants, so how about some leaves blowing on the wind?

Time for action – cueing mother nature

Let's add a blowing leaf particle effect to the scene then adjust it to meet our needs:

1. Click on the **Set** tab.

2. Click on the **Particle** button.

3. Select the **Fall** leaf particle found in the top folder of the **Content Manager** on the left panel.

4. Drag the **Fall** leaf particle to near the base of the tree to the right of the porch and release to drop it into the scene.

5. In the left panel **Scene Manager,** click on the **Show** checkbox to turn on the dummy and the green bounding box so we can see where this particle effect will work.

6. Save your project and preview your work to see where the leaves are at and how they are falling.

What just happened?

We added another environmental element to our scene, the leaf particle, in an effort to boost the scene's potential. As long as we don't clutter the scene other animated objects can bring a sense of fullness.

Time for action – configuring particle settings

The effect is a bit overblown so let's make some basic adjustments to the particle settings:

1. Click the checkbox to show the particle so we can see the green bounding box.

2. With the **Fall** particle selected change **Emit Volume** X to 300, then Y to 300, and the Z to 200.

3. Under the **Position** section, enter X=0, Y=26, Z=450.

4. Under **Emitter Setting** change the **Quota** to 1 and the **Emit Rate** to 1.

5. Under **Gravity** change axis Z to 6.

6. Under **Wind** change axis Y to 1000.

The following image shows the effect before and after adjustment. Experimentation is highly encouraged:

What just happened?

We were able to control how the leaf particles interacted with the scene so we wouldn't over power the scene with the particle effect.

We changed the direction of the particle to blow towards the house and we only wanted a few leaves to fall. We changed the **Quota** and **Rate** to 1 to reduce the number of leaf particles falling. Even though you won't see the leaves in many shots they are ready to add movement to distance shots. We'll discuss adjusting particles in more detail later in this chapter.

One of the problems facing amateur animation concerns scenes that are almost void of movement. You can load up a scene with static props but if you only have limited movement in the scene such as the movements of one or two characters, then the scene can seem empty or artificial. It's a balancing act of too little versus too much.

Time for action – coloring mother nature

The particle still looks out of place. Let's change the color of the leaf particle to better match the season and colors of the environment.

This can be accomplished in two ways: we can exchange the leaf particle images for a green leaf and/or we can use the diffuse and ambient color setting to shade the existing leaf particle. In this case, we are going to do both.

We will be working in the **Particle Key** section of the right menu panel. And we'll start by changing out the particle diffuse and opacity images to change the actual particle itself:

1. Either double-click on the diffuse image or click on the diffuse image and press the button with the open folder icon to invoke the popup image dialog.

2. Navigate to and select the diffuse leaf image (leaf_diffuse.jpg), then click **Open**. The images are provided in the downloadable code bundle located on the book page at www.packtpublishing.com.

3. Either double-click on the opacity image (leaf_opcaity.jpg) or click on the opacity image and press the button with the open folder icon to invoke the popup image dialog.

4. Navigate to and select the opacity leaf image (leaf_opacity.jpg), then click **Open**. The images are provided in the downloadable code bundle located on the book page at www.packtpublishing.com. The following image shows before and after the image imports:

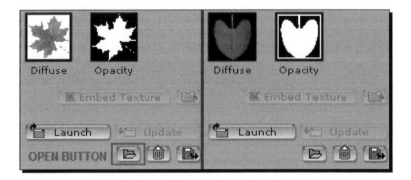

5. With the **Fall** particle selected click on the first particle key marker to select it.

6. Click on the colored square just below the particle keys to invoke the color popup dialog.

7. Pick a light green color for the first marker. We will use progressively darker shades of green to replace the fall colors of the particle.

8. Click on the second particle key and click on the color window to invoke the color dialog.

9. Choose a darker shade of green.

10. Click on the third particle key and invoke the color dialog.

11. Again choose a darker shade of green.

12. Click the fourth and final particle key and you guessed it... invoke the color dialog and choose an even darker shade of green.

The following image shows the before and after results of the particle key. Be sure to *change all four* particle keys. They can be the same color if that suits your needs:

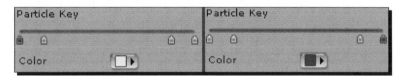

What just happened?

We customized the particle by replacing the diffuse and opacity images and changed the leaf structure and altered the particle. Then we further colored the particle with the diffuse and ambient color selectors. This changed our fall leaf particle color to more of a warm month leaf color.

Attaching iClone particles to props

To effectively use particles we need to know a few things about working with them, such as the fact that particles can be attached to anything except Terrains and Skies. We can also place, attach/link, and change the particle settings to fit the situation.

Let's save our current project and use a new project to learn the basics of particles, then we will work on adding particles such as fire and smoke to the grill of our ongoing project.

This particle primer will demonstrate how to work with the basics of particles and provide you with a cool prop and accessory when we are finished.

Creating a torch

An effective example of attaching or linking particles would be to create a torch with a flame. We will use a cylinder for the torch handle and a particle flame for the torch flame.

Time for action – creating the torch handle

Every torch needs a handle so we will use a cylinder as the base for this handle:

1. Click on the **Actor** tab and the **Avatar** button.

2. Double-click on the **Jana** character to load her into the workspace.

3. Click on the **Set** tab and the **Prop** button.

4. Load **Cylinder_001**.

5. With the cylinder selected, click on the scaling button on the top toolbar.

6. Press *Ctrl + Q* to turn on the gizmos if they are not already on.

7. Use the gizmo handles to make a long, thin cylinder or type the following settings into the scale input boxes (X,Y,Z) of the **Transform** section on the right panel: X=4, Y=4, Z=73. This will be the torch handle.

8. Click on the **Particle** button under the **Set** tab to show the particle menu on the right panel.

9. Click on the **Fire and Smoke** folder under **Particle**, under the **Content Manager** in the left panel.

What just happened?

We loaded a cylinder into the workspace and scaled the axes until we had a long thin cylinder to use as the torch handle. We loaded the character for scale to know approximately how large we needed to make the torch.

Time for action – loading and manipulating the particle

It's time to fit our torch fire particle to the torch handle:

1. Double-click on the **Torch Fire** thumbnail to load the particle or drag-and-drop it into the scene.

2. Click on the **Show** checkbox for the **Torch Fire** particle in the left panel of **Scene Manager** to show the location and range of the particle.

3. With the **Torch Fire** particle highlighted, click on the **Pick Parent** button in the **Attach** section and then click on the cylinder to attach the particle.

 Using the **Attach** feature can create a new object from the attached objects and can merge those attached into one object. Attached objects can also be saved with the parent object, whereas linking is temporary and subject to the current scene only.

4. Click on the **Attach To** button under **Attach** to invoke the **Attach to Sub-Node** popup window.

5. Click on **Positions and Rotation** then click **OK**.

6. With the **Torch Fire** particle still selected, click on the **Move** tool in the top toolbar.

7. Use *Ctrl + Q* to turn on the gizmos if necessary.

8. Use the blue axis handle to move the particle to just above the top cylinder.

What just happened?

We really got the fire going with these steps. We loaded the torch fire particle then attached it to the handle. We then moved the torch fire particle to the upper end of the handle where the flame would normally be located.

Time for action – adjusting and texturing the torch

Save the project and play your animation to view the particle location:

1. Adjust the **torch fire** particle to properly fit the cylinder if necessary.

2. Select the cylinder.

3. On the right side panel click the **Load Material** button in the **Material & Texture Settings** section.

4. Select **Wood04** to use as a texture for the torch handle.

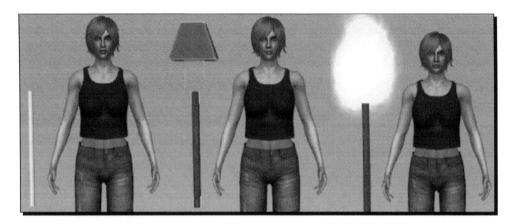

What just happened?

We textured the torch handle with a wooden iMaterial that looks like tree bark and overall we just covered the basics of attaching a particle to a prop. Think about the possibilities!

When the torch is attached to a character it becomes an accessory and inherits the motion of the character. If the character moves the arm then the torch fire will travel back and forth as it moves with the torch handle.

We can adjust the torch fire particle to encompass more of the handle or we can send it the other direction, leaving it perched just on the tip of the handle.

Particles can be adjusted to certain degrees but in some cases they cannot be scaled down in size past a certain point without losing its shape.

The character was placed in the scene as a visual reference for approximate scale which leads us to another tip:

Use a character or prop for scale

When we create a prop from building blocks within iClone we will need to know what scale (size) to build towards. That is easily determined with a character or prop in the scene as a reference.

Even though we can continue to scale objects in iClone they may not scale like you want them to when grouped depending on which axis or groups of axes are scaled. This really becomes a problem when multiple props are merged and we lose the ability to focus our tools on the individual props.

Creating the prop near or at the necessary scale eliminates these problems.

Have a go hero – save the torch!

Attach the torch to one of the hands and save it as an accessory or leave the torch unattached and save it as a prop.

Torch lighting tip

Attach a light on the end of the torch and a light source will follow the character around, moving with the torch. Makes for great ambience in a dark castle hallway!

Better yet... save it both ways! You never know when you may need to combat the darkness of a medieval hallway or a cave in a future adventure!

Time for action – setting up the smoke and fire particles

Now that we've learned how to attach particles let's put this knowledge to use by attaching smoke and fire particles to the grill. Let's open our project file and play with fire!

1. Pick a decent preview camera angle to be able to clearly see the grill and part of the male character.

Review: Home key orientation tip

Remember the home key on the top toolbar represented by a house icon? Click on the **Grill** then the **Home** key for a quick jump to the grill. Adjust the camera to your liking. The home key will quickly frame a selected object in the viewport.

2. Click on the **Scene** tab.

3. Click on the **Particles** button.

4. Double-click on the **Fire and Smoke** folder in the left side **Content Manager** panel.

5. Double-click on or drag-and-drop the **Small Smoke** particle from the left panel or near the grill prop.

6. Click the **Pick Parent** button under the **Attach** section of the right panel.

7. Select the grill.

8. Click on the **Attach To** button and from the **Attach to Sub-Node** popup window select **Charcoals**.

9. Click the selector for **Postion and Rotation**.

10. Click **OK**.

11. Save your project.

12. Click the **Play** button to review the smoke particle in action.

The following image features the particle on the grill with **Show** checked in the **Scene Manager**:

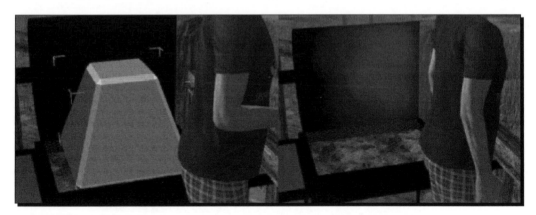

What just happened?

We loaded and attached the small smoke particle to the grill. Then we drilled down into the sub-nodes of the grill to attach the smoke to the charcoals while using the position and rotation options to position the particle for us.

Time for action – adding the fire particle

You know it has to be said. Where there's smoke... there's fire! So as not to disappoint we'll add just that. We will be using the same torch fire particle we used earlier:

1. Drag-and-drop or double-click on the **Torch Fire** particle to add it to the scene.

2. With the **Torch Fire** particle selected, click the **Pick Parent** button in the **Attach** section of the right panel. Click on the grill to parent the fire to the grill.

3. Click on the **Attach To** button

4. Select the charcoals as the sub-node.

5. Select the **Position and Rotation**.

6. Click **OK**.

7. Preview your work.

What just happened?

Just as we did building the torch prop we brought the torch flame particle into the scene. The particle was then attached to the grill, after which we used the **Attach To** button to select the sub-node, position, and rotation of the particle.

We now have a flame but the problem is the flame is a bit too much and looks like it's scorching our character; but before we solve this problem let's test our particle knowledge so far.

Adjusting iClone particles

iClone provides a set of controls to modify various parts of the particle. This is quite possibly another vastly underused and underappreciated feature of iClone.

The particle keys, of which iClone provides four, can be used to shift from one color to another, or to shift from opaque to transparent, and vice-versa. The manipulation of color and opacity teamed together provides us with a lot of customization possibilities. Keys two and three can be dragged up and down the slider to adjust the timing of these adjustments.

Controls like **Softness** will soften out where fog collides with a ground plane or object making the distinct border between them fuzzy. The **Face To** feature makes the particle billboards face the camera so you can use them for above or below shots.

Time for action – controlling the fire

Since we have too much fire, we are going to have to dial some of it down with the controls that the iClone particle system provides:

1. Click on the **Torch Fire** particle to select it.

2. Set the **Life** input to **Min**=10, **Max**=10.

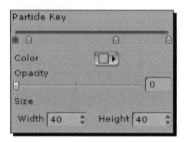

Make the following changes in the input boxes on the right panel:

1. Set the second particle key to **Width**=5, **Height**=5.

2. Set the third particle key to **Width**=5, **Height**=7.

3. Set **Emit Rate** to 200.

4. **Emit Volume** X=5, Y=5, Z=15.

5. Set Z to 0 under the **Position** section.

These setting are highlighted in the following image:

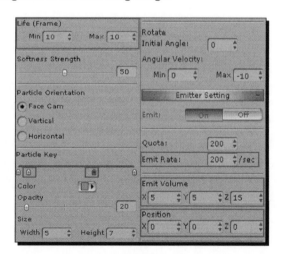

What just happened?

We tamed the fire! By reducing several of the settings we were able to change the flame from a roaring fire to just a hint of fire as you would expect in an outdoor grill.

First we reduced **Life** minimum and maximum frames, which kept the flames from being displayed as long. Then we changed the size and number of particles emitted for two of the four keys. Keys one and four were set to zero opacity and not in use. The other two particle keys were reduced in size on the width and height. After that we moved the particle down on the Z axis to better fit the grill cooking area.

Now when the male character closes the top of the grill only smoke will come out and you won't see any fire. While it is normal for outdoor grills to smoke we'll use the **Visibility** feature to control when the smoke is generated.

Time for action – adding a smoke particle to the smoke stack

Our goal with the smoke and the visibility toggle will be to shut off the main grill smoke when the top is closed and turn on a smoke particle in the top of the smoke stack:

1. Double-click or drag-and-drop the small smoke particle in the **Fire and Smoke** folder.

2. Click on the **Attach To** button and attach the smoke particle to the grill smoke stack.

3. Select the **Smoke Stack** and use the **Position** option, then click **OK**.

4. Select the small smoke particle in the **Content Manager** on the left panel.

5. Change the second particle key to **Width**=13, **Height**=13.

6. Change the third particle key to **Width**=13, **Height**=13.

7. Click the **Off** button under **Emit** to turn the smoke particle off since the grill is open at the start of the scene.

8. We can keep track of visibility by referring to the timeline, which will show when the object is visible. Adjustments to timing can be made on the timeline as well.

What just happened?

We added another smoke particle and attached it to the smoke stack of the grill. We changed the size of the second and third particle keys (again the only particle keys in use) to reduce the size of the smoke effect. We did not change any other settings as we still want the smoke to be thick and rolling.

We then used the **Emit Off** button to turn off visibility of the smoke particle since the grill is open when the scene starts.

Time for action – positioning the smoke stack particle

We added the particle and adjusted its size. Now we need to set the position of the smoke stack particle and set on and off timing for the particles:

1. Move the time scrubber down to a point on the timeline when the grill is closed. This needs to be as soon as the grill top makes contact with the bottom of the grill as timing is critical here. In this case, it is frame 803 but your starting point will vary.

2. Click on the **Show** checkbox for the small smoke particle in the **Scene Manager**. Don't worry about orientation. The smoke will go up with the current settings.

3. Position the small smoke particle dummy towards the end of the smoke stack, similar to the following image:

What just happened?

We moved the time scrubber to the point on the timeline where the top closes down. We then toggled on the particle dummy so we could see where the particle was actually located. Then we simply moved the particle to a likely place for smoke to exit a smoke stack! We may have to adjust the final position later. Moving the emitter at frame 803 generated a key frame on the timeline too.

Using visibility with particles

Another great feature of iClone is the ability to turn particles on or off with the Emit buttons. These buttons are critical to timing with particles, which like the visibility track can be seen and manipulated on the timeline.

The following image shows the particle **Emit On Off** toggle button in the right side panel. Get to know this button well. Experimentation is highly recommended but as always... save your file before attempting anything for the first time!

Time for action – setting the timing for the emitter

Timing for this action is critical but also very simple. We are going to use the **Emit On Off** button to toggle the particles on and off as timing calls for it:

1. Uncheck the checkbox in the **Show** column of the small smoke particle to toggle off the visibility of the particle dummy.

2. Turn the smoke stack small smoke Particle **On** in the Emit section.

3. Turn the small smoke particle attached to the grill (charcoals) **Off** in the **Emit** section.

4. Click on the torch fire particle attached to the grill.

5. Click on the **OFF** button in the **Emit** section.

What just happened?

We set the on and off timing using the emit button to show the grill smoke and fire until the top was closed. With the top closed we turned off the main grill smoke and turned on the smoke stack smoke particle. We also turned off the fire particle attached to the grill so flames wouldn't poke through the grill top when closed.

Using particles with paths

Another fantastic feature of iClone is the ability to attach a particle to a path. We have just scratched the surface of what can be done with paths. As we learned earlier, if you want it smooth, use a path and smooth is the name of the game in animation.

Attach the Shrink or Jet particle to the Helix path and you'll have quite an effect on your hands so let's do just that.

Time for action – creating a magical swirling effect

Let's save our main project and open a new blank project. This type of effect is not needed in the scene we are creating but once you see it in action you will be glad you learned how to do it.

We are going to create a magical swirling effect that can be used on many projects, from magic to animated logo creation.

The assets we need are already provided in iClone so let's get started:

1. Create a new project.

2. Click on the **Stage** tab then the **2D Background** button.

3. Uncheck the **Active** checkbox to turn off the 2D background in the **Image Background** section of the right menu panel.

4. Set the background color to black in the **Color Background** section of the right menu.

5. Click on the **Animation** tab then the **Path** Button.

6. To load, double-click on the **Helix01** path in the **MotionPath** folder of the **Content Manager** in the left panel.

7. Pull your camera back and down far enough to see the entire **Helix01** path.

8. Click on the **Set** tab then click the **Particle** button.

9. In the root folder of **Particle** (left side menu) double-click on the **Shrink** particle to load it into the scene.

10. With the **Shrink** particle selected click on the **Pick Path** button in the **Path** section of the right menu panel and select the blue waypoint that signifies the start of the path.

11. Move the time scrubber down to around 500 frames.

12. Use the **Pick Path** button to click on the last waypoint. This will be the waypoint immediately behind the starting waypoint that is blue.

13. Under **Emit Volume** change the Z axis from 165 to 0. This is in the **Emitter Setting** section of the right menu panel.

14. Uncheck the **Show** checkbox for the Helix01 path in the **Scene Manager** to hide the path.

15. Let's save and then preview our work.

Nice little effect you did there! The following image show the particle as it traverses the **Helix01** path:

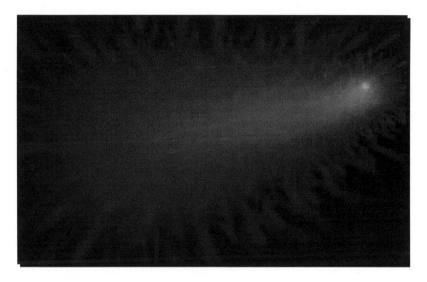

 If your particle only traveled a short distance then you picked the wrong waypoint as the end waypoint. Go back to the end of the path keyframe and click the waypoint on the *other side* of the starting waypoint from the one you clicked originally, or click any other waypoint as you don't have to use the entire path depending on what effect you want.

What just happened?

We combined the particle with the path to get a smooth special effect that would be hard to match with manual key framing techniques.

Simple, smooth, effective... three words that most animators love to hear!

There is also a sample particle project in the default project folder that was installed with iClone you may wish to explore.

Congratulations! You have just reached a major milestone in the progression of this scene and the learning curve in general, so give yourself another pat on the back. So far you have created a scene with sky, terrain, water, props, characters, animation, and particles.

Wow! You ARE a fast learner! Now that you've made it this far, it's time to see what you can do on your own again. Take a shot at the following section. It not only plays off of what we have learned but also makes a cool effect and hopefully will demonstrate just another tiny fraction of what a path and a particle can do together.

Have a go hero – creating a fireball

In animation, fireballs have a lot of uses. Comets, weapon projectiles, and magical or sci fi combat effects are just a few of the uses. With that in mind, we have a very simple challenge here.

Make a fireball streak across the sky!

That's right. It's time to step up and take a crack at creating a simple animation of a fireball moving across the sky and arcing down into the terrain.

The stock iClone assets can provide the objects you need. To get you kick started we'll list the scene objects:

◆ Ball Prop and texture (use the charcoal texture in the downloadable code bundle if necessary)

◆ Path

◆ Terrain

◆ Sky

◆ Some type of fire and maybe a smoke particle

Where to get textures

There are several great places on the Internet to get textures but a favorite is www.cgtextures.com. Read their terms of service before you download any textures.

You can also purchase procedural texture creation software like FilterForge or Genetica. These are great programs but do have a learning curve. Investigate them wisely before purchasing.

While you can do an Internet search for textures you need to be careful of the use of copyrighted material. One of the worst things that can happen is to create a hit video that we can't monetize because we used copyrighted material to which we held no license or right to use commercially.

By progressing this far you have proven that you have the talent and skills to create this scene so take a break from the book project and put some fire in the sky!

Oh yeah... don't forget to save your cool new fireball for later use should you ever need it. If you create a generic path across the sky, then you can save that to Paths for future use too.

Saving prop animations

You can use the **Collect Clip** feature to collect animations to be included as perform motions with the prop for future use. To do this, activate the collect clip button, drag your cursor across the timeline, right-click and select add to library, and save the prop. When reloaded the right-click perform menu will be available to trigger the built in animation.

It cannot be stressed enough to keep a copy of all objects and projects you create for possible use in future projects.

A busy scene makes focusing on the area of interest (the actors or action) very difficult and the viewer could miss an important part of the story by not seeing it in time. Always ask yourself if the particle FX you are going to use will move the story forward or are you just using it because it's there?

Summary

While this chapter might have been a bit thinner than previous chapters, we still covered quite a bit of ground. We even played with fire and didn't get burned! Not many people can successfully make that claim.

Specifically, we covered:

◆ Loading particles into the workspace

◆ Attaching particles to other objects

◆ Modifying particles for our own use

◆ Utilizing visibility to reproduce special effects

Now that we are on our way to becoming the master of particles and illusion it's time to move on to an extremely important and exciting chapter... cameras!

Pop quiz – particles

Let's see how we're doing so far. Time for a particle pop quiz!

1. iClone particles are a billboard type of particle based on what type of images?

   a. Diffuse and Bump

   b. Bitmap and Opacity

   c. Bump and Bitmap

   d. Diffuse and Opacity

2. Particles can be altered by which of the following actions?

    a. Use the Color Selectors to change color

    b. Altering the particle image with an image editing program

    c. Importing new images for the diffuse and opacity maps

    d. None of the above

    e. All of the above

Pop quiz – attaching particles

Let's see what we've learned so far:

1. The following image shows an iClone particle interface button. Identify the button:

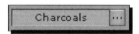

    a. Diffuse Channel Map

    b. Particle Selection

    c. Attach To

    d. Link To

    e. None of the above

2. Particles in general can be attached to:

    a. All objects

    b. All objects except skies and terrains

    c. All objects except accessories

    d. All objects except sky, terrains, and accessories

    e. None of the above

6

Working with Cameras

When iClone first hit the scene, cameras were not selectable and the only camera shots available were pre-packaged camera shots that came with iClone. No custom camera work at all in those days. It wasn't until a later version that free cameras were introduced.

We still have to use a few of the pre-packaged cameras for large scenes or very long shots but we can now create, name, manipulate, and animate cameras to meet our needs.

Looking for that killer shot? Reallusion has made sure that iClone provides us the tools to create just that. Think of using the camera combined with the timeline and one begins to grasp the possibilities.

In this chapter, we shall do the following:

- ◆ Create and name cameras
- ◆ Use specific cameras such as Actor or Face Cam
- ◆ Discuss the lens to set field of view
- ◆ Camera clipping (filming through objects or walls)
- ◆ Use depth of field to focus on an object or character
- ◆ Using the camera switch for multiple camera shots

The best feature to come out of iClone development for a lot of users has been the camera system. It's hard to believe now that this system wasn't always in place. In fact, the current camera system is so powerful in terms of user control that the system is suitable for almost any shot or sequence of shots a director might need. I've yet to encounter a situation or script where camera work became a problem. In fact, iClone gives us the ability to create up to 16 cameras.

So let's move on to an exciting part of any animation project—working with cameras!

Creating cameras

Creating a camera in iClone is a very simple operation so let's get back to our main project and create some cameras to demonstrate just how simple it is.

Time for action – creating our first camera

We are going to use the **Preview Camera** to set our view, then we will save the view as a new camera:

1. Select the grill.

2. Click on the **Home** button on the top toolbar to move the grill into the focus of the preview camera.

3. Rotate the camera until you have the following image:

4. Click on the **Stage** tab.

5. Click on the **Camera** button under the **Stage** tab.

6. On the right side menu panel under **Camera** click on the **Add** button.

What just happened?

We just created our first custom camera! If you look at the camera description on the top-right of the workspace you will see that we are now using Camera 01 instead of the Preview Camera, as referenced by the following image:

We can now select the **Preview Camera** and move it without losing our shot, since **Camera01** will remain in place.

Creating a camera from the current view

If you like or want to keep the view or shot angle of the preview camera then use the above method to create to a new camera to leave in place then switch to the preview camera to work with and look around the scene.

Pay particular attention to what camera is in use. If we move any camera other than the preview camera, then we may have lost that shot unless we can use the undo feature to get back. Whether we want to use undo or not depends on how much work we did in the interim before we noticed we accidentally moved the camera! We can also freeze the camera in the **Scene Manager** to avoid this common mistake.

Renaming your cameras

We discussed the importance of discipline in animation work, and this is another area where a little discipline in naming cameras after they are created will make them much easier to work with than just leaving them with generic names like Camera01, Camera02.

If you only have one or two cameras then you may not need to rename them but scenes can have many cameras and it's faster to identify them by name than to click on them to see the view. When the time comes to learn about and use the camera switch tool we will discover how proper and descriptive naming can speed up that task.

Time for action – naming the camera

It is much easier to keep up with assets by using descriptive names. The cameras are no exception so let's rename our newly created camera:

1. Select **Camera01** by clicking on its icon in the workspace or selecting it in the **Scene Manager**.

2. Double-click on the **Camera01** name in the **Content Manager**.

3. Replace the name **Camera01** with **Grill Right**.

What just happened?

We renamed Camera01 to Grill Right so we can have a descriptive name we can recognize at a glance.

 You may have a better camera name that is more relevant to you but for the purpose of this project let's use the names provided here so we won't get confused when a specific camera is called for in future steps.

Time for action – creating and renaming another camera

This time let's create a camera for a water view off of the deck:

1. Select **Preview Camera** in the camera drop-down box in the upper-right corner of the workspace or select the camera in the **Content Manager** (yes, you can double-click the camera icon if it is in view).

2. Select the grill.

3. Click on the **Home** key to place the **Preview Camera** focus on the grill.

4. Move the camera around to show some of the water, as in the following image:

5. Click on the **Stage** tab.

6. Click on the **Camera** button.

7. In the right side panel under **Camera** section, click on the **Add** button.

8. Double-click on **Camera01** in the **Content Manager** and rename the camera to **Water Shot**.

What just happened?

We now have another new camera. Since we renamed the previous camera this new camera is now **Camera01**, which we promptly renamed to **Water Shot** camera.

We should now have a list of cameras as shown in the following image:

Camera icon visibility

By default, the camera icons are visible in the workspace but are not rendered in the final output. These icons were created in response to user requests to help visualizing their placement or movement. The can also get in the way of another view or be seen moving around the workspace when viewing with another camera. The visibility of the camera icon can be turned off in the **Scene Manager**.

Have a go hero – creating and renaming more cameras

Now would be a good time for you to flex your camera creation and naming skills by creating a few more cameras. We won't be using these cameras in our project but you will sharpen your camera shot framing and positioning skills.

Framing the shot

Framing a shot is very important. So much so that it is outside the scope of this beginner's guide; so when you have a shot you like, save a custom camera for it then go back to the preview camera and swivel it around, turning it this way and that until you have covered most of the available angles. You may be pleasantly surprised by what you discover and end up keeping as another camera.

Using character/object cameras (Follow Cam)

Welcome to a very simple and cool concept, the Follow Cam. The character and object oriented cameras do just that, follow the target and keep that target in the focus of the shot. We will go into detail on the various follow cams but remember that to use a follow cam, you have to select a character first.

Saving the Follow Cam

If you like the particular follow cam shot (actor, face, or bird), create a camera from that shot and link it to the object or character for the camera to follow and you will have a permanent camera instead of a follow cam that is only active when the character or object is selected. The linking action creates an event on the camera **Constrain Timeline** that can be edited.

One negative effect of using a follow cam is that when you see an object which you need to change in the scene, and you click on that object, the camera will jump back to the previous camera shot leaving some users scratching their heads as to what happened. Think about it. It's an object's or character's follow cam so if you click off that object to another object then the follow cam will disappear.

Follow Cam tip: removing the jerky movement

When you use a follow cam, the movement can be very jerky as the camera is parented to a moving object so it will move with the object. To use a follow cam or any camera that is linked to follow, make sure you link it to the *ROOT* of the object or character for smooth recording, unless you want it to be a jerky movement shot.

Using the Actor Cam

The Actor Cam is available when the actor is selected and can be accessed by the camera toggle menu in the upper-right corner of the workspace.

The following image shows the drop-down camera selection menu in the iClone workspace:

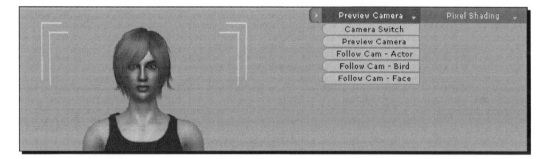

For the purpose of this project we are going to convert our follow cams to normal cameras. We don't always need to do this, however, we need to know how to if we want to keep the camera shot active when we click off of the actor to another object or character.

Time for action – setting up the Actor Cam

To learn the basic usage of the follow cams we will use a blank project:

1. Create a new project.

2. Load the Jana character.

3. Select the Jana character.

4. In the camera selection menu, in the upper-right corner of the workspace, click on **Follow Cam - Actor** (Actor Cam).

Your view should change to be similar to the following image:

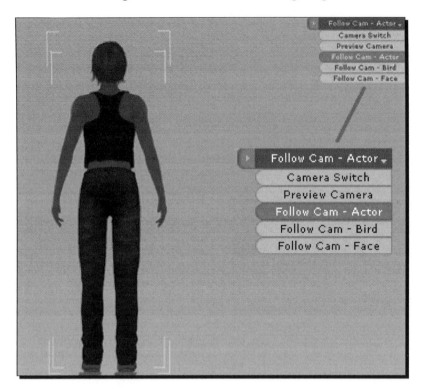

5. Twirl and move the Actor Cam around to see the different angles and views from the camera. Set the camera to a shot like the one in the following image:

6. Click on the **Set** tab.

7. Click on the **Terrain** button.

8. Load the **Community Stage** terrain for reference.

9. Select the character.

10. Right-click on the character to invoke the right-click menu.

11. Choose **Move** then select **Walk_Forward.**

12. Click on a place in front of the character like the grass.

What just happened?

By using the Actor Cam we were able to follow the action as the actor moved. Notice, the camera angle stays the same as the character walks toward the spot we clicked on.

The Actor Cam is a great way to get a close up of the actor in the shot but now let's convert the Actor Cam to a regular camera, or rather let's use the Actor Cam shot to create a new camera with the same view.

Time for action – converting Follow Cam to a permanent camera

We want to keep this shot active even when the actor isn't selected, so we do the following:

1. Click on the **Follow Cam - Actor** (Actor Cam) in the camera selection menu located in the upper-right corner of the workspace.

2. Click on the **Add** button in the **Camera** section of the right menu panel.

3. Double-click the camera name in the **Scene Manager** in the left side menu panel.

4. Rename the camera to **Jana Cam1.**

5. In the **Jana Cam1** control area of the right menu panel, click on the **Pick Parent** button then click on **Jana**.

6. Click on the **Attach To** button in the right menu panel and select **BoneRoot** as the sub-node attachment.

What just happened?

We created a new camera using the view from the Actor Cam then renamed the camera to a description we could understand. After that we linked the camera to the bone root of the Jana character, recreating our own Actor Cam that will stay active even when the Jana character is not selected.

This also gives us one important advantage.

We can now use the Jana Cam in the Camera Switch feature which we will learn about shortly.

 From time to time, the follow cams may break and cease to follow the object or actor for no apparent reason. If this happens to you then restart iClone and reload the project, as that usually solves the problem for most of us.

Time for action – setting up the Face Cam

The Face Cam is the second type of follow cam but as the name implies it is initially close to and focuses on the face. Let's take a look at using this follow cam:

1. Click on the Jana character if not already selected.

2. From the camera selection menu choose **Follow Cam - Face**(Face Camera).

3. Play the animation.

4. With the character selected and using the Face Cam, click on the **Add camera** button.

5. Click on the **Pick Parent** button in the **Link** section and select the Jana character.

6. Click on the **Link To** button of the link section and link the camera to the character's **BoneRoot**.

7. Rename the camera to an appropriately descriptive name.

The following image shows the Face Cam view in our scene with the Jana character selected:

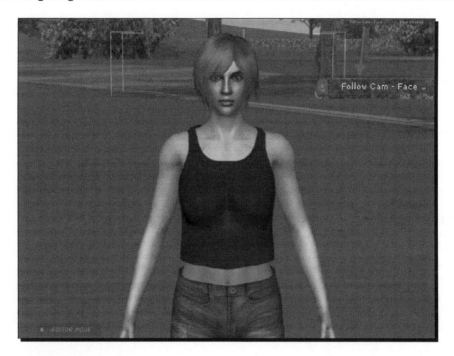

What just happened?

We not only used and previewed the scene through the Face Cam but we also converted it to a permanent camera by creating a new camera from the same view and linking it to the character.

You will notice that the Face Cam is not only focused on the face but is also a smooth camera parented to the root, so when you convert the Face Cam to a permanent camera you will want to parent the new camera to the bone root or root, whichever is available for the particular model.

Time for action – viewing the character from above

The Bird Cam is a smooth camera that views the character from above and to the side.

1. With the Jana character selected choose the Bird Cam view from the camera selection menu in the upper-right corner of the workspace.

2. Play the scene.

3. Add a new camera to the scene.

4. Play the scene.

5. With the Bird Cam selected, add a new camera to the scene.

6. Click on the **Pick Parent** button in the **Link** section and select the Jana character.

7. Click on the **Link To** button and select **BoneRoot**.

8. Rename the new camera to an appropriately descriptive name.

The following image demonstrates the bird view follow cam:

What just happened?

We previewed the scene through the Bird Cam, then we converted the Bird Cam to a permanent camera by creating a new camera and linking it to the bone root.

Pop quiz – using follow cams

1. Which of the following cameras is not a smooth cam as it inherits its motion from the parent?

    a. Face Cam

    b. Actor Cam

    c. Bird Cam

    d. All of the above

    e. None of the above

2. How is a follow cam actually converted to a permanent camera?

    a. Select the camera, right-click and select the Convert button

    b. Create a new camera from the follow cam view

    c. Create a new camera from the follow cam view and link the camera to the root

    d. Create a new camera from the follow cam view and attach the camera to the root

    e. None of the above

Understanding the camera lens

The camera lens has a variable focal length that helps in manipulating tight shots or creating a close up without moving the camera. In fact, using the focal length to move in for a close up produces one of the smoothest camera movements in iClone, since, only the focal point of the camera moves.

iClone cameras come with several pre-set focal points such as:

◆ 20 mm

◆ 35 mm

◆ 50 mm

◆ 80 mm

◆ 105 mm

◆ 200 mm

◆ A variable slider that will create any focal length from 12 to 800 mm

The 50 mm focal point is default for iClone cameras when they are created. An extreme focal point such as 12 to 20 mm will contort the camera view of the scene as it stretches away from the camera.

Animating a camera close up or pull back with the lens

The camera lens can be animated using the timeline. We can set the beginning of a shot to have a focal length of 35 mm and the ending of the shot to have a focal length of 20 mm. This will create a continuous lens movement from 35 – 20 rendering a view that will move away from the camera as the scene progresses without any physical camera movement.

The following image displays the difference in 35 mm, 50 mm, and 80 mm focal points in these series of shots taken from the same camera position:

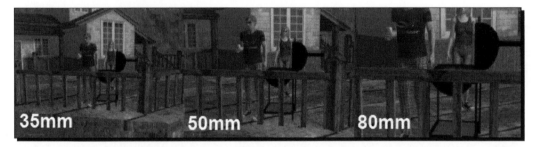

Time for action – creating new cameras and picking the lens

It's now time to return to our main scene so we can set the lens focal point for the best view:

1. Load our main project.

2. Select **Preview Camera**.

3. Select the male character.

4. With the male character selected, click on the **Home** button.

5. With the camera selected, click on **35 mm** button to set the lens.

6. Use the camera controls to position the shot similar to the following image:

7. Click on **Preview Camera** in the camera selection box in the upper-right corner of the workspace.

8. Click on the **Add** button in the camera section of the right side menu panel.

9. Double-click on the new camera name in the **Scene Manager** and rename the camera to **Grill 1**.

10. Select **Preview Camera** again from the camera selection menu in the upper-right corner of the workspace.

11. Once again with the camera selected, click on the **35 mm** button.

12. Rotate the camera until the shot is framed similar to the following image:

13. Click on the **Stage** tab and the **Camera** button to active the camera menu or select **Preview Camera** from the camera selection list.

14. Click on the **Add** button in the camera section of the right side menu to create a new camera.

15. Rename this camera to **Grill 2**.

What just happened?

We created a camera with a shot angle that will show some of the movement of the beer can being placed down on the rail. Since this movement has few problems with the built-in Actionscript, we are using this angle to mask that from the viewer but still show enough of the movement to implant the thought. If done properly the viewer's mind will fill in the blanks. We don't have to animate everything but we do need to create the impression that we have done just that.

We then created another camera with a unique view of the grill. This view hides the lack of animation when we rotated the character but will still show enough of the character to impart the motion to the viewer.

We should now have two new cameras named Grill 1 and Grill 2. We will use these views with the Camera Switch when we set up the final shot sequence in the Camera Switch section of this chapter.

Properly used camera angles can disguise a lot of problems when we first start learning how to animate. Progression of these skills will find us relying less on camera angles and more on animation skills.

Time for action – setting up our main camera angle

When writing this I was tempted not to use the term *Main Camera* as this scene doesn't really have a main camera, but this will be our *go to* camera when we need a good wide angle shot of both characters on the deck. We should already have another wide angle shot from when we created our Water Shot camera in a previous chapter, so this will give us two wide angle shots.

1. Activate a camera so the camera section of the right menu is available.

2. Use the camera selection drop-down menu in the upper-right corner of the workspace or select a camera in the camera section of the **Scene Manager**. It doesn't matter which camera as we just need to activate the camera menu.

3. Click on **Add** in the camera section to create a new camera.

Keeping up with your camera

Always check your camera drop-down box after creating a new camera to make sure you are on the right camera before you move or rotate view.

4. Rename the camera to **Main Camera**.

5. Set up the camera shot so that it looks similar to the following image:

What just happened?

We selected a random camera in the scene to activate the right side camera menu then created a new camera based on the view of whichever camera was chosen. The view didn't matter because we were going to change it. We could have used the preview camera to accomplish the same task.

We renamed the camera to Main Camera to better describe it for future use, then we framed our shot. This gives us a good view of the characters with the house in the background. We will use this shot with the Camera Switch later in this chapter.

Time for action – setting up a lens only camera close up

We are now going to use the Grill 1 camera to create a smooth lens only close up without moving the camera:

1. Select the camera **Grill 1**.

2. Turn on the **Timeline** if it's not already on.

3. Click on the **Object-related track** button to make sure we have the timeline focused on the **Grill 1** camera.

4. Move 200 frames down the timeline from the scene's starting point. In our example, the scene starts at 320 so we will move the time scrubber down to frame 420 or type in 520 in the **Frame** section of the timeline menu. Your scene may vary. We will adjust these key frames later when we use this camera in the Camera Switch section.

 Use the Zoom Slider on top of the timeline to move up and down or expand or contract the timeline.

5. With the **Grill 1** camera selected, click on the **50 mm** button in the **Camera** section of the right side menu.

6. Click on the **Play** button to preview the close up.

 Camera speed

If the camera moves too fast or too slowly, you can speed up or slow down the movement by moving the key frames closer together (speed up) or further apart (slow down).

The following image shows our timeline for the Grill 1 camera with the starting and ending key frames (in the red squares) at 320 and 420, respectively. Disregard the key frame at frame 1 as it is before our scene will start:

What just happened?

We used the existing Grill 1 camera as the basis of our lens based close up. After moving two hundred frames down the timeline we clicked on the **50 mm** button in the **Camera** section to change the lens from 35 mm to 50 mm. This resulted in a very smooth close up shot homing in on the grill.

We accomplished this close up very quickly and easily without moving the camera!

Have a go hero – creating a lens only pullback shot

Time to test our skills again! We created a very smooth *Lens only* close up using the Grill 1 camera which made for a nice shot.

Duplicate the Grill 2 camera and use the newly created camera to create a *pullback* shot using only the lens setting and timeline.

Rename this camera to something that makes sense to you, like Pullback, or if you want to get more technical... *dolly shot or dolly zoom out*.

This will give us an opportunity to learn about creating a new camera from an existing camera and changing some of its parameters to suit our needs.

Pop quiz – testing our lens knowledge

1. Which lens is the default lens of for the iClone cameras?

    a. 35 mm

    b. 200 mm

    c. 50 mm

    d. 80 mm

    e. None of the Above

2. The 200 mm lens would place the focal point further away than a 35 mm lens.

    a. True

    b. False

3. The lens size and focus can be animated with the timeline.

    a. True

    b. False

Focusing with depth of field

Depth of field is a very cool feature that allows us to use a camera to focus on a specific part of a scene no matter how busy or complicated that scene may be. This is accomplished by setting up a point in the scene's 3D workspace that the camera will focus on while blurring the objects outside of that pre-set focal field.

The best part of this feature is that it truly is point-and-click! Make a few adjustments and you have a very nice and professional looking effect that can make a good shot great.

Time for action – creating a depth of field camera

Our depth of field (DOF) camera will be created from a new camera, so let's get started.

1. Select a camera, any camera, to invoke the right side panel **Camera** menu.

2. Click on the **Add** button to create a new camera.

3. Rename the camera to DOF 1.

> It doesn't matter if you put a space in between DOF and 1 or not. This is strictly descriptive for our own use.

4. Frame the shot similar to the following image:

5. Click on the **Depth of Field** checkbox in the camera section of the right side menu. The scene will blur until after the next step.

6. Pick your target and select the grill.

In the following image, notice the sharp contrast between the characters and the grill versus the blur of their surroundings. This is depth of field in action:

What just happened?

We just created an advanced camera effect! We set the focus of the depth of field on the grill which was near the characters in the scene. This made these characters and the grill come into focus with everything else remaining blurred.

The grill was chosen strictly for its proximity to the scene's characters to bring both of them into the focal point of the scene. Had one of the characters remained outside of the focal point we would have made adjustment to the DOF settings till it was inside.

Have a go hero – exploring depth of field

Save your project and use the newly created DOF camera to experiment with its settings in the right side control panel. Experiment with focus and range. Click on different parts of the scene with the **Pick Target** button to demonstrate its effects.

The following image shows the depth of field control panel in the **Camera** section of the right side menu. Like almost all of iClone, the menu is context sensitive so a camera needs to be selected before the camera controls become available:

Picking a target creates an event on the timeline that can be controlled. The target and the timing can be manipulated like any other event on the timeline.

When you are finished, reload the project you saved before you started experimenting. This will put us back on track for the next section.

Creating more cameras

In order to have enough cameras for our Camera Switch section, we need to create more cameras for different shots. Mainly, we need to set up a follow cam on Benny for his stroll and a good wide angle shot of Benny and the house with our two other characters.

Time for action – creating the Benny cams

1. Select the Benny character from the **Avatar** section of the **Scene Manager**.

2. Select the Actor Cam from the camera selection menu in the upper-right corner of the workspace.

3. Click on the **Home** button to home in on Benny with the preview camera.

4. Frame the shot similar to the following image:

5. Click on the **Add** button in the camera section of the right side menu to create a new camera.

6. Rename the camera to **Benny Cam1**

7. Link the camera to Benny with the **Pick Parent** button.

8. Click on the **Link To** button and select the **BoneRoot**.

What just happened?

We used the built-in Actor Follow Cam as the basis for this new Benny cam. We linked the new camera to Benny and linked specifically to the bone root, so the camera won't inherit the character's motion as he walks but will follow Benny as he strolls along.

The resulting camera is the same as the Actor Cam it replaced but this camera is permanent and is available even when the character is not selected.

As always we renamed the camera so we could keep up with our camera shots at a glance. Now that we have created several cameras you can understand why we rename them.

Time for action – creating a wide angle camera shot

We need a wide angle shot so we can see Benny, the house, deck, and the two other characters at the same time:

1. With **Benny Cam1** still selected, click on the **Add** button in the **Camera** section of the right side menu to create another camera.

2. Rename this camera to **Wide Angle 1**.

3. Frame the shot similar to the following image:

What just happened?

We used the newly created **Benny Cam1** as the basis for our new camera that we reframed and renamed to **Wide Angle 1**.

The new camera gives us a great wide angle shot of the house, the deck ,and all the characters as well as the gazebo we made from building blocks.

We should now have several new custom cameras to use with our Camera Switch section, as shown in the following image:

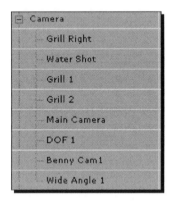

We will be using all of these new cameras with the Camera Switch.

Selecting cameras for filming

The **Camera Switch** is a very powerful tool that allows us to pick the camera we want for filming at any time on the timeline. This tool switches to and from the cameras selected as their markers are reached on the timeline.

Each little triangle tick mark on the **Switcher** line is where a camera becomes active and begins to film from its point of view. As you can see in the following screenshot, there are several camera views set up in the **Switcher** line of the example:

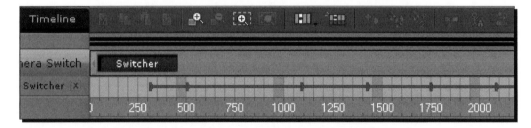

We will learn how to use this tool and switch between custom camera shots for an interesting and flowing scene.

> **Convert follow cams for use in Camera Switch**
>
> The follow cams *are not available* in the **Camera Switch** tool so convert the follow cams to normal cameras by creating new cameras from the follow cam views. Do not forget to link your new cameras to the subject or they won't follow the subject.

Creating a shot list

No... not a short list but a shot list! Just as the name implies, this is a list of shots and the order in which those shots are used. In a commercial project, the shot list is usually provided by the director of photography, the principal photographer, or the creative director. This list is created with a lot of input from the director and the creative team.

Guess who creates this list in most of our projects with iClone? That's right... us! We don't have the luxury of having a list handed to us if we are working on our own project late at night after the kids are in bed and the spouse has given up on any attempt to communicate with us. Maybe if they followed this guide and used iClone to create a video clip then we would pay attention, but they would still need a shot list!

In this case, the shot list will be used to set up the camera switch. In fact, we can think of the camera switch as an animated shot list.

Imagine the scene in your mind as we go through the timeline. Which shot will work better for the first shot,...the last shot, and so forth.

In this case we will set up our shot list as follows:

1. Grill 1
2. Grill 2
3. Main Camera
4. Water Shot
5. DOF 1
6. Grill Right
7. Benny Cam1
8. Wide Angle

Before we go any further, we need to discuss the fact that a shot list doesn't have to be set in stone but can be used as a guide to getting started. We may very well find out that a different sequence of shots gives us a better scene but we need to start somewhere, so writing out our shot list either on paper or in Notepad will help with the task, especially when several cameras are involved.

We do not have to create our shot list first, but I never worked on a commercial project that did not have a shot list created before work started. We will most likely create this shot list when brainstorming or planning out the project in its very early stages but for the purpose of this beginners guide we are discussing it this late in the project to introduce the concept in a more orderly flow.

Understanding camera cuts and timing

When to cut away from one camera to another and timing between camera changes are very critical and important factors when using the camera switch. The success of any scene with multiple cameras can hinge on these factors. Time spent setting up your camera switch is always time well spent and certainly makes for a better production.

Time for action – setting up the camera switch

We are now going to set up multiple camera shots as the scene progresses using the Camera Switch:

1. Click on the **Timeline** button in the bottom toolbar of the main workspace to make it visible if it's not already.

2. Make sure the **Object-related track** button is clicked OFF.

3. Click the **Track list** button on the **Timeline** toolbar to open the **Track list** menu.

4. Select **Camera Switch** from the menu choices.

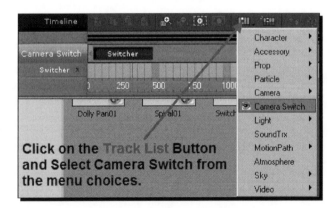

Click on the Track List Button and Select Camera Switch from the menu choices.

5. Click the **Switcher** button to open its **Timeline**.

6. Make sure the time scrubber is set all the way back to the start of the scene, which in this case is frame 320.

7. Right-click on the red line in the timeline at frame 320 and choose **Camera List** and select the first camera in our list, **Grill 1**, as the starting camera.

8. Play the scene or move the time scrubber until just after the male character sets the beer can down. In this case it was around frame 485.

9. Right-click on the red line again in the timeline and select our next camera in the shot list, **Grill 2**.

10. Play the scene until our character closes the top of the grill. This was frame 888 in our example.

11. Right-click on the red line in the timeline again and choose **Main Camera**.

12. Play the scene or move the time scrubber down 200 frames.

13. Right-click on the red line in the timeline and choose the **Water Shot** camera

14. Move the time scrubber or play down another 300 frames.

15. Right-click on the red line in the **Timeline** and choose the **DOF 1** camera.

16. Move the time scrubber or play down another 300 frames.

17. Right-click on the red line in the timeline and choose the **Grill Right** camera.

18. Move down another 300 frames.

19. Choose the **Benny Cam1** camera.

20. Move down the **Timeline** 200 frames.

21. Choose **Wide Angle 1** camera.

22. Save the project.

The following image shows the **Camera Switch** as set up by the proceeding steps:

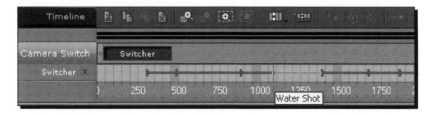

What just happened?

By moving down the timeline in two to three hundred frame blocks then selecting the camera, we set up one continuous scene shot between several cameras. Play the scene through and watch how the camera switches from one camera to the next.

There are a few advantages while using the **Camera Switch**:

- ◆ One render featuring several shots instead of one shot per render
- ◆ Quick and seamless switching of cameras
- ◆ Ability to adjust timing and order of cameras
- ◆ Continuity of action within a scene between characters

Have a go hero – adjusting the camera switch settings

Save the project and experiment with different camera orders and timing to get a good feel of what the **Camera Switch** is all about.

Move the camera ticks up and down the timeline and replay the scene to see how each movement changed the dynamics of the scene. You could also load music into the scene and time the **Camera Switch** to the dynamics of the soundtrack.

You have a saved copy of the project file to this point so be fearless and create your own shot list then set it up in iClone. When you are finished experimenting, reload the main project and continue to next the section.

 Change the order of cameras anywhere on the timeline by selecting the camera tick mark on the timeline and deleting it, then right-clicking and choosing a new camera from the camera list.

Filming through walls and objects with camera clipping

We did not have a need to use camera clipping in our project but it is a very important tool that we need to be aware of and use properly. Camera clipping cuts out part of the scene in front of the camera so you can film through an object such as a wall, roof or door.

To demonstrate the use of camera clipping we will be using a new blank project so that we don't interfere with our ongoing project.

Time for action – Using camera clipping

We'll be using a couple of the primitive building block props to complete this exercise:

1. Save our continuing project if you haven't already done so.

2. Create a new project.

3. Go to the **Set** tab.

4. Click on the **Props** button.

5. Double-click on **Box_001** in the **3D Blocks** folder of the **Content Manager** in the left side menu to load it into the center of the workspace.

6. Double-click on **Ball_005** to load it into the workspace.

7. Select **Ball_005** in the **Scene Manager** and move it directly behind **Box_001** where the box blocks our view of the ball.

8. Set up the ball prop behind the box prop as shown in the following image:

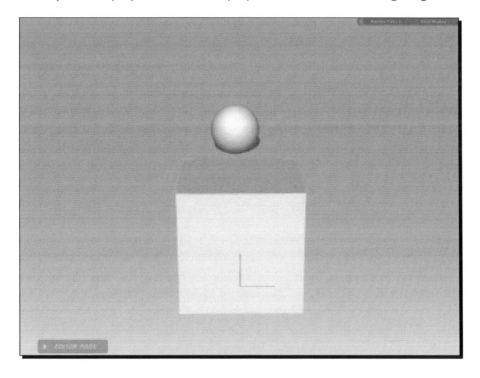

9. Select the **Preview Camera**.

10. Click on the **Add** button to create a new camera.

11. Frame the shot with the new camera similar to the following image, where the ball is blocked from view by the box:

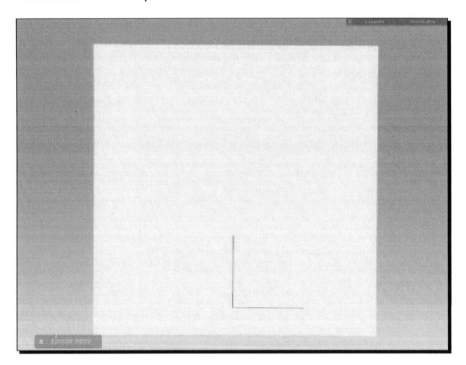

12. With the new camera selected type in or dial up the arrow till the **Near** setting is on 29, as referenced by the following before and after image:

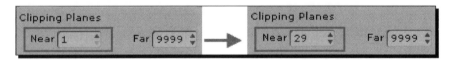

We will now be presented with the view in the following image that shows the shadow of the box but not the box:

What just happened?

When we dialled up the **Near** setting of the **Camera Clipping** section from 1 to 29 we cutaway the objects in front of the camera until we could see the ball behind the box.

Camera clipping allows us to film in a tight room like a small bedroom, office, or even a closet. Combine this with the Lens settings and we can position a camera in a very tight space and still film effectively from it.

Summary

Well now... we have been through another chapter and you are one step closer to being a better animator and iClone filmmaker. Cameras could be the subject of complete books but we have touched on most of the important aspects of basic camera usage.

iClone has demonstrated time and again that it provides us with great tools and features to accomplish by ourselves what would have needed an entire team of animators years ago.

Specifically, we covered the following:

◆ Creating cameras and framing the shot

◆ Using the follow cams and converting them to permanent cameras

◆ Renaming cameras for ease of use and identification

◆ Understanding and using the lens feature of the cameras to change the focal point of a scene or make a very smooth *zoom in* or *zoom out* shot

◆ Using depth of field and how it can add focus to a scene no matter how busy that scene may be

◆ The importance of camera cuts and timing

◆ Using the Camera Switch to amp up the dynamics of a scene and create a multi-shot single render project

◆ Discovered camera clipping which allows us to film in very tight spots

We have covered a lot of ground in this chapter, just as we have done in previous chapters, and while we could go on and on discovering the nuances of cameras and their proper use, we must now continue on to our next chapter... *Using Video with iClone*.

7

Enhancing Scenes with Images and Videos

Reallusion has provided us with some powerful tools in iClone as we've seen in past chapters. These tools help us to complete complex tasks or add special effects. The tools in this chapter not only stand out in a group by themselves for pure ease of use, but also add maximum eye-candy effect with little or no strain on the iClone engine.

The proper use of these tools can enhance a scene as much as any factor other than lighting, and can have an effect on dynamic atmospheric lighting too.

In this chapter we will be doing some light duty work with heavy duty results as we discover the following:

- ◆ A right-click menu system for bringing in assets quickly and easily
- ◆ What billboards are all about
- ◆ How image planes enhance our scenes with little overhead
- ◆ Image layers and some of their intended uses
- ◆ Using video in a scene
- ◆ Attaching video to a prop
- ◆ Using and creating pop video

So let's get started by taking a look at the general use of video in an iClone project.

Using the 2D drag-and-drop menu

We have discovered a few possibly unnoticed or underused gems among the iClone toolset and this is another one. The right-click 2D drag-and-drop system does all the work for us when we add an image plane, image layer, billboard, or video. In fact, all we have to do is choose were the 2D asset will be placed in the scene and what type of asset it is.

This system is pure drag-and-drop-from an open explorer window into the iClone 3D workspace and works with the basic 2D assets such as:

♦ Image Layer

♦ Plane

♦ Billboard

♦ Background

 You must *RIGHT-CLICK* and drag the assets to the 3D workspace to trigger this menu.

The following image shows dragging a 2D asset such as an image from an open window into the 3D workspace. In this example it was used as a background texture.

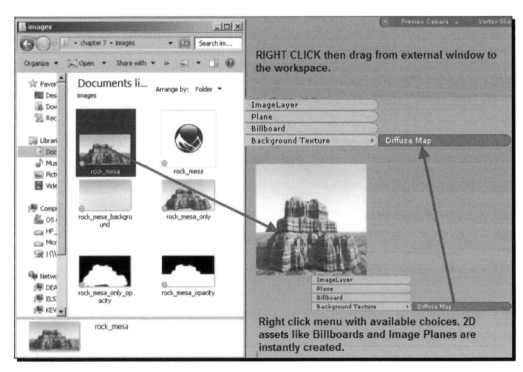

We will be using this system to add a few more objects to our scene to enhance the overall look of the scene and to add enough detail to make the scene interesting.

We can use 2D assets with its opacity channel to create a realistic background object from an image or from a video if the video has an opacity channel or separate opacity video.

Our first step will be taking a look at Image Planes and their function within the iClone 3D workspace.

Adding details with planes

Planes are primitive, flat 3D rectangle objects that have all the mapping channels such as Diffuse, Opacity, Bump, Specular, Glow, Reflection, and Blend. The channels allow us to use 2D assets such as images to make realistic props for our scene. These planes can also be manipulated by the usual means of Move, Rotate, Scale, and so forth.

The following image shows a primitive wall prop on the left that could be used as an image plane but iClone does the work for us by using the right-click drag-an-drop system. The image plane on the far right has the diffuse image but no opacity image. The image plane in the center is a duplicate of the same image plane, with an opacity map to mask out anything other than the rock mesa from being visible.

Time for action – creating an image plane

We are going to work with a blank project once again to learn the basics of using the right-click drag-and-drop system while creating image planes with opacity:

1. Save our ongoing project.

2. Create a new blank project.

3. Click on the **Set** tab.

4. Click on the **Props** button.

5. Click on the **Import** button on the right side menu.

6. Browse to and select the **Grass Floor** prop located in the code bundle on the book page at www.packtpub.com. We could drag-and-drop but importing will place the **Grass Floor** prop in the proper location.

7. Open a Window or right-click on the Windows Start button and choose **Open Windows Explorer** to open an explorer window.

Multiple monitors

If at all possible, using a second monitor will allow you to have direct drag-and-drop access to your iClone content. Better search features in newer operating systems also allow for a search then drag-and drop-method, saving valuable time and reducing the frustration of finding certain assets.

8. In this window, navigate to the folder holding the contents of the code bundle.

9. Left-click on the **Packt Overview Camera** file and drag it into the workspace then release.

Your active camera should now be the Overview Camera.

10. In the code bundle explorer window, right-click and hold on the **green_ mountains1024.png** file then drag the mountain image to the workspace and release to trigger the menu.

Remember to use RIGHT-CLICK!

11. Select **Plane** from the menu choices as shown in the following screenshot:

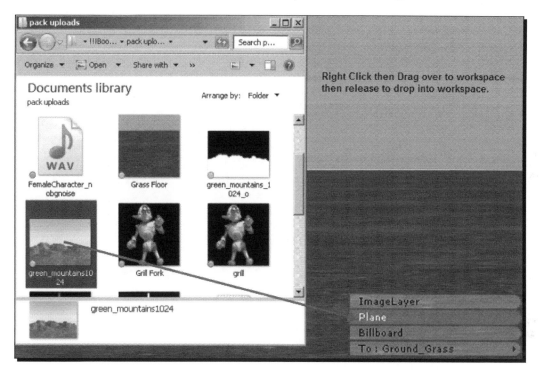

12. Move the newly created image plane into view. Don't worry about size or exact placement yet.

13. Right-click and hold on the image **green_mountains_1024_o.png** (the opacity image) and drag it onto the Image Plane we created in the preceding step.

 Opacity images are created with tools like Photoshop or the open source Gimp image editor. Search the web for creating opacity maps for more information.

14. From the menu select **Opacity** to place this image in the opacity map channel:

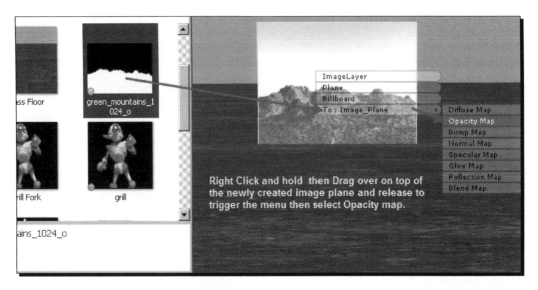

15. Select the newly created image plane of the mountain and move it towards the back of the workspace.

16. Use the scale tool to stretch the horizontal and vertical axes of the mountain to fill the screen, similar to the following image:

17. With the **Set** tab selected click on the **Sky** button.

18. Double-click on the **Clear Day 00** sky to load it into the workspace.

19. Set the height of the sky to -5000.

20. Locate the **Animated Clouds** prop in the code bundle and drag-and-drop it into the scene with the usual *left-click* drag-and-drop method.

21. Position the animated sky to your liking with the **Move** tool.

The end result of our 2D image plane work is shown in the following image:

What just happened?

After loading a terrain floor, we used the right-click drag-and-drop system to drop an image into the workspace as a 2D image plane. We then used the same drag-and-drop method to place the opacity image on top of the newly created image plane, which triggered a pop up menu giving us a choice of map channels. The opacity channel was chosen as we wanted to only show the mountain as the final image plane.

Using the **Move**, **Rotate**, and **Scale** tools we then moved the mountain prop towards the back of the terrain then down till it went slightly into the terrain. We then stretched the horizontal and vertical axis until the mountain prop suited our needs.

The animated cloud prop is an animated image plane made in Studio Max. We could have also used the **One Way Movement UV Base** prop turned white with an opacity map to create a similar prop in iClone without Studio Max.

Have a go hero – adding another mountain

It's once again time for you to strike out on your own and try out your skills. This challenge is another simple but effective method of adding a little more depth to the scene.

Duplicate the mountain image plane and turn it around 180 degrees (so it will be the opposite of the original) then move and rotate the mountain back until you get an angle that is to your liking that lends more depth to the scene. Scale this second mountain horizontally to cover the entire screen side-to-side then scale it up to make it taller so it can be easily seen over the first mountain image plane. This should give us some depth with the space between mountain props.

Add a fog particle or particles between the mountain props. This will make fog boil between the mountain peaks when the particle(s) is properly placed between them.

The following image shows a straight on and an angled overhead shot of the props and the fog particle:

Billboards

Billboards are image planes that always face the camera. Billboards are great tools for trees, plants, and flowers, and when used properly they can mimic an entire army or group of people while using very little computer resources. They can also be used to mimic structures and other objects that will be away from the camera. These assets usually work better the further the 2D object is from the camera, but with proper placement and clear sharp maps you can use them up close in certain situations.

For our scene we will be adding some structural billboards to add some detail to the far end of the scene.

Time for action – working with billboards to add an old barn

We are going to add a group of old barns to our scene but we need them to always face the camera in this case so we will use a billboard:

1. Open the code bundle in an explorer window if it is not already open.

2. Right-click on the **old_barns** color image in the bundle and drag it into the workspace, choosing **Billboard** as the method of placement.

   The following images shows right-click drag-and-drop to create a billboard:

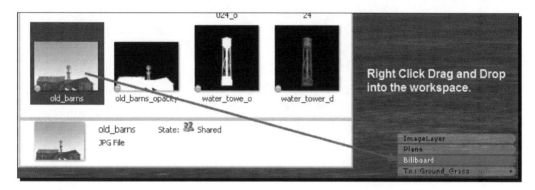

3. We may need to move the image up since the floor prop is elevated so if you can't see the billboard then select the Move tool and move it up until it is visible.

4. Drag-and-drop the **old_barns_opacity** image with a right-click onto the existing **old_barns** image in the workspace and choose opacity from the submenu.

   The following image shows right-click dragging and dropping of the old barns opacity map onto the same billboard using the **Opacity Map** channel:

5. Move the old barns billboard and rescale it till it's similar to the next image.

 Remember that no matter how you turn it, the billboard will always face the camera.

What just happened?

By using a billboard with our old barns diffuse and opacity maps, we were able to drag-and-drop in a detailed building for the background of the scene. We dragged and dropped the diffuse image first with the right-click menu, creating a billboard for us. We then dragged and dropped the old barns opacity image onto the same billboard using the **Opacity Map** channel.

This extremely low poly count 2D asset gives us a visually rich building to place into the background.

 Using billboards and with appropriate shots

Since a billboard always faces the camera, they are generally used in simple and short time frame stationary shots that add character or richness to a scene. You will have to take care in planning a moving camera shot to take into account the fact that the billboard will swing to face the camera as the camera moves. With trees and plants this presents no problem but buildings will look very strange moving with a curving camera shot. Experiment with the camera lens and depth of field to enhance the scene.

Time for action – working with billboards to add a water tower

We added our old barns, now let's add an old water tower to the opposite side of the scene:

1. Using a right-click, drag-and-drop **water_tower_d** (diffuse map) in the workspace near the barns.

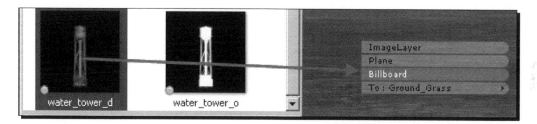

2. Using the same right-click method, drag-and-drop **water_tower_o** (opacity map) onto the same billboard we just created and choose the opacity map channel:

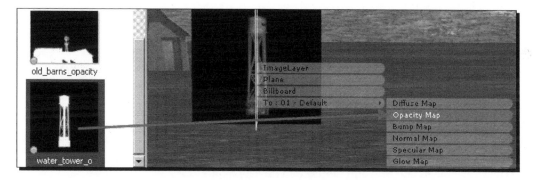

3. Place and scale the water tower billboard similar to the following image:

What just happened?

We added another high detail object to the scene with the right-click drag-and-drop system. By placing this object just slightly behind and to the side of the first billboard, we can add a little more depth and volume to the scene.

Had we actually been using this scene in production, these 2D billboards would be placed in the far distance at the back of the scene to provide detail, but not so close as to give away the 2D aspect of the asset.

Pop quiz

1. To properly use a billboard or image plane, which of the following image maps are required?

    a. Diffuse and Bump

    b. Diffuse and Opacity

    c. Diffuse and Glow

    d. Diffuse and Blend

    e. Diffuse and Reflection

2. An image Plane always faces the camera.

    a. True

    b. False

Have a go hero – adding the wishing well

In the code bundle, you will find diffuse and opacity images for a wishing well prop; drag-and-drop then position this wishing well as a billboard in the current scene near the front of the old barns billboard. Use both the diffuse and opacity maps on the same billboard, as we have with previous billboards.

Image layers

An image layer is a very simple overlay that stays on top of your scene like an airplane cockpit or an automobile interior. They can also be used for messages to the viewer.

Multiple image layers can be placed from front to back so they can be layered in any desired order. Image overlay properties such as opacity are keyable on the timeline and therefore can be animated. These multiple image layers can then be combined and saved as one custom image layer if need be.

Time for action – driving down the street

For image layers, we are going to use a new, blank project to learn the concepts, then we'll apply what we learn to our ongoing project just as we have in past chapters:

1. Create a new, blank project.

2. In the **Set** tab under the **Terrain** button, load the Community Stage terrain.

3. Click on the **Stage** tab, then click on the **Image Layer** button.

4. Double-click on the car image layer to load it on top of the workspace.

5. Select and hold down the left mouse button and move the entire image overlay up towards the top of the screen as shown in the following image, then release the left mouse button:

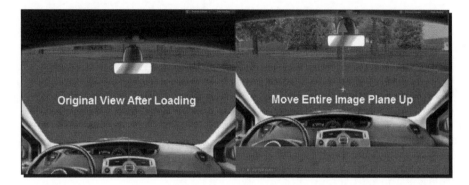

6. On the bottom-right corner of the overlay you will see an area where the yellow boundary flares out. Move your cursor over this area and it will change to an arrow.

7. Hold the left mouse button down and drag the corner of the image to just off the screen, and cover the entire screen before releasing the mouse button:

8. Click on **Preview Camera** in the upper-right corner of the workspace.

9. Click on **Add** in the **Camera** section of the right side menu to add a new camera.

10. Click on the **Animation** tab.

11. Click on the **Path** button.

12. Click on the **Create Path** button.

13. Draw a short curving path then select the path and move it up off the ground, similar to the following image:

14. Click on the **Set** tab then click on the **Props** button.

15. Load **Ball_001** prop.

16. Reduce the ball prop to 10 percent in the scale input boxes located in the right side menu.

17. With the time scrubber at the start of the scene, click on the **Pick Path** button.

18. Select the first waypoint on the path.

19. Move the time scrubber down to around frame 500.

20. With the **Ball_001** prop selected click on the **Pick Path** button and select the last waypoint on the path.

21. Select **Camera01** from the **Scene Manager** or use the camera selector menu in the upper-right corner of the workspace.

22. With **Camera01** selected, click on the **Attach** button in the right side panel.

23. Select the **Ball_001** prop to attach to.

24. Use the **Move** and **Rotate** tool to position the camera as you desire.

Using a dummy object to attach cameras/objects to paths

Cameras attached to paths are locked to the path and cannot move, rotate, or deviate from the chosen axis. By using a dummy object to attach to the path then attaching your camera or other object to the dummy, you can move or rotate your camera or object as needed.

25. Select prop **Ball_001**.

26. With **Ball_001** selected, move the opacity slider in the right side panel to zero to make the dummy ball prop invisible.

The following image shows our scene to this point:

27. Uncheck the **Show** box for the path in the **Scene Manager**.

28. Save our scene and then play it to see what we have accomplished.

What just happened?

In first part of this exercise, we added an overlay to the camera view. We then moved and resized the image layer to fit our needs, which was to give us a better view out of the windshield.

After the image layer alterations, we added a curved path for the image layer to follow and we created a camera just for this layer. We also added a dummy primitive ball prop, scaled down to 10%, which we attached to the path.

We then attached our camera to the ball object and oriented the camera to the desired position.

 By parenting to a dummy prop we are able to move or rotate the camera freely when using a path.

We then turned off the *show* properties of the path and used our overlay to "drive" down the road.

Time for action – using multiple image layers

Multiple image layers can be loaded and stacked on top of each other. You can send selected image layers towards the front or the back to change the order in the workspace:

1. Click on the **Stage** tab.

2. Click on the **Image Layer** Button.

3. To load, double-click on the **Air Fighter** image layer located in the **Content Manager** on the left side panel.

4. Rename the **ImageLayer** to **Cockpit** in the **Scene Manager** on the left menu panel.

5. Double-click on the **Scope Image Layer** to load it into the 3D workspace.

6. Rename the Image Layer to Scope.

7. With **Scope Image Layer** selected, we need to hover our cursor over one of the bottom corners until the cursor changes into a double arrowed cursor.

8. Move the cursor up and towards the center of the workspace to resize the **Scope Image Layer**.

9. With the **Scope Image Layer** selected, change the **Contrast** to 60 in the right side menu panel.

10. Move and place the **Scope Image Layer** similar to the following image:

11. With the **Scope Image Layer** selected, click on the **Move Backward** button to send the scope image behind the cockpit image layer.

The following image shows part of the image layer control menu and the result of sending the scope image layer backward behind the cockpit image overlay:

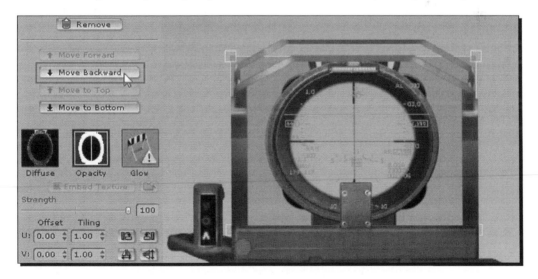

12. In the **Content Manager,** use your left mouse button while holding down the *Shift* key to select both the Cockpit and Scope Image Layers.

13. Click on the **Custom** tab in the **Content Manager** on the left side of the menu.

14. With both image layers still selected, click on the PLUS icon at the bottom of the **Content Manager** section to save the two images layers as one.

15. Click on the **Set** tab.

16. Click on the **Sky** button.

17. Double-click on the **Clear Day 00** sky to load it into the workspace.

18. With the sky still selected, set the height to -5000 in the right side menu.

19. Set the **Scale** to 200.

20. Click on the camera selection menu in the upper-right corner of the workspace to activate the right side camera menu.

21. Click on the **Add** button to add a new camera.

22. In the **Scene Manager,** rename the camera to **Fly**.

23. Click on the **Time Setting Panel** button.

24. Change the number of frames to 1000 and click **OK**:

25. Move the time scrubber all the way to the end of the **Timeline,** to the last frame.

26. Click on the **Zoom** key in the upper toolbar and zoom in few times.

27. Save the file and press the play button to review our work.

What just happened?

We loaded two image layers and renamed them to identify them easily. Next, we resized the scope to fit into the Heads Up Display (HUD) of the cockpit image overlay. Since we wanted the scope to be behind the cockpit we used the Move Backward button to move the scope layer behind the cockpit layer, allowing all the HUD lettering to show.

In case we ever needed this custom image layer again, we selected both image layers and saved them as one into the custom image layer folder.

To add a little more pizazz to the scene and test what we've learned in previous chapters, we added a new camera and a sky. We then moved the time scrubber to the last frame of the time line and used the Zoom tool to move the camera forward, mimicking forward travel in the clouds.

Have a go hero – adding more clouds

Add the **Animated Clouds** prop that we used earlier in this chapter to the cockpit scene. This prop is located in the code bundle. Make copies of the **Animated Clouds** prop and set them at various heights to experiment with the effect.

 For best results, it is recommended that you turn off the shadow property of the Light source by clearing the Shadow checkbox on the active directional/spotlight in the Scene Manager.

Experiment with the following:

♦   UV Mapping by changing the tiling of the opacity map

♦   Rotate the prop to change cloud movement direction

♦   Use the Adjust Color panel on the right menu to experiment with the sliders and witness their effects

The following image shows the two image layers with the sky and Animated Clouds prop:

Using 2D with special effects

Like a lot of tools we've covered, two dimensional image assets are deceptively simple and powerful. In the case of creating a space scene, we need to have a volume of stars that seem to engulf and fill space instead of just a star field image for a background. And for color there needs to be a nebula or cosmic cloud that breaks up the void of space. Just a bunch of stars can get boring very quickly.

Time for action – using planes to mimic volume effects

We will be making a simple space scene with nebulas and star fields created with image planes. This scene will also be the basis for our space scene in *Chapter 9, Animating Outer Space*, so be sure to save it and keep it on file for use when we get to the final chapter:

1. Open a new, blank scene.

2. Click on the **Stage** tab.

3. Click on the **2D Background** button.

4. In the right side menu, uncheck the **Active** box to turn off the 2D background.

5. Select black in the **Set Color** section above the **Active** box.

6. In the code bundle, drag-and-drop the **Star Globe Glow** prop into the 3D workspace.

7. With **Star Globe Glow** selected, click on the **Glow** channel in the **Material & Texture Settings** section of the right side menu.

8. Set the **Strength** slider all the way to 100.

9. In the code bundle, right-click and drag the **red_nebula.bmp** image into the workspace and select **Plane**.

10. Also in the code bundle, right-click and drag **red_nebula_o.bmp** onto the same image plane as the opacity map.

11. Rename the **DefImagePlane** to **Nebula** in the **Scene Manager**.

12. Resize and move the Nebula to fill the screen.

13. Rotate the Nebula to 31 on the Z axis or type 31 into the Z axis input box.

14. Set the Nebula opacity to 25 in the right side menu panel.

15. Double-click on the **Glow** Channel and select the **Cold** glow from the Reallusion supplied glow maps.

16. Move the **Glow** slider to 2.

17. In the code bundle, locate then drag-and-drop via right-click the **red_starfield.bmp** image as a billboard.

18. In the same code bundle, locate then drag-and-drop via right-click the **red_starfield_o.bmp** onto the same billboard as the opacity map.

19. Place the **red_starfield.bmp** image plane a good distance behind the angled nebula prop and rescale to fill the screen with the starfield.

20. In the code bundle, locate then drag-and-drop via right-click the **starfield.bmp** image as a plane.

21. In the code bundle, locate then drag-and-drop via right click the **starfield_o.bmp** image to the opacity channel of the starfield image plane.

22. Move the starfield image plane in front of the other planes and put some distance between the red_starfield plane and the starfield plane.

23. Rotate the starfield image to around 348 on the Z axis.

The final results should look similar to the forward shot on the left side of the following image. The right side of the image is an angled shot of the scene with the background lightened up to show the planes at their angles:

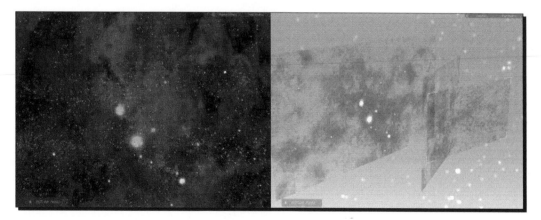

What just happened?

Who said space had to be dull? We took a lifeless space scene and spiced it up with some images combined with image planes to create an almost volumetric area of space. While it is true that this is not volume in a real sense, the angled planes will give a sense of realism as a spaceship or comet streak through the stars. Parts of the angled planes will pass by at different times giving the illusion of stars or nebula clouds surrounding the space craft.

The image layers were layered with the red_starfield billboard the farthest away. This way the red_starfield will always face the camera as it moves. The red_nebula image plane was next in order, followed by the starfield image angled opposite the nebula plane with plenty of space in between the planes.

 Remember to keep this scene as it will be the basis for *Chapter 9, Animating Outer Space*.

Time for action – adding mountains

In this section, we are going to use what we've learned so far to add the mountains to our ongoing project:

1. Open our ongoing project.

2. Open an explorer window that displays the contents of the code bundle for this chapter.

3. Using right-click, drag-and-drop the **green_mountains1024** diffuse image into the workspace.

4. Using right-click, drag-and-drop the **grenn_mountains_1024_o** opacity image onto the newly created image plane as the opacity map.

5. Scale and place the 2D mountain prop behind the island terrain. Position it to your liking or similar to the following image:

 Images and texture map quality are determined by the Max Real-Time map size parameter in the preferences panel. The default value is 512x512 but should be set to the highest value available for clearer sharper textures.

What just happened?

We enhanced the visual aspect of the scene by adding the green mountain two dimensional image plane behind the island.

This not only gives us a separator between the sky and the island terrain for depth but also adds a nice touch of continuity and quality to the scene.

Using video to enhance scenes

iClone gives us the ability to load a video clip on almost any surface depending on how that surface was originally mapped. If we have a television in a scene such as a living room or bedroom, we can animate that prop by adding a video clip to the screen area.

How the clip works with a prop is dependent upon how the prop was built. As long as the area of the prop you want to use for video is independent of the rest of the prop in terms of texture mapping, the video will attach and play as anticipated. However, should the TV prop have been created without a separate UV mapping area, the video would play over the entire surface of the prop instead of just the screen area.

The following image shows an example of the same video clip dropped onto the center display area of two merchandising marquees. The left marquee had separate textures for the display area and the surrounding marble so the drag and dropped texture could be applied to the center area with the outside marble untouched. The right marquee was created as a single texture object:

Add a wall prop to an incorrectly mapped monitor or television prop

You can simulate the screen of a monitor or television by using the wall prop in the 3D Blocks prop folder. Scale the wall to fit where the screen should be, then cover the screen with the wall prop and attach. Drag your video onto the attached wall prop.

Video clips can also be used to create moving objects such as birds, airplanes, and just about anything the user can imagine, even crowds!

The same powerful right-click drag-and-drop system we used with images works with video clips too! If you have a video clip with built-in alpha channel (opacity) or created your own alpha channel clip, you can combine them with the original clip to mask out unwanted areas. Reallusion has also given us the ability to render our own separate alpha clips if we need to use AVI format by checking the **Alpha Video Only** checkbox before rendering.

Time for action – adding video to props

Adding video to props is as simple as adding the prop then using the right-click drag-and-drop menu to place the video onto the prop. When placing a video a bounding box will appear around the entire prop. The video, however, will be placed in the area of the cursor when released:

> *1.*   Open our Main project.

2. Make sure the time scrubber is set to the first frame.

3. Click on **Preview Camera**.

4. Click on the grill and press the **Home** key to center the grill area in the **Preview Camera**.

5. In the code bundle, you will find the TV Cabinet prop. Drag-and-drop the prop into the workspace and place it as shown in the following image:

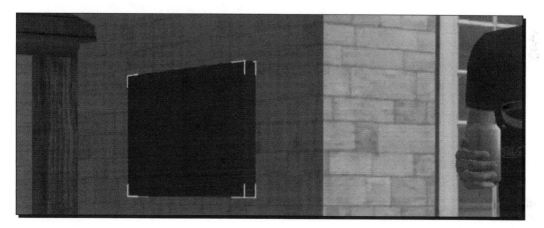

6. Right-click on the TV Cabinet prop and choose **Open Doors** from the **Perform** menu.

7. Click on the **Set** tab.

8. Click on the **Video** button.

9. Using the right-click drag-and-drop method, drag the **TV04_Rockband** video over to the **TV Cabinet** prop and hold your cursor in the middle of the prop screen.

10. Release the mouse button to drop the video onto the video screen. Your first attempt may take a couple of tries. Use the **Undo** key and set the time scrubber back to the beginning then try again.

11. Select the TV Cabinet prop.

12. Under the Materials and Texture section on the right side menu, select SCREEN in the **Select Material** drop-down box.

13. In the **Color** channel, change the **Ambient** and/or **Diffuse Color** to a lighter color or to white.

14. With the TV Cabinet selected, right-click on it and choose **Remove All Animation**.

If you drag a clip onto a surface and you know the clip is there but you can't see it, check the color channels. If ambient or diffuse are a black or a dark color you won't be able to see the video through the color. Lighten the colors till you can see the video.

The following image shows the open **TV Cabinet** prop with the rock band video running:

What just happened?

First we moved our preview camera to a workable view, then we imported the TV Cabinet prop. The prop was scaled and placed into the scene, then we triggered the built-in animation so the cabinet doors would be open. After dragging and dropping the video onto the video screen area of the TV Cabinet prop we then lightened up the screen colors so the video would be clearer.

We finally removed all animation so the prop would be open and stay open during playback or rendering.

Video clips can be dragged to a variety of surfaces. Applying an almost transparent water video to the outer glass walls of an aquarium will give it a watery look. A flock of birds or an airplane can be done with video instead of the actual models eating up resources in the iClone engine. There are many more uses for video in iClone than just monitors, televisions, or view screens.

 Using iClone movies in iClone scenes

Since iClone is movie making software, we can always render simple iClone scenes to use as video clips in other iClone scenes or for use with props.

As in all things... your imagination is the limit!

Creating and using popVideo

Reallusion introduced popVideo to a user base that really didn't know what to make of it for the most part and like other iClone tools it has become invaluable over time to many users. A popVideo is a video with an alpha channel. According to the documentation, the advantage of using popVideo over just using the diffuse and opacity channels on a plane is that the videos are perfectly synchronized.

The formats available as per the iClone manual: "iWidget to be used for live Flash Media publishing, or output in iClone's popVideo format. popVideo for HD resolution 3D virtual set productions. You may also export your own video masks (.AVI) for use with other video compositing tools."

popVideos are great for placing a live actor into an animated background. If you film the actor with a green background, you can then use the popVideo converter to do the keying work for you. The green background will be keyed out and all you see is the actor. This footage can then be layered in with other footage using planes and 3D space to set up the scene.

There is also an **Export Alpha Video Only** option during AVI rendering to create a separate alpha video which can be used with other editing software.

 The PopVideo Converter is a one click Chroma-key product from Reallusion that keys out (removes) the blue or green background of a scene. You can create a character on a blue or green background in iClone then use the PopVideo Converter to make the background transparent for use as an overlay on other videos. Visit the Reallusion website for more information.

The following image is a mixture of actor and animation:

Time for action – playing with popVideo

To grasp popVideo, let's throw together a quick scene using basic props and assets:

1. Start a new project and click on the **Set** tab then on the **Props** button.

2. Double-click on the **Floor_001** prop in the **Wall and Floor** subfolder of the 3D Blocks prop folder to load the prop into the workspace.

3. Double-click on **Podium_005** in the **Podium** sub-folder of the **3D Blocks** folder.

4. Click on the **Video** button in the top toolbar.

5. Drag-and-drop **B_19** (male actor) from the **Intro** folder in the **Content Manager** on the upper-left menu panel into the workspace.

6. Position the B-19 video plane behind the podium.

7. Frame the camera shot to your liking and press the play button to review.

The following image shows the video plane in from a front and angled side view:

What just happened?

We used the video image plane with 3D props to create a very quick scene. This type of prop is completely dependent upon camera angle.

Summary

We've learned quite a bit about 2D assets and how they can enhance a scene with little overhead.

Specifically, we covered the following:

- What image planes are and how to use them
- What the difference is between planes and billboards
- How to use layer and save image layers
- How to use diffuse and opacity with planes for special effects
- How to add and use videos/popVideos in a project

So let's move on to the next chapter, *Rendering our Work*, which involves formatting and outputting our work for all to see.

8
Rendering our Work

Rendering... we used the term many times getting to this point and now we are going to discuss it in detail as we have arrived at the point in our ongoing project where rendering will be one of the next steps.

 Rendering out our scene is only the next step for most of us in making a video, as it would afterwards be used in a video editor to complete a movie. Very rarely are complete movies rendered out of any 3D application including iClone.

In this chapter we shall discuss the following:

- ◆ What rendering is in general
- ◆ What rendering is to iClone in particular
- ◆ Rendering controls and options
- ◆ Single image and Image Sequence renders
- ◆ Video and popVideo renders
- ◆ Stereoscopic Rendering

So let's get started on this crucial part of the process.

Understanding rendering

Rendering in essence, at least to most of us, is exporting our work to an external file. This may be a video format like AVI or Windows Media for use in a video editor or upload to the web or a number of reasons as the formats available to export vary and we will cover each of those formats in their appropriate section.

In actuality, according to Wikipedia, rendering is:

> *...the final process of creating the actual 2D image or animation from the prepared scene. This can be compared to taking a photo or filming the scene after the setup is finished in real life.*

> *...rendering may take from fractions of a second to days for a single image/frame. In general, different methods are better suited for either photo-realistic rendering, or real-time rendering.*

As you can see within the venue of rendering there are real-time applications like iClone that instantly render lighting, shadows, atmosphere, and other components or there is standard or non real-time rendering that that can take hours, days, or even months to render a project depending on the final quality of the output.

Rendering in iClone

iClone straddles the world of real-time and non real-time rendering by doing both. We see the real-time render as we work. This is what is displayed in the 3D workspace. However, when we render out (export) the video, we are using the more traditional non real-time method but the video is rendering very fast and video files can be exported quickly in iClone depending on your hardware. However, iClone rendering is hardware dependent.

You could screen capture the workspace output with a program like FRAPS but that would only be a more difficult way of accomplishing the same task since iClone has built-in rendering.

One thing to keep in mind is that a screen captured image or video is a second generation capture of what your screen displays up to the limits of the capture software or your screen. If, for example, you are using a free capture utility that only records in 256K of color then you will not have a high quality video.

By rendering out the video in iClone, we are creating a high quality, first generation video file. The render quality and speed is completely hardware dependent. A good video card, a lot of RAM, and quality components with multiple core processors provide fantastic performance as a platform for the iClone engine. On the other hand, there are users running iClone on laptops and desktops that barely meet the minimal requirements of the program and are able to use it successfully and create nice final renders.

Some artists, traditional and digital, refer to 3D applications as "The Artist in a Box Concept" or "Instant Artist" but that is not really true as there is much more to creating digital art than just throwing together a scene and rendering it out. We have covered many of the basics of iClone but we have not covered topics like *composition and framing* because those skills are complex topics unto themselves and beyond the scope of this guide. As you grow and your skills increase, you will develop your style from hands-on experience but it's important to know that these two items, at minimum, should be researched further by the serious digital artist.

What we are about to discuss will take our work outside of iClone and into the realm of digital art starting with single image renders.

Exporting single images

Almost everyone that looks at iClone realizes it exports videos but some do not realize that we can export any frame from any video or a scene created specifically for single image renders.

It is difficult to tell, at times, whether any particular digital image you are looking at was photographed, filmed, or animated with a 3D application. In fact, this can be said for many images found in print too. Higher end applications costing thousands of dollars and the free open source Blender application can render photo-realistic results if you have the time, skills, and computational processing power.

There are many prime examples of single image renders from 3D applications all over the web. From very futuristic science fiction to sunny meadows filled with flowers, the various 3D applications have blossomed into artistic tools and iClone is no exception.

The iClone community is full of digital artists like Stuckon3D and Wolf (from the Wolf and Dulci Hour) that are masters at lighting, composition, and framing making their single image renders works of digital art that can compete on almost any level with any application. Famed and highly skilled machinimists like Anima Technica rely on single image renders for posters and to promote their works.

Programs like iClone give us an opportunity to show that we too can create digital art.

Reallusion has provided us several formats for exporting single images. These formats are as follows:

- BMP: Bitmap
- JPG: Joint Photographic Experts Group
- TGA: True Vision sometimes called TARGA

- ◆ GIF: Graphics Interchange Format
- ◆ PNG: Portable Network Graphics

Items such as dummies, helpers, and paths will not be rendered in the final output.

The following image shows the options for single image renders under the **Export** tab:

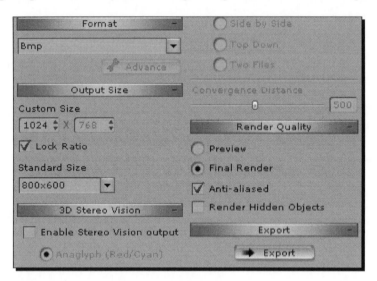

So now that we have discussed the basics, let's try some hands on exporting from our project.

Time for action – rendering our first image

We aren't going to become the next digital Picasso overnight so let's just concentrate on getting that first single image render completed:

1. Open our ongoing project.

2. Select the **Water Shot** camera from the camera selection menu in the upper-right corner of the workspace or from the **Scene Manager** on the left menu.

3. Click **Add** in the **Camera** section to create a camera from the Water Shot view.

4. Rename the Camera Still 1.

5. Double-click on the grill to select it or select it from the **Scene Manager**.

6. Click on the **Orbit/Roll** camera control on the top toolbar.

Position the camera shot similar to the following image using the grill as the pivot point:

7. Select the **Export** tab.

8. Click on the **Image** button.

9. Drag the time scrubber to around frame 500 to produce smoke rising up from the grill. You can play the scene then stop it or you can move the time scrubber to get the particles and special effects up to speed.

 Particles are visible only when the animation is playing and can be captured for a single image as the effect will freeze when the playback is stopped.

10. Select **PNG** in the drop-down menu of the **Format** section in the upper-right menu panel.

11. Select **800 X 600** in the **Standard Size** drop-down menu if it's not already selected.

12. Skip the **3D Stereo Vision** section as we'll cover that later in this chapter.

13. Make sure **Final Render** and **Anti-aliased** are checked, click the **Export** button.

14. Browse to a location of your choice, name the image, and click on the **Save** button:

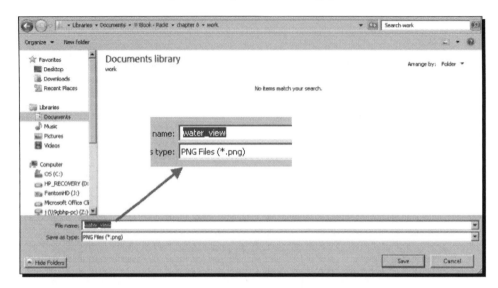

After clicking on **Save**, a pop up window will display the results of the render as shown in the following screenshot:

What just happened?

After loading the scene, we selected the Water Shot camera as a starting view for our render. We then clicked on the grill to use it as the pivot point of our scene. After selecting the Rotate/ Orbit tool, we framed our shot then clicked on Export to save our single image render.

We can use this rendered image as part of other projects, part of a portfolio or as a gallery piece to show the world we are digital artists in our own right!

Time for action – rendering an action shot

For the next single image render we will be moving down the timeline to catch some action in the image:

1. Select the **Water Shot** camera.

2. Move the time scrubber down the timeline until after the beer is set down and just before he actually touches the grill handle to close it, as shown in the following image:

3. Select the **Export** tab and click on the **Images** button.

4. Select **PNG** format.

5. Select **800 X 600**.

6. Press the **Export** button.

What just happened?

We used an existing camera, Water Shot, as the view and then moved the time scrubber down to a particular point in the animation to make the smoke visible for the still image render.

Have a go hero – rendering more images

Time once again to strike out on your own. As in the past, be sure to save the main project first before any experimentation.

Create one or more shots by creating more camera views then render those views into single images. Create at least a six shot portfolio as if you were creating a sales brochure for the property.

Exporting image sequences

Image sequences are just as the name implies—a sequence of images that taken together in sequential order make up a movie or scene. Individual single images are created and automatically named in sequential order instead of creating a single video file.

Image sequences are old school. Very old school and still very much in use as most high end video production applications have an option to import image sequences. This allows very precise artistic control over every image (frame) for post render editing or manipulation in other programs such as Photoshop™ or After Effects™.

iClone provides the following formats when exporting image sequences:

- ◆ BMP: Bitmap.
- ◆ JPG: Joint Photographic Experts Group. Options include quality adjustment from 0 to 100%.
- ◆ TGA: True Vision sometimes called TARGA (recommended). Options include 24-bit and 32-bit export with the 32-bit having an alpha channel.
- ◆ GIF: Graphics Interchange Format. Simple animation format with a transparency option.
- ◆ PNG: Portable Network Graphics with optional 24-bit and 32-bit depth settings.

 Consider what the final use is to help determine the format, as JPEG and GIF use compression and can lose quality in the production pipeline as it goes from application to application.

Time for action – exporting our first image sequence

We'll use our ongoing project to learn about exporting image sequences:

1. Open our main project and select a camera for the view.

2. Select the **Export** tab.

3. Click on the **Image Sequence** button.

4. Choose **PNG** sequence.

> A lot of users export in TGA (TARGA) sequence at 32-bit to preserve the alpha channel for use in other external applications and retain high graphic quality.

5. Select **640 X 480** as the size.

6. Under **Output Range** in the right menu panel input frame 320 to frame 500.

7. Click on the **Export** button.

> **Export image sequences to their own folder**
>
> Since there may be several hundred to several thousand images created, it is highly recommended to create a new folder just to hold that entire image sequence when exporting.

8. In the pop up dialog, browse to the location where you wish to save the image sequence and click the **Save** button.

The following image shows some of the image sequence renders created in the preceding steps:

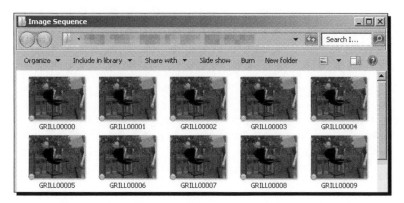

What just happened?

Instead of a video, we rendered a sequential group of images representing each frame. iClone will open a new explorer window displaying the image sequence after it finishes the rendering process. You can see by the naming of the files that each file starts with our file name of GRILL and is then sequentially numbered.

Post process third-party applications like After Effects and Photoshop then uses this naming sequence to load the image sequence in the proper order for editing.

We exported as a PNG sequence so we could see the thumbnails and more easily view the image sequence output from an explorer window.

Exporting videos

Exporting video is no more complicated than exporting still images, as iClone simplifies the process with its video export menu choices.

There are some underlying differences in video though that must be understood to get a good video render in the proper format for the job at hand.

Understanding video

Reallusion has given us several choices when it comes to output formats for our video renders. Each format has its good and bad points depending on how the video will be displayed, including the device and screen ratio. There are also several different codecs available depending on which format and what codecs are installed on your computer.

Codecs and formats are constantly being confused by users and misrepresented on the internet. They are two very distinct items.

Codecs versus formats

A *codec* is a computer program that compresses/decompresses audio/video from very large files to smaller files capable of being streamed over the internet or stored on a computer or device for playback.

Popular codecs in use today are H.264, MPEG-4,MPEG-2, VP6 (On2), VP7 (On2), VP8 (On2), Cinepack, and Indeo.

A *format* describes the type of container the file uses to transport the video. This container might be AVI (Audio-Video Interleave), WMV (Windows Media), RM (Real Media), or one of the many other formats available.

To better understand this concept, let's consider the fact that AVI is not a codec but a format and as such can run under different codecs. You could render out an AVI with a Cinepack codec or an Indeo codec but it would still be an AVI file.

The codec has a definite effect on the size and quality of the file. This is another excellent area for experimentation when you have time. Getting to know the differences in codecs concerning playback quality and file size can pay dividends later.

Video editing tip

If the video is to be used in another application, such as an editor, then it is recommended to produce a high quality uncompressed format at a large resolution such as 1280X720 (720p) at minimum. Even when playing on the web at 640X360 you can use the larger size in the editor and set the render to 50% while maintaining quality. Going down in render size versus original size is not a problem but going up is not recommended as the quality will decrease as the size increases.

Formats available in iClone

Reallusion has made several of the popular formats available to us. Options within each format will vary.

AVI

AVI is an old multimedia format and the personal favorite of this author for use in other applications and video editors. I also choose to render out these files uncompressed instead of using a codec like Cinepack or Intel IYUV.

A word of caution is warranted here. While an uncompressed AVI has great quality, it also creates huge files with just a few minutes of output easily equalling a gigabyte or more of file size. Should you choose to render out work in uncompressed AVI then make sure you have plenty of data storage on hand. The advantage to uncompressed AVI or AVI, in general, is the superb quality of the render when it is imported into a video editor for further processing.

Every re-render is a subsequent generational step down from the original render so keep editorial rendering to a minimum. If you use footage created in iClone then render it in a special effects editor then render again in a final video edit with soundtrack you will have a third-generation render. While it still may be a render of excellent quality it is generationally removed from the original render.

Digital re-rendering is not as destructive as analog copying was in its time, but if you throw a piece of software in the pipeline that isn't up to par you can get substantial degradation over the original render. Using uncompressed AVI provides for a quality original render that can stand the test of re-rendering in subsequent applications.

AVI format videos are more apt to be recognized and imported by third party video editors than some of the more obscure formats or even some of the older formats. There are very few video applications that will not import the AVI format. You have a choice of codec options with this format and in turn the chosen codec may have its own options. Note the lack of profiles. A pop up window will allow us to choose the codec after you press the Render button.

High Definition rendering in both 720p (1280X720) and 1080p (1920X1080) are available with the AVI file format as shown in the following image of pre-set resolutions available, as well as setting a custom resolution:

- 320 X 240, Multi-Media
- 640 X 480, Multi-Media
- 800 X 600, Multi-Media
- VCD NTSC (352 X 240) North America and Japan
- VCD PAL (352 X 288) Europe
- SVCD NTSC (480 X 480) North America and Japan
- DVD NTSC (720 X 480) DVD Disk Format
- DVD PAL (720 X 576) DVD Disk Format – European
- HD 720p (1280 X 720) High Definition
- HD 1080p (1920 X 1080) High Definition

The following image shows the render options menu for the AVI format:

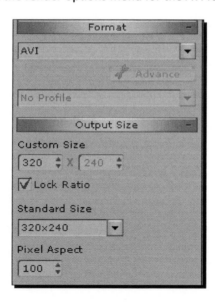

RM

Real Media. What can you say about this ground breaking media format that hasn't already been said? Much has been written about it too. Real Media holds a soft spot in this author's heart as it was one of the early media formats back in the infancy of the internet that could stream audio and video from a dial-up internet connection!

And as fond as this author is of the format, in my own productions it has been relegated to the dustbin of digital technology that may never see the light of day again unless needed to fill some niche only RM could reach. Hard to imagine that niche right now as there are many other great formats available.

Quick select render profiles available for the RM format are:

- 128k Dual ISDN
- 150k LAN
- 12k Substream for 28k Dial Up
- 16K Substream for 28k Dial Up
- 26k Substream for 56k Dial Up
- 256k DSL or Cable
- 384k DSL or Cable
- 512k DSL or Cable
- 768k DSL or Cable
- 28k Dial-up
- 56k Dial-Up
- 64k Dial-Up

The following image shows the output size options available for the Real Media (RM) format:

WMV

Windows Media Video files are very popular on the web and play in the native Windows Media Player that is installed on a large base of computers worldwide. WMV format is a streaming format created specifically for streaming video and audio over the internet. Next to the AVI format, this is my second favorite format and the format in which most of my final renders to clients or uploaded to the web are streamed with. While my final production renders are from a video editor I do find myself using WMV in iClone at high quality for preview work as it renders faster on my system than uncompressed AVI.

WMV is a good general choice for streaming over the internet while maintaining high quality. I upload my YouTube™ and Vimeo™ videos to the web in this format. This is a very versatile streaming container file. It is also used for DVDs and Blu-ray Discs since the adoption of SMPTE standards with version 9.

The following image shows the quality settings sliders pop up activated by the Advance button for the WMV format:

High Definition rendering in both 720p (1280X720) and 1080p (1920X1080) are available with the WMV file format. You can also set a custom size resolution:

- ◆ 320 X 240, Multi-Media
- ◆ 640 X 480, Multi-Media
- ◆ 800 X 600, Multi-Media
- ◆ VCD NTSC (352 X 240) North America and Japan
- ◆ VCD PAL (352 X 288) Europe
- ◆ SVCD NTSC (480 X 480) North America and Japan
- ◆ DVD NTSC (720 X 480) DVD Disk Format

- ◆ DVD PAL (720 X 576) DVD Disk Format – European
- ◆ HD 720p (1280 X 720) High Definition
- ◆ HD 1080p (1920 X 1080) High Definition

MP4 for PC

The MP4 file format, also known as MPEG-4, was touted as an alternative to MP3 but still lags behind in adoption and usage, which is surprising considering its higher quality AAC (audio) codec. It is another excellent container file for streaming audio and video over the internet that was born out of an earlier Apple QuickTime file format.

MP4 formats also include 3GP and 3G2 used by 3G phones. iTunes and iPods use the MP4 file format and it can be replayed in several popular players such as QuickTime, Windows Media Player and the Real Player.

The following image shows the Render menu and options for the MP4 container file format:

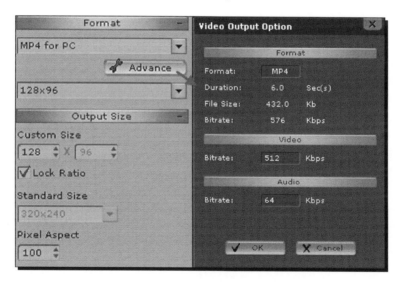

Quick select render profiles along with custom options available are:

- ◆ 128 X 96
- ◆ 176 X 144
- ◆ 352 X 288
- ◆ 704 X 576

Flash video

Flash video, FLV, has become so popular that sites like YouTube, Vevo, and Hulu use flash as their native video format. If you're not familiar with Flash then you're probably not aware of how much flash video you have watched over the internet.

While it has been argued for many years that Flash is a mature platform soon to start fading to obsolescence, it simply hasn't happened yet. Flash has an enormous installed base of flash players out there.

The following chart is taken from Adobe's research concerning the market penetration of the Flash player(`http://www.adobe.com/products/player_census/flashplayer/ version_penetration.html`):

	Flash Player 9 & below	Flash Player 10	Flash Player 10.1
Mature Markets	99.6%	99.0%	85.3%
US/Canada	99.9%	99.5%	87.4%
Europe	99.7%	99.5%	86.2%
Japan	98.6%	97.4%	78.6%
Australia/New Zealand	99.1%	98.3%	83.3%
Emerging Markets	98.8%	97.0%	82.4%

This type of installed base and market penetration makes the Flash format a very attractive option for streaming quality audio and video across the web. The chances that Flash Players are installed on the computers of your target group are greatly enhanced with the dominating market position.

Flash, as a web video delivery format, is an excellent choice due to its ability to produce high quality video and audio with small file sizes and play on a larger number of computers than the WMV format. The Flash player itself is compact in size and overhead and will auto-install when used with the proper code. Being vector based the flash output is scalable allowing it to play on almost any size of player or webpage.

For use as a temporary editing media flash has its drawbacks due to a lack of importing FLV capabilities in most editors so it is not used as often as a media for re-rendering in pipeline applications such as special effects or video editing.

The following image shows the Flash format menu and **Quality Settings** panel:

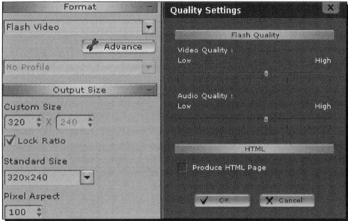

Some options for the Flash format are as follows:

- Custom quality sliders to 100%
- Custom options for size

Using good video rendering habits

Like everything else, it's good to start early on creating good work habits, particularly when rendering out our work.

Determining end usage

What is the video going to be used for?

- The Internet
- Mobile phones
- Desktop applications
- DVDs
- Some or all of the above

Knowing all the possible end uses for the video will be helpful in determining what format to use. For just the web, Flash and WMV are great choices. For the web and desktop applications I'd give the nod to Flash. For phones we'd probably want to use MP4 at the appropriate resolution of the target phone.

If, as we discussed earlier, we will be using this footage in other video applications in our production pipeline, then we want to go with AVI.

Setting screen resolution as soon as possible

It is generally better to choose our project resolution when we start the project if at all possible. Old style television is at a 4:3 screen ratio, whereas the newer High Definition televisions are 16:9 ratio. There is a drastic difference in visible screen area from the same camera spot between these two standards.

Changing mid-stream in the project could result in the loss of camera work to that point by having to reposition the cameras again. Choosing the resolution as early as possible can eliminate this problem.

> 720p in uncompressed AVI provides a good starting point and balance in terms of quality and resources.

Time for action – rendering our main project video

We've discussed the various formats and codecs available, so it's now time for us to render out the video from our main project:

1. Open our ongoing project.

2. Select the **Camera Switch** with the camera selector drop-down in the upper-right corner of the workspace.

3. Select the **Export** tab.

4. Click on the **Video** button.

5. Select **AVI** in the format drop-down menu.

6. Select **HD 720p (1280X720)** in the **Standard Size** drop-down menu.

7. Make sure **Final Render** is checked and **Anti-aliased** is selected.

8. Choose your render output range. In this example, we will end the render at frame 2530, which is after they say hi to Benny. Your ending point may vary.

9. Leave the frame rate at 30.

> Frame Rate can vary as film runs at 24 frames per second (fps) whereas NTSC TV is 29.97 fps. PAL format uses 25 fps. In the early days of the Internet, Flash videos were created at 12 to 15 fps to save time and overhead. Now 30 fps is widely used and provides a much smoother video. This author uses 30 fps when rendering out of iClone.

10. Click on the **Export** button.

11. Navigate to the location you wish to store the video at.

12. Name the video and press the **Save** button.

What just happened?

We have just rendered out our first iClone video! Rendering time depends on the hardware, the scene, and other variables and can take from seconds to hours.

You probably noticed on step 5 that the camera view changed significantly when the HD 720p option was chosen. This demonstrates the difference in view when working in 4:3 ratio then rendering in 16:9 ratio. While it had little effect on this scene, it could have a major impact on screens that are dependent on camera angle, prop placement, or mattes. This further demonstrates the need to choose resolution size as early in the project as possible.

The final rendered video showcases a lot of what we have learned to this point. While it is not perfect animation, it is a great starting point for novice animators.

Rendering popVideo

As stated earlier, popVideo is a video with an alpha channel. These videos can then be layered from front-to-back to achieve a certain look or effect. 3D assets in the scenes can also be changed out with popVideo planes to lower the face count of the scene and reduce any lag issues.

popVideo comes in two formats: *iClone.popVideo* and *WidgetCast.iWidget*. Both are Reallusion proprietary formats for use with iClone, and the latter is also used with their WidgetCast product.

Rendering out a popVideo is basically the same as rendering the AVI and other formats. Choose video and audio quality, size, and other options then click the **Export** button.

If you are rendering out in the iWidget format there is an optional button available that will open Reallusion's WidgetCast product after the render is over. This makes the operation seamless between creating a video in iClone and getting it to the Web in WidgetCast.

3D rendering... got glasses?

Ok... now we're really confused. What do you mean by 3D render? Isn't that what we've been doing? Afraid not, at least not in context to this type of 3D rendering, which refers to stereoscopic or channel rendering. We've all seen the funny glasses a viewer must use to see the effect and most of us will remember the blue and red tints.

The following image shows some of the different 3D effect glasses available. The glasses on the top row are for Anaglyphic, with the top left being the proper lens combination for iClone. The glasses on the top right will not work with the iClone 3D render. The bottom glasses are for other methods such as Side X Side or Top Down, which may require active shutter technology or other types of polarized lens:

Understanding 3D stereoscopic rendering

As it turns out, there is a lot to know about stereoscopic rendering or 3D Stereovision as it's referred to in iClone. The way in which a scene is set up and how the action is framed are key to the success of this render method.

Chief among the important points in setting up a scene for this type of render concerns the convergence point, as everything in front of the convergence point will pop out and everything behind the convergence point will "go deep" according to Reallusion. Any character, prop, or any item in focus that partially or completely leaves the viewing area will lose the stereoscopic effect so keep this in mind when determining the convergence point.

Reallusion has some excellent information in their **Help** section with links to the various requirements for viewing 3D successfully.

The following image demonstrates how the objects will appear depending on the scene setup:

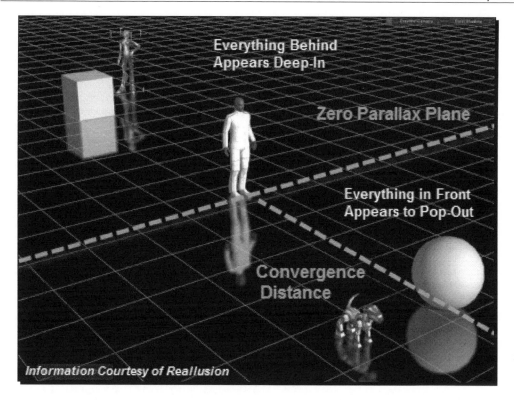

While doing some research on this topic, I was very surprised to find out that Stereoscopy, in general, was invented by Sir Charles Wheatstone in 1838! To say it's been around a while is certainly an understatement. In that time, we have discovered a lot about how our vision works and what techniques work best to present images to us in something other than a flat plane.

What Sir Wheatstone discovered was the method of presenting a slightly different image to each eye. According to Wikipedia this early version did not define depth very well due to a lack of an important visual clue, Accommodation of the Eyeball (focus).

Since that time great strides have been made in understanding the eye and how it reacts with this type of 3D technology.

There are several types of stereoscopic rendering available in iClone:

- Anaglyph
- Side X Side
- Top Down
- Two Files

Anaglyph

Anaglyphic 3D uses the stereoscopic method with one image for each eye. The left image being red and the right image cyan, which according to Wikipedia provides better color than the blue used in times past. Animations, DVD's, films, and video can all be produced and displayed economically making it a popular choice of available formats.

> There are two standards of colored anaglyphic glasses. iClone uses the RED/ CYAN combination with Red on the LEFT eye and cyan on the RIGHT eye.

The following image demonstrates an anaglyphic render. The electronic version of this book will show the effects. A full color image is included in the downloadable code bundle if you are using the print version. Red and Cyan 3D glasses are required to view the effect:

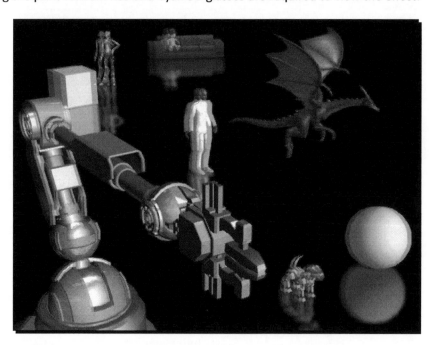

Time for action – setting up the scene

We are going to set up and render a simple scene to showcase the power of stereoscopic 3D via the anaglyphic method:

1. Create a new scene.

2. Use *Ctrl + G* or go into the preferences to turn on the grid.

3. Select the **Set** tab and click on the **Water** button.

4. In the **Content Manager** on the left side menu, click on the **Still Normal** folder.

5. Double-click on the **Water 9** in the **Still Normal** folder to load it into the workspace.

6. Set the water height to zero in the **Basic Water Parameters** section of the right menu.

7. Click on the color and select **Black** as the color (the water will not be black yet).

8. Select the **Stage** tab and click on the **2D Background** button.

9. Select **Black** as the color.

10. Uncheck the **Active** box under the **Image Background** section.

11. Select the **Set** tab and click on the **Props** button.

12. Click on the **Plus** icon next to the **iProps** folder in the **Content Manager**.

13. Click on the **Home** folder within the **iProps** folder.

14. Double-click on the sofa to load it into the workspace.

15. Move the sofa forward to the middle of the scene and rotate it 180 degrees.

16. Double-click on the bed prop in the **iProps** folder to load it into the workspace.

17. Move it towards the couch and to the left with part of the bed off screen.

18. Select the **Actor** tab and double-click on the Jana character to load her into the workspace.

19. Move the Jana character back and to the right beside the couch then rotate her towards the camera (see the following image).

20. With the Jana character selected, right-click on her and choose **Move_Forward** from the **Move** menu.

21. Click on an area forward of the couch, in front of the camera, to have the Jana character walk towards the camera and stop just before she actually gets to the camera so she will be fully framed by the shot (see the following image).

22. Select the couch then right-click on the couch and under the **Operate** menu choose **Sit_Down**.

23. Select the Jana character then right-click on the Jana character and from the **Operate** menu choice select **Sofa-Sit1**.

The following image shows the results of the previous steps where Jana moves to the camera then back to sit down on the couch:

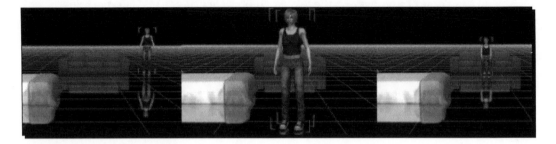

What just happened?

We set the scene up with the couch and bed to give us some perspective and to help with distance. The character gave us our focal point and by animating it towards the camera then back to the couch, we could observe the difference in how the character stood out from the props.

The combination of props and character movement which stayed within the frame of the camera demonstrates the effectiveness of the anaglyphic render process.

Time for action – rendering the scene

We've set up our stage area and now we need to start the actual 3D render of the scene:

1. Select the **Export** tab

2. Click on the **Video** button.

3. Select **WMV** format from the drop-down menu on the right menu panel.

4. Select **HD 720P (1280X720)** from the **Standard Size** drop-down menu.

5. Check the **Stereo Vision Output** box.

6. Click on the **Anaglyph** option to select it.

7. Leave the **Convergence Distance** at 500.

8. Set the **Range** from 1 to 1400 or just after the Jana character completes the motions we assigned.

9. Click on the **Export** button.

10. Navigate to the location where you wish to store the rendered video.

11. Name the video and press the **Save** button to begin the render.

What just happened?

We selected the proper settings and rendered out our first stereoscopic video! Now put on those funny 3D glasses and enjoy!

Have a go hero – experimenting with the convergence distance

Now that we've set up and rendered our first stereoscopic 3D scene, it's time to experiment with the convergence distance to see what affect it has on our scene at various settings.

Render out tests at 250, 500, 700, and so forth to discover the effects of each distance on the scene.

Side X Side

In this method, left and right images are exported together. It also requires special equipment such as a 3D Player and glasses.

This would be exported in the same manner as the anaglyphic render while choosing Side X Side in the render options. Shutter or polarized glasses are needed for this method.

The following image shows a Side X Side 3D render:

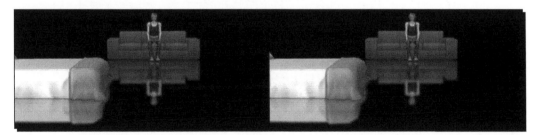

Top Down

Top Down is yet another method requiring special equipment such as a 3D player and specialized glasses. As you can see in the following image, it creates a dual image above and below each other:

 Side by Side and Top Down are typically supported by the higher end players for 3D capable monitors and glasses systems.

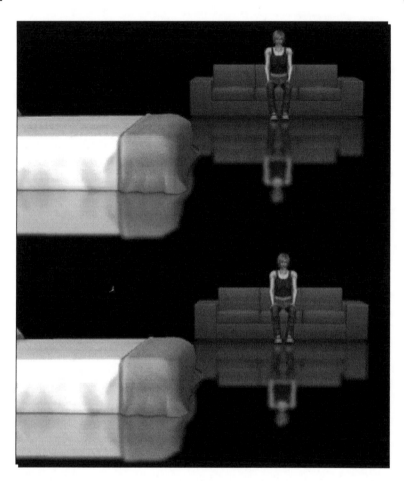

Two Files

The Two File or DualStream method part ways with the previous methods, in that it creates both a left channel and right channel file when rendered. These files are then used with specialized equipment to replay in the 3D format.

 Be very careful when first adopting 3D stereoscopic rendering methods other than anaglyphic due to the cost, including the need for specialized equipment (and video cards, in some cases) then there are the specialized glasses to consider. Do your research before jumping off into these other techniques. Your choices will vary depending on whether it's a 3D capable TV or a computer monitor. The cost of active shutter glasses can be a show stopper in some cases.

Summary

Rendering is a rather dry subject. More technical than hands-on but knowing the available options and how to best manipulate them to your needs is an added bonus to your skillset. We've also discovered that rendering isn't just about videos. In fact, videos are just a small part of rendering, as still images and image sequences are a very important part of the entertainment arts industry today.

In this chapter, we covered the following:

- What rendering is and its importance to the animation process
- How to render single images for use in print or artwork
- How to render out image sequences for use in third-party tools and editors
- Formats and codecs, what they are and what they do
- Formats available for different uses
- Good rendering habits
- 3D Stereoscopic rendering

We've put a lot of work behind us and it's time to put all those new found skills to use in the next chapter's space project that will test what we've learned in our journey along the iClone animation skill path.

Pop quiz

1. A codec is:

    a. A video container file.

    b. A program that compresses/decompresses an audio/video file.

    c. A scripting language.

    d. An audio/video editing tool.

2. Which of the following would be a codec?

    a. WMV

    b. RM

    c. MP4

    d. VP8

    e. All of the above

    f. None of the above

3. MP4 for PC is:

    a. A codec

    b. A video container file

    c. An audio container file

    d. All of the above

    e. None of the above

9
Animating Outer Space

The hard work is behind us and now we are going to have fun animating an outer space scene with custom 3D assets created for this project. In this chapter, we are going to put to use what we have learned up to this point to create a visually pleasing outer space scene.

In this chapter we shall:

- Plan and layout our outer space scene
- Create the scene by building it out from our star and nebula filled project, which we created in an earlier chapter
- Set up multiple cameras for use with a camera switch
- Tweak the scene and adjust final lighting, if necessary
- Import, place, and animate scene assets
- Render the scene

So let's get on with it...

Reviewing the project assets

The downloadable assets for this project are located in the code bundle on the book page at www.packtpub.com.

These assets include the following:

- space scene created in earlier chapter
- space freighter prop
- shuttle craft prop

We will be adding these elements to the already existing space scene but for the sake of efficiency we need to take some time now and plan out our scene. What are we going to do with the assets and which assets will be animated or static?

Laying out and planning the scene

To layout the scene we just have to ask ourselves a few questions. The first questions are generic to any scene, then we'll follow up with specific questions for this project. The following sub-sections will highlight those questions with their own section.

Whether you choose to use a more disciplined method or not, is entirely up to you. That's one of the great things about machinima—we get to do what we want, not what someone else tells us to do.

If you are animating strictly for fun, friends and family, or co-workers, you might just want to dive right in and start building out the scene. Many machinimist/animators do this. In some cases, good machinima could have been great, had it been planned out. In other cases, spontaneous creation was the key to success.

The great thing is we have a choice in how we do each project and for the sake of this project we are going to plan it out.

Determining the purpose of the scene

If this was a professional project, we would have a tightly scripted scene with exact instructions to convey the message/purpose of the scene. In the case of machinima, we may have a script where a scene calls for dialog that may or may not give us direction and instructions or we may just have an idea that needs to be quantified to be realized.

Whether we have a script or not, this first question is very important and will stay with us for the entire project, so we have to make sure we get it right. This is also the starting point of just about any type of creative project as you have to plan and brainstorm before you can write a script!

What are we trying to accomplish here?

The idea is to have a space freighter moving across the screen horizontally, perhaps at an angle, until it reaches a certain point on the screen where it will explode. The craft will start off screen on the left and continue towards the right side of the screen until it reaches about three-quarters of the way across where we will launch an escape shuttle and trigger the built-in explosion for the large freighter prop.

Determining render resolution

We have already briefly discussed how determining resolution should be done early in the project to prevent any unnecessary grief as the project matures to the render stage. This brings to mind another very important question in which the latter part of the question is determined by the answer to the first part of the question.

What are we going to use this for and what resolution suits that purpose?

We want to show our creation off on the web on one of the video sharing sites like YouTube and Vimeo or we might want to post it to our own website. This tells us basically everything we need to know, in this case to set up our project resolution.

Time for action – setting the resolution

Time to jump right in, so let's get started:

1. Open the space background project we created earlier in Chapter 7, *Enhancing Scenes with Images and Videos,* or open the Red Star field project provided in the code bundle.

2. Select the **Export** tab.

3. Click on the **Video** button.

4. Choose **WMV** (if for some reason WMV is not available on your computer you can choose another format to continue the project).

Changing file types later

We can change file types anytime later, but we must set the resolution to the same size after changing file types to recover our scene for render in another format, like AVI or RM, without having to make adjustments to cameras.

5. Set the **Custom Size** in the **Output Size** section of the right panel to 640 X 360 which is the 16:9 screen ratio used in high definition.

6. Select **Preview Camera** in the camera selection drop-down menu.

7. Delete any custom cameras other than the preview camera to make sure we have the same initial scene. You can delete these from the **Scene Manager** or **Camera Manager**.

8. Save the project under any name you find appropriate.

What just happened?

We re-used a previously created scene and we also did a little housekeeping to clean up any unnecessary items left over when we created the scene in Chapter 7, *Enhancing Scenes with Images and Videos*. We will frame new camera shots for this project.

Since we decided this is for the Web, we picked a web-friendly size that will fit most web-based players and show off our work with clarity and quality. We chose 640 X 360 because it is half of the standard 720p (1280 X 720), which gives it the proper screen ratio for HD playback on a smaller scale.

We can also render at 1280 X 720 (720p) and reduce the final render in our video editor to 640 X 360. This gives us the option of using both sizes without affecting our camera shots when we change sizes.

Downsizing is not a problem with quality during a re-render, but increasing the resolution from the original render size is not recommended as it will have poorer quality and possibly pixilation when rendered out of the third part video editor.

Determining the scene animation

We know at this point, the space freighter and shuttle props will be animated as they need to move across the screen. The space freighter will plod along horizontally across the screen and the shuttle will escape at an angle to the ship.

Both could be animated with or without paths. We will animate the space freighter without a path as it is only across the screen movement. We will, however, use a path for a smooth escape trajectory with the shuttle.

Determining the particle effects required

This will be fairly simple. We know we have an explosion, so we will probably be using the fire particles. The duration will be short since it's in the vacuum of space.

There are some great special effects in additional content packs by Reallusion at the Content Store that would work great with this scene, but we will rely on what comes with the stock iClone installation for this project.

Laying out the scene tasks

Now we have the purpose, the resolution, the animation required, and preliminary particle effects, which we may expand usage of as the project progresses. Now we need to organize how we are going to build out the scene:

1. Tweak the project to fit the new resolution.
2. Animate outer space to live space.
3. Set the atmospheric lighting.
4. Add the space freighter prop.
5. Animate the space freighter movement.
6. Add the shuttle prop.
7. Add the shuttle path.
8. Animate the shuttle to the path.
9. Determine the explosion frame and trigger explosion animation.
10. Attach and adjust particle effects.
11. Set up the shot list.
12. Add camera according to the shot list.
13. Set up **Camera Switch.**
14. Render out project.

Tweaking the project assets

Now that we have set the project resolution we need to adjust the placement of scene assets for use in this project. You never want two projects to look alike, so when re-purposing assets it is generally a good idea to present them in a different manner.

Time for action – adjusting the existing scene

To work on our scene, we need to get a camera view and then setup our assets in a way that intersect with each other to fill the void space:

1. With the **Preview Camera** selected, zoom out and move the mouse to the right of the screen to rotate the view so we can see the 2D planes clearly.

The following image shows the 2D planes and **Star Globe Glow** prop. The background has been lightened to see the planes more clearly:

2. With the Red Star image plane selected, use the input box on the right side menu, set the Z rotational axis to zero.

3. Set the scale to 1000 with the **Lock XYZ** box checked to scale all three axes.

4. With the Nebula image plane selected, use the input box on the right side menu, set the z rotational axis to zero.

5. Set the scale to 1000 with the **Lock XYZ** box checked to scale all three axes.

6. With the Starfield image plane selected, use the input box on the right side menu, set the z rotational axis to zero.

7. Set the scale to 1000 with the **Lock XYZ** box checked to scale all three axes.

8. Select the Star Globe prop and set the scale to 1000 with the **Lock XYZ** box checked.

9. Move the planes to positions similar to the following image, which shows the project from an angled side view and front view. The planes are in front of each other:

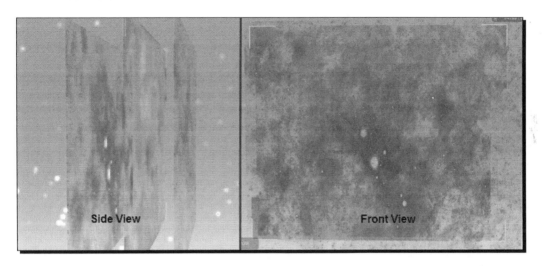

10. Rotate the **Preview Camera** to a front view similar to the right side of the previous image.

What just happened?

We removed the Z axis rotation from the 2D images planes, putting them all on the zero axis. We then resized each image plane to 1000 on all three axes so we would have plenty of room to work with as the scene develops.

We then moved the image planes to a more orderly layered position with the Star field image at the front, or forward of the other planes, followed by the Nebula and then the Red Star image planes.

We are now set up to start development of our scene with some basic movement animation for two of the three image planes in the scene. If you lightened up your background color to see the planes more easily, then set the color back to black before we proceed.

Time for action – turning outer space into live space

We are going to be using very simple and short horizontal movement of the image planes to give outer space a little more pizazz. In essence, we will be turning dead space into live space.

1. Select the **Preview Camera**.

2. Click the **Add** button in the camera dialog to add a new camera.

3. Center the image layers in the camera shot and zoom in until the image layers fill the viewer similar to the following image:

4. Select the Nebula image layer.

5. Click on the **Move** tool in the top toolbar and press *Ctrl + Q* to activate the gizmo, if it's not already visible.

6. Move the time scrubber all the way down to the last frame or click on the **End** button on the bottom toolbar (frame 2000 unless you changed the frame count).

7. Move the Nebula image layer to the left about an inch or two at the most. Just a subtle movement. A keyframe will be generated on the timeline.

8. Select the Starfield image layer.

9. Select the **Move** tool.

10. While still on the last frame, move the Starfield layer about an inch or two to the right of the workspace just opposite the Nebula movement.

11. Return the time scrubber to the first frame and playback the scene. If the movement is too much or not enough, then go back and adjust how much the two image layers move off the screen. Make this adjustment in the last frame for each image layer.

12. Save the project and play the animation.

What just happened?

Instead of having a rather dull and lifeless space scene, we animated two of the three image layers to move slightly off screen in opposite directions. Even with a static camera, there is now animated motion involved that brings space to life and makes it pop out at the viewer.

We wanted this type of motion to be more subtle, therefore, very little horizontal movement was required and in fact the less movement the better, as long as the viewer can discern movement.

In fact, during the previous two action sections we have improved outer space quite a bit over the static background/backdrop type of space scene. The image planes are layered as they are can give the viewer a feeling of volume compared to a 2D background and the slight movement of the image layers draws the eye in to the scene.

Movement adds appeal

Slight or hinted image plane movement can add depth and make the scene more interesting and more alive to the viewer. Create a depth of space between layers.

Time for action – lighting the scene

Let's add some basic atmospheric lighting to our outer space scene:

1. Select the **Stage** tab.

2. Click on the **Atmosphere** button.

3. Click on the **HDR** checkbox to activate HDR lighting.

4. Click on the **Tone Map** checkbox to activate the tone map.

5. Turn the **Exposure** down to around 20 or to your liking.

6. Set the **Glare** type to **Spectral Cross**.

7. Set the **Scale** to 1.

The following image shows the scene after adding atmospheric lighting:

What just happened?

We took a few minutes to set up the atmospheric lighting. We might have to adjust these settings as we add assets and set up camera angles. We may eventually choose not to use atmospheric lighting at all, but by setting it up now we will have the opportunity to see how the scene develops with HDR lighting.

Always keep in mind not to blow out the lighting of a scene by using settings that are too extreme. Many animators consider too much light to be almost as bad as not enough.

 When using HDR lighting we will need to review our scene after changes, adding new scene assets or moving existing scene objects. These all have direct effects on HDR lighting.

Time for action – importing scene assets

It's now time to import our scene assets, the Packt Freighter and the Escape Shuttle props. We must use the import feature for this action so the props will import at the proper location in the workspace for us to prep them for the scene.

1. Select the **Set** tab.

2. Click on the **Props** button.

3. Click on the **Import** button in the right menu panel.

4. Locate the Packt Animated Freighter prop in the code bundle.

5. With the Packt Animated Freighter prop highlighted, click the **Import** button on the right side menu.

6. Locate the Escape Shuttle prop in the code bundle.

7. With the **Escape Shuttle** prop highlighted, click the import button to load the shuttle which we will not be able to see yet.

8. Select the **Escape Shuttle** in the **Scene Manager**.

9. Select the **Preview Camera** from the camera selection dropdown menu.

10. With the Escape shuttle selected, click on the **Home** icon in the upper toolbar to focus the camera view on the shuttle prop.

11. Select the **Stage** tab.

12. Click on the **Atmosphere** button.

13. Turn off the **Tone Map** on the right side menu in the **HDR Settings**.

14. With the Escape shuttle still selected, click on the **Pick Parent** button in the **Linkage** section of the right side menu and click on the freighter near the shuttle prop to link it to the freighter prop. Once again this creates a controllable timeline event.

15. Select the Packt Freighter prop.

16. Set the scale to 10% with the **Lock XYZ** box checked in the **Scale** area of the **Transform** section.

17. Save the project under a different file name. Choose whatever filename is relevant or comfortable to you.

The following image shows the shuttle loaded onto the freighter prop with the **Import** button. This is after linking, but before it is scaled down to 10% of the original size:

What just happened?

We loaded our main props, the Packt Freighter and the Escape Shuttle into the scene. We switched cameras so that Camera 1 would keep our shot and used the Home icon to frame the shuttle prop in the preview camera so we could attach it to the freighter prop. We used the **Link** feature instead of **Attach** so we could animate de-linking in the timeline.

By selecting the freighter prop and scaling this large prop down to 10% of its original size the attached shuttle craft scaled with the freighter prop. We could have made these props at the proper scale in Studio Max, but we need to polish our skills in working with different sizes of props when imported.

Since this scene will have no characters in it, we do not need the props to be large scale or even character scale. Smaller scale assets are easier to work with in the iClone workspace. At its native size we may have to use a Large Scene camera to film with, so scaling it down just makes sense in terms of working with the scene.

Storyboarding with iClone

We have our scene and we have our assets loaded, so now would be a good time to think about how the scene will flow and storyboard it, with a few single image renders.

When some people think of storyboards, they think of elaborate hand drawn artwork that depicts the scene's action at certain points in the story. In reality, storyboards are anything from the aforementioned elaborate artwork to scribbles and stick figures on paper.

iClone was built for storyboarding. You can render out still images from the project to give you an idea of the flow of production. Storyboards aren't always an exact visualization of the final scene but they are visual aids that work particularly well with teams.

You might think that working alone won't need storyboards and that could be largely true, but if you use storyboards, you just might find out things about your project you wouldn't normally know about until you started the actual animation work. It's always better to know about any potential problems long before you start animating the scene and storyboards are a valuable tool for discovery.

In many cases, you may find your preconceived shot list needs some adjustment, as some shots may not frame out as visualized. A render for a storyboard shot will demonstrate this. A storyboard is also a great visual aid to voice actors for understanding the scene.

Now that we have our assets in the scene it would be a good time to create some simple storyboards to help determine our preliminary shot list which we will create in another subsection of this chapter.

Since this is just the conceptual stage we won't concern ourselves with getting everything perfect. We just want to get a good sense of prop position and camera angles.

Time for action – creating our initial storyboard frame

The opening of any storyboard sequence usually shows the first bit of action, so we are going to position, at least initially, our freighter prop and render out the initial action shot of the scene:

1. Select **Camera01** for our initial view.

2. Select the **Packt Animated Freighter** prop.

3. Make sure the time scrubber is at the beginning.

4. Rotate the prop and move it slightly off screen to the right of the screen.

The following image shows the Packt Freighter prop rotated and moved to the right side of the screen before being moved completely off screen to the right:

5. Click on the **End** button located on the bottom toolbar.

6. Move the freighter prop across the screen towards the left until it is just out of view.

7. Preview the movement. If you like it, save the file under a new filename.

8. Move the time scrubber down a few hundred frames until the freighter is about one-third of the way across the screen.

9. Select the **Export** tab.

10. Click on the **Image** button.

11. Select **JPG** as the format.

12. Set the size to 640 X 360 (or 1280 X 720, if you prefer).

13. Click the **Render** button to render the image.

14. Navigate to the location of your choice and save the image as `space_freighter_001.jpg`.

 We can change export sizes easily when the ratio is the same, such as 1280 X 720 to 640 X 360. It's only when we change the aspect ratio of the render that we may have to reframe our camera shots.

What just happened?

We rotated the freighter prop so it could be animated from right to left horizontally across the screen during the scene. We then moved the freighter prop completely off the screen to the right in the first frame, jumped to the end frame and moved the freighter just off the screen to the left.

We then rendered out our first storyboard image in jpg format as shown in the following screenshot:

Time for action – storyboarding the action at mid-scene

Now that we have the freighter moving, we need to set a close-up shot of the shuttle just before it leaves the craft:

1. Move the time scrubber about one-third of the way towards the end (around frame 570, in this example). This should put the freighter in front and just slightly past the larger red stars in the center of the background.

2. Select the **Preview Camera**.

3. Select the shuttle prop.

4. Click on **Home** to move the **Preview Camera** to the shuttle.

5. With the **Preview Camera** selected, click on the **Add** button in the right menu panel to add a new camera.

6. Rename this camera to Shuttle Cam.

The following image shows the Camera01 shot on the left and the newly created Shuttle Cam on the right:

7. Click on the **Link** button and select the shuttle to link the Shuttle Cam to the shuttle prop.

8. Select the **Export** tab.

9. Click on the **Image** button.

10. Click on the **Export** button.

11. Navigate to a location of your choice and save the image as `space_freighter_002.jpg`.

12. Select **Camera01**.

13. Select the **Export** tab.

14. Click on the **Image** button.

15. Click on the **Export** tab to export the Camera01 image.

What just happened?

We moved down the timeline until the freighter was positioned to our liking, then we created a new camera to focus on the shuttle and used this as the basis for a storyboard shot. This shot represents a time just before lift-off of the shuttle and before the explosion.

We then select Camera01 and rendered an image from it for another storyboard shot to depict the movement of the ship across the screen. We now have a total of three storyboard shots from two cameras.

 The camera icon (and point light icons) can become visible in a scene even after being turned off previously. Simply toggle the visibility in the appropriate section of the scene manager to correct.

Time for action – storyboarding the shuttle escape

This shot will be fairly simple and will take place just at a short distance down the timeline:

1. Select the Shuttle Cam camera.

2. Move the time scrubber down the timeline 200 frames (frame 770 in this example).

3. Select the Escape Shuttle prop.

4. Click on the **Unlink** button in the right side menu.

5. Move the time scrubber forward by five frames (775).

6. Move the shuttle straight up to where it clears the freighter.

7. Move the time scrubber down the timeline to 900.

8. Raise the shuttle prop straight up again, where it will clear the dishes and antennae of the freighter prop.

9. Move the time scrubber back about 120 frames (779).

10. Select the **Export** tab.

11. Click on the **Image** button.

12. Click on the **Export** button to export the image.

The following image shows our storyboard shot at this point in the action:

What just happened?

We unlinked the shuttle then moved it abruptly up to simulate a launch so the shuttle prop will clear the freighter prop. By using the Link feature, instead of the Attach feature, we are able to link and unlink in the timeline, giving us precise control over unlinking the shuttle prop from the freighter prop.

We then moved down the timeline about 120 frames for the shuttle escape launch to play out.

Time for action – storyboarding the explosion

We've launched the escape shuttle, so our next task will be to blow up the freighter. Did you bring some high explosives? Don't worry... I've built it into the prop for a no fuss, no mess explosion of near planetary proportions:

1. Move the time scrubber to a point on the timeline where the shuttle has already launched and the freighter is just starting to pass beneath it. In this example, that is around frame 800.

2. Click on the **Time Setting Panel** icon near the counter on the bottom toolbar.

3. Change the frame count to 3000.

4. Select the Packt Animated Freighter prop.

5. Right-click and from the **Perform** sub-menu, click on **Explode** and let the animation run until it stops.

 Prematurely stopping an animation from completing its run can truncate the animation. Delete the animation, return to the proper time, and reload.

6. Select **Camera01**.

7. Move the time scrubber back to a point on the timeline where the shuttle has launched and the freighter has started to explode (around frame 872, in this example).

8. Select the **Export** tab.

9. Click on the **Image** button.

10. Click on the **Export** button to render the image.

What just happened?

After moving the time scrubber down the timeline to a point where the shuttle has launched, we triggered the built-in animation of the prop to blow it up. This prop was custom-built just for this book and demonstrates the ease of using my destructible line of props. All of the tedious hard work in animating and simulating the explosion has been taken care of, where all we have to do is trigger the explosion from the right-click menu. Now how easy is that?

The following image depicts the explosion of the freighter and makes a nice storyboard shot:

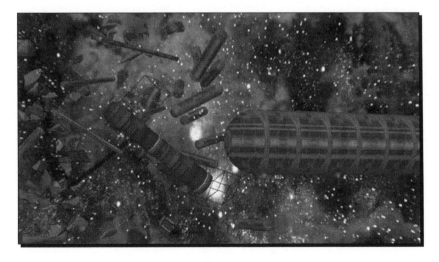

Time for action – storyboarding the shuttle leaving

In just a few frames, after we trigger the explosion, the shuttle is actually hit by a large piece of debris. We can correct that while we set up the shuttle escape:

1. Move the time scrubber down the timeline around 50 to 75 frames from the beginning of the explosion.

2. Select the **Shuttle Cam**.

3. Select the Escape Shuttle prop.

4. Right-click on the Escape Shuttle prop.

5. Select **Timeline** from the menu.

6. Move the time scrubber to the last key frame we created for the Escape shuttle earlier. That's frame 900, in this example (the last movement of the shuttle).

7. Move the shuttle forward towards the left side of the screen. Because the camera is linked to the shuttle, it will not go off screen. Continue to move the shuttle until you are satisfied it has moved enough.

8. Save the file under a new filename.

9. Select the **Export** tab.

10. Click on the **Image** button.

11. Click on the **Export** button to export our last storyboard frame.

    The following image shows the shuttle escaping the explosion. If we actually use this shot in our final version, we will need to adjust some of the image planes as we can already see some of them no longer covering the background of our shot on the left side:

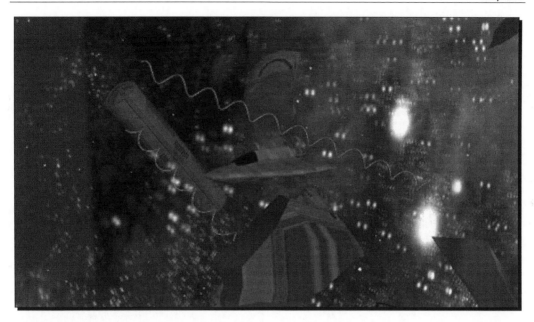

What just happened?

We went back to the last animated key frame of the shuttle and moved the shuttle forward giving it the illusion of escaping through the debris.

This provides us with our last shot in the storyboard, and along the way as we created these shots, we also did a lot of our animation work for the final production. It makes for a great starting point to tweak the scene further.

Analyzing our storyboard

As we review our storyboard, we can see that we have a solid line of progression starting from beginning to end of the scene. Nothing is out of order so all we have to do now is improve and clean up our scene.

The following image shows the storyboard we have created for our scene. iClone is a natural storyboarding tool with its ability to render out different camera angles at lightning quick speed:

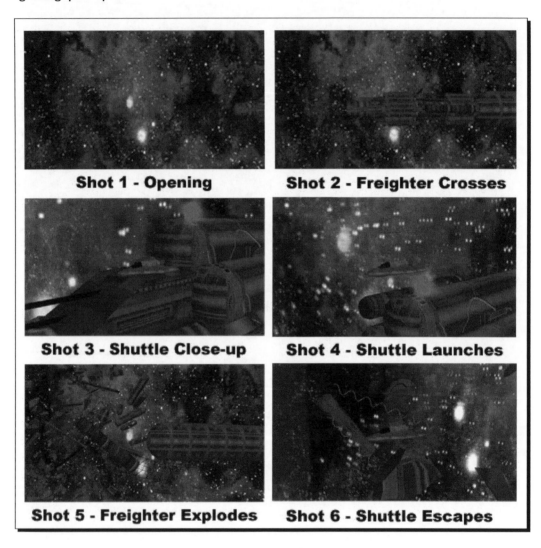

Shot 1 - Opening

Shot 2 - Freighter Crosses

Shot 3 - Shuttle Close-up

Shot 4 - Shuttle Launches

Shot 5 - Freighter Explodes

Shot 6 - Shuttle Escapes

Time for action – setting up the animated shuttle path

We will now animate our shuttle escape that will most likely be our most difficult segment to animate as it all depends on timing. This segment could be animated without a path and would be easier to accomplish but wouldn't be as smooth a trajectory leading to a worse end result:

1. Move the time slider down the timeline until you reach the point where the shuttle moves up from the freighter. We want to stop somewhere near the point where the shuttle ends its upward movement and before it starts its forward movement. This is around frame 779 in our project.

   The following image displays the point on the timeline where we will add and connect to a path. The shuttle prop has just lifted off from the freighter:

2. Draw a path out and up away from the freighter. Try to create a smooth curve. Delete the path and try again if you have difficulty with the curve.

As was stated earlier in this book, drawing a path in 3D space can be difficult. You can turn on the grid and the points will snap to the grid to draw out your path then edit it with the move and rotate tools. Reallusion recommends drawing the path in either the camera view or by grid on the ground plane but not to draw the path using both, or you will get unexpected results. This author also uses a top view to draw paths then adjusts the path markers as necessary.

If you don't like your shuttle path use the Edit Path tool with the Rotate and Move tools to move a group or individual path markers to the desired locations.

3. Detach the shuttle prop from the freighter by clicking the **Detach** button in the right side menu panel.

4. Attach the shuttle prop to the first waypoint on the path (the different colored waypoint).

5. Move the time scrubber down the timeline 100 to 200 frames. The less frames, the faster the shuttle will travel. In this case, we moved to frame 901.

6. With the shuttle prop highlighted, click on the **Pick Path** button and select the last path marker:

What just happened?

We drew an escape route using the Create Path tool and adjusted it to our needs. In this case, the path arced up and through the debris making the shuttle race away from the freighter as it explodes.

The number of frames between the first marker on the path and the last marker on the path determine how fast or slow the shuttle will move away from the freighter.

Have a go hero

We've created the path and set up the escape movement, but to further test our skills, edit the course of the path to as smooth an arc as possible. You can do this by using the Move and Rotate tools in combination with the **Edit Path** button to change, delete, add, or manipulate path markers to smooth out the path.

You can also adjust the escape shuttle speed by adjusting the keyframes closer or further apart in the motion timeline, along with moving the path constraint markers. The following image shows the last **Transform** key frame and the last path Constrain key frame that can be moved forward to shorten (speed up) or moved back to lengthen (slow down). These two keyframe items must be kept together. You will have to move them one at a time but place them on top of each other with the end result as shown in the following screenshot:

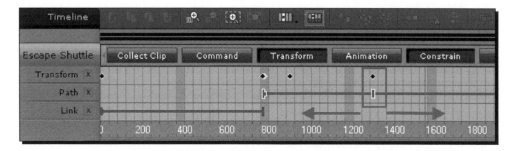

[Viewing the Timeline – In addition to the top slider that can be expanded, contracted, or moved right and left on the timeline, you can also use the zoom buttons on the **Timeline** top toolbar.]

Time for action – adding particles

Even in space, you can't have an explosion without some pyrotechnical effects. Over the years, viewers have come to expect fiery explosions in the vacuum of space, so let's add some pizazz to our explosion so we won't disappoint anyone:

1. Move down the timeline to a point where the explosion starts as shown in the following image. In our example, that was frame 809:

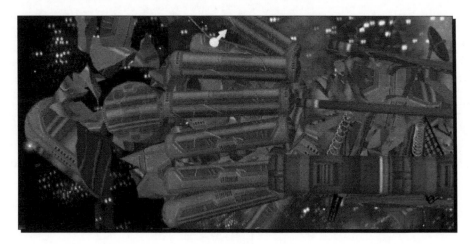

2. Select the **Set** tab.

3. Click on the **Particle** button.

4. Click on the **Fire and Smoke** folder in the left menu panel.

5. Either double-click or drag-and-drop the **Torch Fire** particle into the 3D workspace.

6. In the right side menu panel, use the **Pick Parent** button in the **Attach** section to attach the **Torch Fire** particle to a piece of debris. Click any piece you wish to use.

7. Click the small **Attach To** button and click the **Position and Rotation** option, then click the **OK** button.

8. Repeat steps 3 through 7 three more times to add three more **Torch Fire** particles to three more parts of freighter debris. Choose any part to attach to, but it's recommended that we put them near the actual area of the explosion close to the front, near the freighter tug.

    The next image shows four separate pieces with a **Torch Fire** particle attached to each. The pieces you chose to attach to in your scene will vary:

9. You should now have four **Torch Fire** particles in your scene. Click first **Torch Fire** particle in the **Scene Manager**.

10. Move the time scrubber all the way back to the beginning of the **Timeline**.

11. With the first of four **Torch Fire** particles selected, press the **Off** button in the **Emitter Setting** section on the right side menu.

12. Move the time scrubber forward to the frame in which you want the fire to start emitting from the explosion. For this project, it was frame 800. This can be before or during the explosion. In our example, we will start during the explosion right after it begins.

13. With the same **Torch Fire** particle selected, click the **On** button in the right side menu panel of the Emitter section.

14. Repeat this process three more times until all the **Torch Fire** particles are off at the beginning of the scene, then turned on during the explosion.

The following image shows an example of turning the **Torch Fire** particles off and on:

15. Move the time scrubber back down the line to the same area we were working in after the explosion starts as shown in the previous image.

16. Double-click or drag-and-drop the **Hell Fire** particle into the 3D workspace.

17. Attach the **Hell Fire** particle to a large piece of debris.

18. Click on the **Attach To** button and select **Position and Rotation**.

19. Click the **OK** button.

20. Move the time scrubber back to the beginning of the **Timeline**.

21. With the **Hell Fire** particle selected, click the **Off** button in the right side menu panel.

22. Move the time scrubber forward to the location you want the **Hell Fire** particle to start. We moved forward to frame 809 again, in this example.

23. With the **Hell Fire** particle selected, click the **On** button in the right side menu panel.

24. Save the project and preview the work.

The image below shows a close-up of the explosion with particle fire effects:

What just happened?

We attached a smaller Torch Fire particle to four different pieces of the freighter, causing the particles to fly off with each piece it was attached to.

We then attached a much larger Hell Fire particle to a piece of debris which gave us a larger area of fire. We also timed the visibility of the particles by using the on and off switch.

Have a go hero – adding more particles

Even though we added several fire particles to our explosion, we could use several more to make it look even better. Add at least four more fire particles to the scene that turn on and off at the proper times on the timeline.

We didn't turn off the fire particles towards the end since this was the end of our scene, but for practice, select each fire particle and choose a place on the timeline after the explosion to turn the fire particles off. The duration of the fire is up to you.

You can also go into the particle menu and change colors, particle duration, size, and other features to see what works with the scene.

 Particles that have been turned off will continue to remain visible until their life duration expires.

Setting up the shot list

Now that we have our action animated, we need to start adding some cameras to fill out our shot list we created earlier, keeping in mind how we want to capture the action

Time for action – deleting an existing camera

Delete any cameras we have already created as those were work cameras and even though the shuttle camera could be re-used lets delete it too to take a fresh look at shooting the scene:

1. Select each camera in the camera selection drop-down menu, located at the top right of the workspace or in the **Scene Manager**.

2. With a camera selected, click the **Delete** button in the right side menu for each camera that can be deleted.

What just happened?

We cleaned up the scene by deleting our working cameras. We didn't actually have to delete any cameras as we can have up to sixteen. In this case, we deleted existing cameras for clarity of learning and to practice our camera skills including framing the shot.

Creating cameras for the shot list

The following image shows our shot list we created earlier. Shot 1, 2, and 5 are the same angle. Shot 3 and 4 are the same angle. Shot 6 is unique:

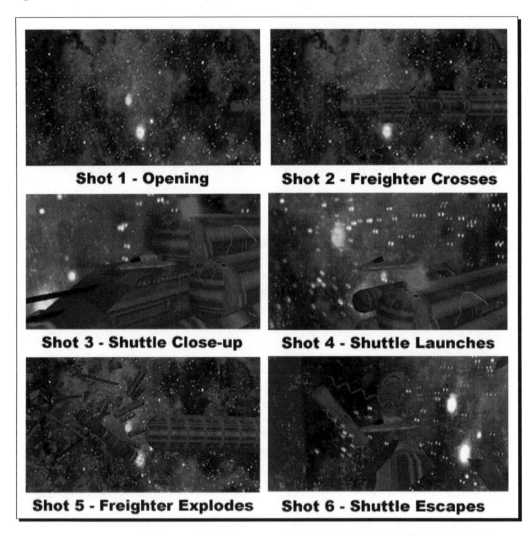

Shot 1 - Opening

Shot 2 - Freighter Crosses

Shot 3 - Shuttle Close-up

Shot 4 - Shuttle Launches

Shot 5 - Freighter Explodes

Shot 6 - Shuttle Escapes

Time for action – creating cameras

Refer to our original shot list above when initially framing each shot as we create cameras for use with our switch in the next section:

1. Select the **Preview Camera** to activate the right side camera menu. Click on the **Add** button to add a camera. Frame Shot 1, as shown in the previous shot list.

Be sure to position the scene horizontally to capture the explosion at the beginning of the ship and also have the space backgrounds fill the frame at all times. You may have to move the time scrubber down the timeline to see where the explosion is but MAKE SURE you return to the first frame before you adjust the camera position.

2. Rename the camera to Shot 1-2-5.

3. Play the scene at least through to the explosion to view the shot.

4. Make adjustments necessary to improve the shot to your liking.

 You do not have to create the cameras to mimic the shots on the list exactly, as you may find out through experimentation that there are better angles or distances to shoot from. Move each camera around to see different views before deciding on a final shot angle.

5. Select the **Preview Camera**.

6. Create a new camera with the **Add** button.

7. Select the **Escape Shuttle** prop.

8. Click on the **Home** button in the top toolbar with the Escape Shuttle selected to frame the shuttle.

9. Use Shot 3 (from the shot list) as an initial guide to frame the camera shot.

10. Rename the camera to Shot 3 shuttle.

 Naming conventions

When working on your projects use names that make sense to you when you are creating assets or cameras; names that are descriptive or easily recognizable. When working in groups use naming conventions understood by the group since members of the group may be working with the project file also.

11. With the **Shot 3 shuttle** camera selected, click on the **Pick Parent** button in the **Linkage** section of the right side menu.

12. Select the Escape shuttle as the parent object linking the camera to the shuttle.

13. With the Shot 3 shuttle camera selected, click on the **Add** button to add a new camera.

14. Frame the shot similar to shot 4, which is above and slightly pulled back from Shot 3.

15. Rename the camera Shot 4.

16. With the **Shot 4** camera selected, click on the **Pick Parent** button in the **Linkage** section of the right side menu panel.

17. Select the Escape Shuttle as the parent object.

18. Select the **Shot 1-2-5** camera.

19. Create a new camera with the **Add** button.

20. Frame the camera shot similar to Shot 6 on the shot list, which is a wider angle shot to show more of the action. It's almost the same as **Shot 1-2-5** except it's pulled back for a wider angle.

21. Rename the camera Shot 6.

What just happened?

We now have four cameras for the six shots on the shot list:

◆ Shot 1-2-5 camera

◆ Shot 3 shuttle camera

◆ Shot 4 camera

◆ Shot 6 camera

The shuttle cameras were linked to the shuttle prop so the cameras will move with the prop as it moves across the screen, making this a moving camera shot, as opposed to the stationary camera shots that fill the rest of the list.

This is at least a great starting point and possibly all the cameras will need to finish out the shot list. We may find as we set up the switch that we need more cameras, but we have enough to complete the shot list as it is.

Setting up the camera switch

We've created our cameras so now it's time to set up the camera switch to shoot the scene. This is strictly a judgement call as to how to setup the order and each director will have their own style or way of doing things.

Time for action – setting the camera order

We'll set the camera order next:

1. Select **Camera01**.

2. Open the **Timeline** window, if it's not already open.

3. Open the **Camera Switch** with the **Track list** button on the timeline toolbar as shown in the following image:

4. Select **Shot 1-2-5** as the first camera on the switcher.

5. Move the timeline scrubber down the timeline to a point before the explosion happens, somewhere around 100 frames ahead of the explosion. In our case, it was frame 650.

6. Right-click on that point in the switch time line and select the **Shot 3 shuttle** camera.

7. Move the time scrubber down to a point where the shuttle moves up off the freighter but before it snaps to the path and changes the camera angle as shown in the following image (frame 778, in this example):

8. Select the **Shot 4** camera on the **Camera Switch** to change to that camera's view.

9. Move the time scrubber down the timeline about 50 or 100 frames (can be adjusted later, if too short or too long).

10. Select the **Shot 1-2-5** camera on the **Camera Switch**.

11. Move the time scrubber down the timeline about 200 frames.

12. Select the Shot 6 camera on the **Camera Switch** to finish out the scene.

The following image shows our example of the camera switch:

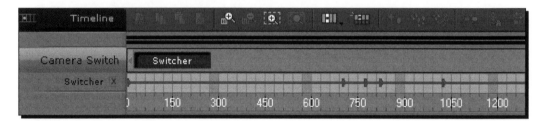

What just happened?

We moved down the timeline to set the point at which the camera view will switch from one camera to another as the scene plays out. We then selected the cameras in sequence to match the shot list. This is a quick and easy task as we know just which camera is next in the sequence.

Shots 1, 2, and 5 were the same angle with the same camera so we didn't have to set up a Shot 2 camera on the switch, as Shot 1 was taking care of both shots at different times on the timeline.

Last minute tweaks

We have one last bit of housekeeping to do and we will be ready to render!

Time for action – adjust the movie length

We added too many frames to our scene so we need to modify the movie length:

1. Click on the **Time Setting** panel button on the bottom toolbar to the right of the frame counter.

2. Set the number of frames to 2000.

We can also use the triangle markers below the workspace to define the output range as shown in the following image:

What just happened?

We didn't need all the frames that we added to the scene so we cut them back to the amount needed to accomplish our task. Changing the length of the movie removed the unused frames.

Have a go hero – making the scene your own

This is a good time to review the scene and make any changes that you would rather see done your way instead of how it was laid out in this project. Try more cameras, different angles. Try different points on the timeline to trigger the camera switches or redo the sequence of camera shots on the switch. Just remember, to save the scene and work with another copy of the project so you can be fearless in your experimentation, but be able to go back to the original file if necessary.

Rendering our scene

Now we are down to the last part of this project in rendering the final movie version. We are going to use AVI as the format.

Time for action

Now let's get on with rendering out our movie so we can see it in action:

 Good rendering habits

Before you render, always make sure you have the right camera selected and the atmosphere turned on. Some animators create their own checklist to consult before rendering begins.

1. Select the **Camera Switch** as the current camera in the camera selection box in the upper-right corner of the workspace.

2. Select the **Export** tab.

3. Click on the **Video** button.

4. Select **AVI** as the format. Select whichever codec you desire at the proper time.

5. Set the **Custom Size** at 1280 X 720 or any size that maintains 16:9 ratio, such as 640 X 360.

6. If you want Stereoscopic 3D, then enable **Stereo Vision** and choose the appropriate format.

7. Check the radio button for **Final Render**.

8. Check the **Anti-Aliased** box.

9. Click on the **Render** button, browse to the location where you wish to store the video and press the **OK** button to render.

What just happened?

We set up and rendered our space project into a movie. We chose a generally available format, set the dimensions, checked the options, and started the render. When the render is finished, we will get to view our work and use it in other applications, such as editors or on the Web.

Have a go hero – promotional stills

We've created our scene and populated it with props and characters. We've animated movement, interaction with props and dialog. We've tweaked it and finally rendered the movie version of it. You even made the project your own with modifications.

Now we need some promotional stills to promote the movie to our viewers.

Your challenge is to render a series of still shots including the existing shot list to use as promotional items. When you create your own projects, you will want to promote them and stills are an effective method.

Summary

Congratulations on a job well done! Give yourself a big pat on the back. You've come a long way in a short time. We've covered a lot of ground since the early chapters and we've been exposed to, or used, many different features and tools of iClone.

This last chapter was a recap of what we have learned in earlier chapters by putting those skills to use in a different environment with a completely different project.

The tips from this book are not all mine as I have learned a lot of them from the iClone community, Reallusion staffers, and anybody that tells me how they did something. I have been fortunate enough to be able to learn from the best in the community such as Stuckon3D, Shygirl, BigBoss, Mike Aparicio, Wolf (of the Wolf and Dulci Hour), AnimaTechnica, Cape Media, Duchess, Alley, and Biggs Trek. These are names you will want to follow as they are the cream of the iClone crop and there are many others too numerous to mention.

If I had any single tip to give, it would be to have fun and don't let anybody keep you from doing what you want to do in your own personal projects, BUT always *receive criticism in a thoughtful and appreciative manner, and LEARN from it.*

A practical last tip would be not to do too much in any one project scene. Chances are very high you will be using this footage in a video editing program so you can always edit together short scenes. For example, if you have a character leaving a room, walking to another room then entering that room, you might not want to do all that in one scene. It could just as easily be three scenes (leaving, walking, and entering). Shorter scenes can create less headaches in terms of timing.

I have also been blessed to work freelance with some of the best 3D artists in the industry and they have taken notice of products like iClone. While it may not turn out Pixar quality renders... it certainly does a great job of animation for the price and the learning curve. It can make anyone with decent computer skills an animator. Whether or not you are a polished animator will be up to you.

Machinima and amateur animation can be quirky and generally not comparable with high-end animation but it is a very fun arena to work and play in. It's a growing area of interest with a wide range of users both in terms of age and background. Plus, the animation is improving in leaps and bounds as dedicated software like iClone puts more tools into the hands of the *want to be/need to* be animator that is in all of us.

I hope that this book has helped you grasp the basics of iClone and its tools. Admittedly, we didn't cover everything because iClone has so much to offer and some tools go beyond basic usage, but we covered quite a bit so be very proud of yourself for making it this far. You don't have to be a whiz kid or gifted to use iClone... you just need the desire to tell a story!

You are always welcome and encouraged to stop by any of my websites for a visit and there are contact forms at www.mdmccallum.com and www.iclonerevolution.com (iClone freebies) with which you can contact me in a manner that will weed its way through the spam we all deal with every day. You can also find easy to use pre-animated destructible props at the iR Store, store.iclonerevolution.com.

Since becoming involved in 3D work, it has become a pleasure to go to work and like a lot of 3D guys and gals... I don't ever want to go home. There are so many stories to tell!

So... if you find yourself up in the wee hours of the night, you can rest assured that you won't be alone as there will be a lot of us fellow iCloners there with you in spirit...creating and animating!

Using Personas, iProps, and Helpers

AML (DramaScript Markup Language) is beyond the scope of this series and has not been discussed with any detail in this guide, as it will take familiarization with iClone beyond the beginners level to fully understand AML. However, there are several AML based Personas, Helpers, and iProps that are installed with iClone that can help with many tasks, so we are going to discuss some of those tasks here.

In this chapter we shall:

- ◆ Have a basic overview of AML
- ◆ Explore character personas
- ◆ Work with AML driven templates
- ◆ Use the AML driven helper for objects such as cars and planes

We'll get started with AML templates so let's just dive right in!

Understanding AML

The best way to describe AML is from the iClone Wiki, which this author originally set up for, and under the direction and guidance of the team at Reallusion:

> *The DramaScript Markup Language (AML) is a general-purpose specification for creating performance interaction between characters and props. It is classified as an XML (Extensible Markup Language) because it allows its users to write individual DramaScripts for either characters or props in iClone4 to interact. Its primary purpose is to create script animations to allow characters and props to interact with each other smoothly. AML Script Editor can be used when modifying DramaScripts.*

— www.iclonewiki.com

 At the time of writing, version 1.0 of AML Script Editor was having issues on Windows 7 systems with the latest version of Direct X.

Where to find and store Motion Files for the Characters?

◆ *C:\Documents and Settings\All Users\Documents\Reallusion\Template\iClone 4 Template\iClone Template\Motion*

What's the difference between Prop's Animation Clips and Character's Animation Clips?

◆ *For Prop's Animation Clips, there are two ways to produce the motion clips. One is using the collect clip method in iClone and the other method is to use 3Ds Max and export it through our Plug-in converter. 3Ds Max can produce both the prop and the animation, but when you produce the motion clips for the props, the animation is embedded within the prop itself.*

◆ *For the creation of the character's motion, the character and the character's motion are always exported separately.*

The following table is also from iCloneWiki:

	Character	iProps
Where is AML Stored?	Persona	AML is embedded within the iProp.
Where to access the motion files.	Animation > Motion files in iClone Template.	in the iProp's right-click menu under Perform
How to export the AML scripts?	Export Persona from the right-click menu.	Export DramaScript from the right-click menu.
How to generate motion files?	In the timeline or Motion Editor in iClone3 Pro or above	In the timeline or Motion Editor in iClone3 Pro or above
	3DS Max 8.0 or above	3DS Max 8.0 or above

Exploring personas to animate a character

A Persona is an editable AML file that is based on the XML specification. A Persona can hold many different motions such as waving, walking, and so forth. These actions are Perform actions that are available from the right-click **Perform** menu when a Persona has been loaded into a character.

Default characters such as Dylan and Jana already have a Persona loaded into them which will differ from character to character. The motions the Persona invokes can also be used as regular motions and are accessed by the **Animation** tab, **Motion** button interface when a character is selected.

Personas can be exported, saved, then imported into another character with the right-click menu under the Persona menu choice. Personas can be edited with an XML editor such as the free XML Notepad from Microsoft. XML Notepad was originally released in 2006 then updated in 2007. There may be other updated versions available.

```
http://www.microsoft.com/download/en/details.
aspx?displaylang=en&id=7973
```

The following image shows the right-click menu with the Perform sub-menu highlighted. Notice the three actions available: **Hey You, Listen Music, Puzzle,** and there are additional commands under the **Move** sub-menu to **Walk Forward** or **Run Forward**.

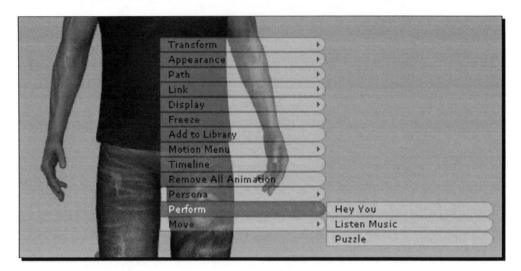

Some Personas will have more commands available than others. It depends on what the Persona author had in mind. Remember that all of these motions are available in the motion library also.

To demonstrate a different Persona we will use the Dylan character to load with a different Persona.

Time for action – loading a Persona

Since Personas can have different motions available, we will add a different Persona to the Dylan character to demonstrate this:

1. Start a new blank project.

2. Make sure the time scrubber is at the start of the **Timeline**.

3. Load the **Dylan** character into the workspace.

4. Right-click on Dylan and hold your mouse cursor over the **Persona** menu item until the sub-menu appears.

5. With the Dylan character selected, click on the **Actor** tab.

6. Select the **Persona** button.

7. Double-click on the **Benny** Persona in the **Content Manager** on the left side menu to load the Benny Persona into Dylan. There will be no visible change when the Persona is loaded.

The following image shows the choices available when the Benny Persona is loaded versus the few choices that were available with the Dylan Persona:

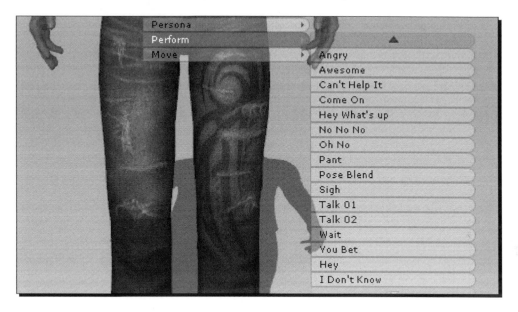

8. Select the Perform motion **Angry**.

9. Select the **Can't Help It** choice when the previous action has stopped running.

10. Select the **Talk 01** choice when the **Can't Help It** motion stops running.

11. Move the time scrubber to the beginning and playback the scene.

The following is an image depicting the three motions strung together in the Perform timeline. Notice the linear designation. Remember our curves? We can change from linear to ease out or any of the available curve choices. In most cases, the curves are slight differences from the default linear curve:

What just happened?

We loaded a character, explored its built in motion based on the characters default Persona file. We then loaded a different Persona to see the difference some Personas have.

After loading the Benny Persona file we then proceeded to add three distinct motions with the simple right click menu system by adding a new perform action when the previous actions stopped playing.

Have a go hero – experimenting with perform motions

Experiment by loading the various Personas into different characters and see how they react. Use different curve settings and blending with the handles. This exercise is for you to become acquainted with the various Personas and their effect on characters.

Female-based Personas will have female characteristics just as male-based Personas will have a male-oriented body language. Mixing these up can produce some unique results.

Using AML templates

In the **Content Manager**, you may have noticed a folder named **AML Templates**. These are helper props that contain AML scripting to help perform a task or function such as sitting down. The AML can be built into props but the helpers can work with regular props such as furniture, downloaded from the web or created in another 3D application.

Implementing character interaction

The following image shows the AML templates available from the **Character_Interaction** sub-folder located in the **Props** folder:

Time for action – placing and using character interaction dummies

Once again we will use a new blank project for this action section:

1. Create a new blank project.

2. Load the **Jana** character into the workspace.

3. Load the **Dylan** character into the workspace.

4. Load the **Hello_Dummy** prop located in the **Character_Interaction** sub-folder of the **AML Templates** folder.

5. Place the characters near each other, in facing the same general direction.

6. Place the **Hello_Dummy** prop, as in the following image:

7. Click on the **Jana** character, then right-click on the **Hello** prop and select the **Operate** menu then **Hello** from the sub-menu:

Select the character you wish to interact with the prop, then use the Hello template perform action to have this character initiate the motion.

What just happened?

We used the Hello AML template to initiate a waving from the Jana character without having to key frame the event.

 The last character selected will be the character whose action is triggered by the AML templates.

Time for action – applying the kick me AML template

1. Load a new blank scene.

2. Load the **Violet** and the **Benny** characters.

3. Load the **Kick Me** AML Template prop.

4. Turn the characters to face each other.

5. Place the **Kick Me** prop in front of Jana at the location in which she will initiate the kick.

6. Select the Jana character to make sure that is the character performing the kick.

7. Right-click on the **Kick Me AML Template** prop and select the **Kick_At** perform command:

What just happened?

We used the Kick Me AML Template prop as a starting location for the kick. Jana started her kick in that area then continued forward to complete the kick at Benny's head.

This will take some practice and modifying the placement of the Kick Me AML Template prop until the proper distance to the object or character being kicked is achieved. The built-in AML triggers the movement and the kick for us.

Have a go hero – using the hit me template

Create a new scene with two characters and try out the **Hit Me** AML Template prop. This prop will work the same as the Kick Me prop, in that you will place it where you want the character to initiate the punch. Follow up by adjusting the placement of the second character to intercept the punch.

Directional adjustment

If you find your character turns the wrong direction when using these templates, then simply rotate the template prop to the proper direction.

Using operate dummy props

The following image shows the Operate Dummy props that help when using a character to perform these functions. All of these functions would be very difficult and time consuming to key frame by hand, particularly while trying to keep them as smooth as possible:Z

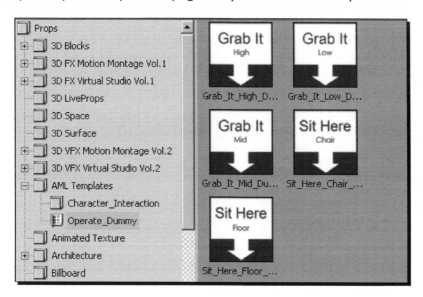

These AML templates are actually very handy helpers with certain tasks such as:

- ◆ Grab It – High, mid, and low for picking up objects relative to those positions.
- ◆ Sit Here Chair – This to be placed in the area of a chair that the character is to sit on.
- ◆ Sit Here Floor – Just as the title denotes, this is placed on the floor where you want the character to sit.

So let's try a couple of these out to see how they work.

Time for action – Using the character interaction templates

To test out these templates, we will use stock characters and props:

1. Load the Jana character into the center of the workspace.

2. Go to the **Home** sub-folder of the iProps folder under the **Set** tab, **Props** button and double-click or drag-and-drop the Sofa into the workspace.

3. Arrange Jana and the sofa as in the following picture. Angle the sofa to demonstrate that this can be done at any angle:

4. In the **Character_Interaction** sub-folder of the **AML Templates** folder, select the **Sit Here Chair** prop and drag it over into the workspace onto the sofa where Jana is to sit:

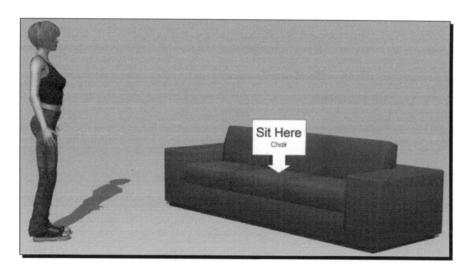

5. Right-click on the **Sit Here Chair** prop and select **Sit** from the **Perform** menu.

The following image shows the **Sit Here Chair** prop, selected with the right-click menu displayed:

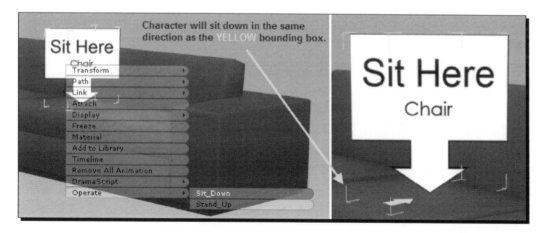

What just happened?

After placing the character, sofa, and **Sit Here Chair** template into the scene, we right-clicked on the template prop and chose the sit down action. The placement of the template prop determines the placement of the character that is interacting with it.

The character will sit down in the direction of the yellow bounding box. Since the Sit Here Chair prop is made out of a billboard, the prop will always face the camera but the yellow bounding box will show the angle at which the character will sit as demonstrated in the following image:

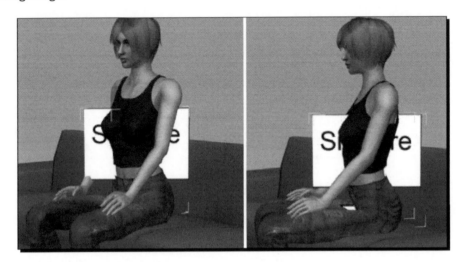

Multiple characters in the scene

When more than one character is present in the scene, we need to select the character first that we wish to interact with the template. Click on the desired character then right-click on the template prop and choose the perform action.

Time for action – using the grab it AML template prop

The Grab It AML Template has three different types, depending on the height of the prop being grabbed, low, mid, and high:

1. Start a new blank project.

2. Load **Ball_001** from the **3D Blocks props** folder.

3. Scale the ball down and place it on the floor.

4. Load the **Dylan** character.

5. Load the **Grab It Low** AML Template prop from the **Operate Dummy** sub-folder, **AML Templates**, and place the visual marker at the bottom of the prop inside the ball prop.

6. Select the ball prop and attach it to the Grab It Low marker.

7. Right-click on the **Grab It Low** AML Template prop and select **Pick Low** from the **Operate** choice.

The following image shows the progression of the scene from start to finish:

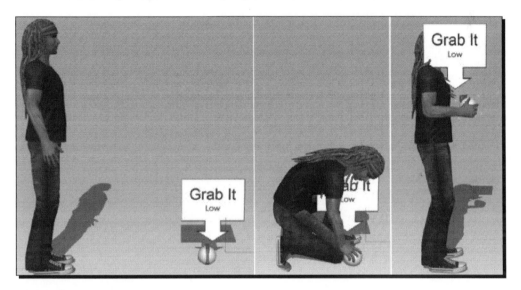

What just happened?

By placing the Grab It Low prop on the ball prop and attaching the ball prop, we used the built-in AML to have the character reach down to grab the ball then return to an upright position.

This is not a perfect solution but it's a great start on a complex action. We will have to make adjustments in position or scale when we use these templates, as conditions such as height will vary from scene to scene and prop to prop.

Have a go hero – using the other operate dummy props

Just as before, with the other AML templates, go through the props in the Operate Dummy folder to familiarize yourself with their usage. Use different characters with them or try different heights to see how you need to adjust the movement built into the AML that is loaded into the prop.

Working with iProps

iProps are script-driven props that with a right-click perform menu, triggers, the built-in animation, and motion of the prop. If we use an iProp drinking glass versus a standard prop or accessory drinking glass, we can use the built-in AML script to call on the animation needed to move to and pick up the drinking glass, whereas this would have to be done manually via separate motions and key framing with a standard prop or accessory.

iProps are not perfect, in that we have to make adjustments in position or scale of some scene assets, but it is a great start from which we can make the necessary adjustments without having to create the entire motion or animation.

iClone has several stock iProps and the City Marketplace has developers that create iProps that can be very helpful to us. iClone installs several iProps for use in the iProps folder within the Props section.

Exploring the home iProps folder

The home folder holds several props such as a door, bed, sofa, remote control, and others. These are all AML driven to interact with the characters. We will take a look at some of them to explain their usage.

 iProps are sometimes position dependent, in that we can't always get a character to do what they are supposed to from just any angle. Familiarizing ourselves with the various iProps will help in building a bedroom or scene in which the prop is properly located.

Time for action – getting in and out of bed

This action can be quite difficult to key frame manually and this iProp helps us to perform the task with little or no difficulty:

1. Create a new blank project.

2. Load the **Bed** from the **iProps** folder into the workplace.

3. Load the **Jana** character into the workspace.

4. Arrange the Jana character away from the bed as in the following image:

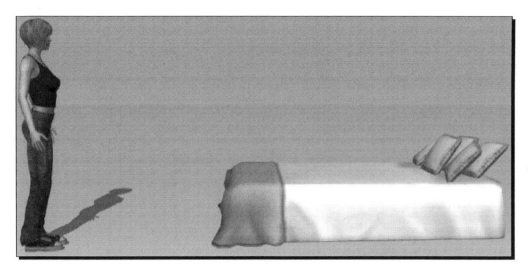

5. Click on Jana to select her.

6. Click on the **Bed** to select it.

7. Right-click on the bed, and from the menu choose **Sit On Bed** from the **Operate** menu choice.

What just happened?

It's not a bad idea to form the habit of selecting the character first even when it is the only character in the scene. We selected the character, then the iProp bed, right-clicked on the bed and chose Sit Down from the menu, which triggered animation and motion that walked the character over to the bed, turned around and sit down with no manual key framing!

iProp adjustments

If an iProp motion walks a character into the prop, we can adjust these motions to some degree by adding key frames in the timeline but when you cannot adequately adjust the position, then use camera shot framing to mask that part by not showing it on camera.

The following image shows Jana sitting on the iProp bed. You can then select any of the other **Operate** commands such as Lie Down or Stand Up to continue the action:

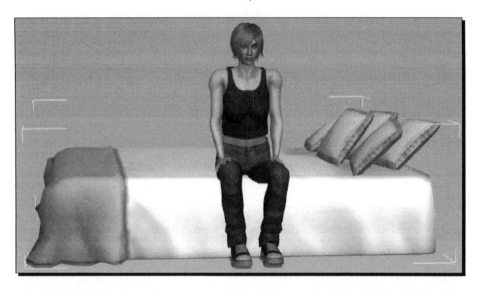

Have a go hero – sitting down on the iprop chair

We used the Sit Chair AML Template earlier with the sofa but now we will use the built-in AML script to accomplish the task.

The Sofa iProp works in much the same manner so give it a try. Place the sofa in the workspace with a character and use the right-click **Operate** menu to issue commands to sit or stand.

Time for action – using the iprop door

Opening and closing a door is also a very difficult movement to animate manually. There are many factors involved in this type of movement that, without the use of AML, would take far longer to accomplish, so we will let the AML do the work for us.

Like any door there are two sides to the door, as listed on the Operate command menu shown in the following image. We will quickly learn when have chosen the wrong side if our character walks through the door then turns around to open it:

 Use the Undo function, reset the timeline scrubber to the appropriate time, and choose a different open command.

1. Create a new blank scene.

2. Load the **Door** iProp into the scene.

3. Load the Dylan character into the scene.

4. Position the Dylan character away from but in front of the door as shown in the following image:

5. Select the Dylan character first.

6. Select the Door iProp and choose **Open Door from Bedroom** to match the side of the door we will be opening.

7. Preview the animation to see the character walk to and open the door.

The following image demonstrates the Dylan character's movement to and opening of the door:

What just happened?

We used the built-in AML script for the door iProp to manipulate the Dylan character into walking over and opening the door. All with a few simple clicks of the mouse button!

The beer iProp we worked with earlier during our main project and the Stein, Remote Control, and Apple (shown in the following image) work in the same manner:

The TV is a bit different from the other iProps, in that it does not interact with a character. Instead, it allows you to load several videos and has an off feature that allows us to turn on the TV, move through channels, and turn it off.

Working with vehicle dummies

The vehicle dummies mimic the movements of several types of vehicles and make our life easier! All we have to do is attach the real prop to the dummy, choose the appropriate command, then click a place in the workspace for the dummy to move to.

The following image displays the available vehicle dummies in iClone starting with the car, helicopter, plane, and arrow:

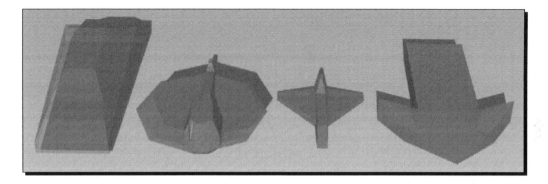

Car	The car dummy mimics a car's movement including turning corners or turning around. It has Move Forward and Move Backward commands available.
Helicopter	The helicopter dummy moves like a helicopter without us having to animate that movement. It has a Move Stationary command where the dummy moves in one spot, such as rotating or turning and the standard Move Forward command where the dummy tilts like a helicopter and moves off.
Plane	This mimics the smooth flight of an airplane that banks on the turns and has a Move Forward command available. The banking can be a bit quick but it's a good start like other iClone helpers.
Arrow	The arrow dummy has two Move Forward and Move Backward commands available and travels smoothly to the selected location.

Vehicle Dummies will not make assets like tires, propellers, or blades spin. They mimic the movement of the vehicle, not the vehicle parts themselves. There are other individual dummies and helpers available from Reallusion and content developers, in addition to the stock dummies we have covered here.

Summary

We have discussed several types of AML driven assets that make difficult animation tasks much easier and quicker. By using these script driven AML templates, helpers, and iProps, we shave time off of completing a project or reduce the complexity of animating some moves and actions.

Specifically, we covered the following:

- Loading and using Personas to drive motion.
- Using AML driven templates for more complex actions such as sitting or grabbing objects.
- Placement of operate dummies.
- Using iProps for complex motions without templates.
- Introduction to vehicle dummies that mimic items such as cars, planes, and helicopters.

While there is still much to be said about AML scripting above and beyond the beginners level, this appendix should give you enough information to get started using the objects that are script-driven and reduce the frustration and hard work of animating certain tasks.

 Depending on the type of animations supported by the object's AML, the right-click commands may be located under Perform, Operate, or Move.

B

Animating with iClone Physics

Do NOT Fear the Physics!

You don't have to understand physics or be a genius to use this fantastic tool that Reallusion has added to Version 5. So, relax, as we don't have to know how it works to use it properly. It can be as simple as checking a box and pressing the play button. This appendix is packed with common sense and basic examples of physics usage.

To grasp physics in a pinch, just think of an iClone character that drops an object to the floor, like a book or a drinking glass. In version 4, we had to release the prop from the character and animate it all the way down to the floor or just forget it and shoot the scene some other way. In version 5, you just make sure the prop isn't linked or attached, make a few settings, press play, and watch the object drop nicely to the floor and even roll around or bounce... all in a few seconds of runtime!

Version 5 brings iClone users a new animation tool that gives us the ability to simulate an object's physical properties, such as falling or colliding with another object. We can control these actions using props and dummies in conjunction with the timeline to get great animation results.

Physics is certainly not new to this author as my destructible line of props would not exist without the ability to simulate them within Studio Max before exporting them into iClone format. The physics within iClone seem to be a natural extension of those found in Studio Max. Maybe not as robust in terms of control, but the physics user interface for iClone is still under development as it's in its infancy with version 5. As a long time user of physics, when possible I can attest to the hours of animation toil saved by this wonderful and powerful tool.

Jason Lin at Reallusion was instrumental in providing the notes and information needed to write this appendix on physics. Most of what is discussed here is a direct result of combing through the various documents, research, and engineering notes. Jason helped by answering any questions I had at the same time as he was preparing for the official release of version 5. It was indeed a busy time and his help was appreciated as this appendix would not have been possible to write this soon without his assistance.

There are just a few basics that you really need to know to get started using physics and we will discuss basic concepts or theory then go through the action sections to start acquainting ourselves with the workings of the physics as we explore other concepts and features of this exciting and time saving tool.

In this chapter we shall do the following:

- Cover the basics of iClone physics
- Discover soft and rigid body objects
- Knock down, over, or drop objects
- Complete many different scenarios for basic physics

So let's get on with it and see what mayhem we can wreak with physics!

Understanding iClone physics

iClone physics provides a certain amount of physical effects such as those resulting from applying gravity and mass to props that allow us to simulate any number of actions and interactions between physics activated props and characters. In the case of character collision and interaction, there are already developers, including myself, working on creating characters that have built-in collision mesh that require no rigging by the user.

I hesitate to use the word rigging as that invokes a mental image that extraordinary skills or knowledge are required and that is far from the case in iClone. We don't even have to rig dummies, which we will discuss later, to use the physics feature but we can create character and prop rigs that make our life easier when needed, so do not let this term scare you. In fact, you will probably embrace rigging as another great tool for the animation toolbox.

As was just stated, we don't have to rig or attach any object to another to see the effects that are provided by the physics addition, and that will be demonstrated soon in our first action section but we need to cover a few basics before we move on to the hands on phase.

One of the great things about physics is the help it gives the animator and the speed in which some things are accomplished. When creating a video to highlight iClone 5 for Reallusion, I had a character going through a system of caves carrying a torch for light. At one point I needed the character to drop the torch to the floor to free his hands. In previous versions of iClone, we would have had to key frame animate that fall, it would have had to be a simple movement and we might even have kept it off camera entirely as a work around. With physics, we can simply allow the prop to fall and, in this case, the torch fell to the ground and rolled out of the scene! You can't get much better help than that and it took less than a minute of simulation to accomplish this task!

We will work with imparting as natural a motion as possible in the following action sections but we also need to be aware that we can use the new Prop Puppet feature to simply grab a physics-empowered dummy and push it into the physics objects to trigger a simulation. This method does remove some of the conditions of an actual simulation by turning it into a forced event.

Working with simulations

First what we need to grasp is the fact the physics are SIMULATING physical laws and any changes we make in object placement can and will have an effect on the simulation. In fact, we can change NOTHING AT ALL and still get a different simulation the next time we press the play button.

Unless you save your favorite simulation and turn off the simulation mode, you will lose it the next time you press the play button. Creating and keeping multiple copies of the file will give you the opportunity to select the best of several attempts. Just remember to always turn the simulation OFF when no longer needing it.

Baking the physics

iClone bakes in (stores) the physics-driven animation, which allows us to modify it for our use. While working with physics, we can rerun the simulation as many times as we need before we bake the physics in to modify or tweak to our heart's content. It's a very simple process. We replay the simulation over and over until we get one we like, then we turn OFF the simulation within iClone and the animation information is stored in a motion segment.

By frames vs realtime

Clicking on the **Realtime** button on the bottom toolbar will toggle the mode to By Frames which will give a more accurate simulation than leaving the preview in realtime mode.

Testing versus saving simulations

So how do we keep the simulation we want... one that we can count on, instead of the unpredictable results of another simulation? We must make sure we **do not reactivate the physics engine without first saving a copy of the project file**. Otherwise, our prize simulation will be overwritten with the next one!

We can control our simulations with the built-in parameters available via menus and with the placement of our props and other scene objects, including hidden objects and dummies.

Duplicating physics activated props

Props with physics activated will retain the attributes of the original prop when duplicated.

Touring the physics menu

Like most new tools and toys, there are parts of a new interface to learn. These pop-up menus provide access to the parameters that must be set for the physics to be properly simulated. The depth in which you choose to explore these options will decide the level of interaction your scenes will have with the physics engine and if that interaction is smooth and plausible.

Clearing the animation

Anytime we find ourselves facing an expected baked physics-based animation that persists, then we can clear that animation by using the right-click menu with the **Remove Animation** option when the object in question is selected or use the **Reset** button on the bottom toolbar. Chances are, this was a baked in animation from a previous simulation.

The **Physics Object Settings** pop-up menu works for rigid and soft body objects and holds the input boxes, drop-down menus, and other selections concerning the physics properties of our object.

The following image displays the **Physics** section of the top toolbar:

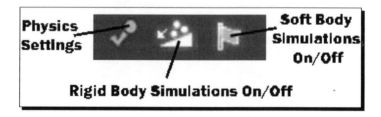

The following image shows the **Physics Object Settings** pop-up menu with the **Rigid Body** parameters on the left and the **Soft Body** parameters on the right:

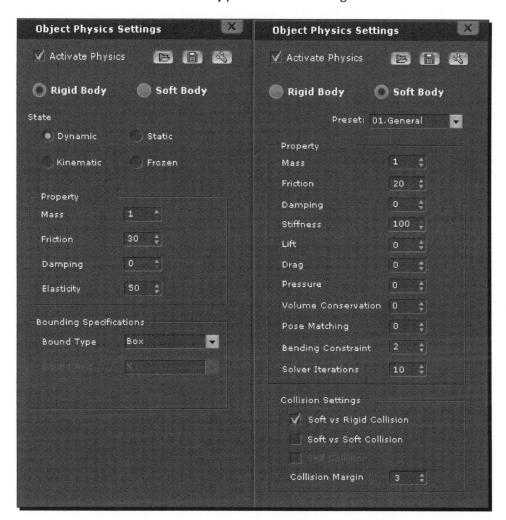

 Saving physics object settings

Once you have achieved the desired results, you can save your settings by clicking on the disk icon located to the right of the **Active Physics** checkbox. The folder icon will invoke an open dialog to load these saved settings.

Understanding soft bodies versus rigid bodies

In iClone physics, we already discovered the two main types of objects, the Soft and Rigid Body objects. These objects behave very differently depending on which option is chosen. Collisions are rigid body objects with dynamic or kinematic attributes.

From Wikipedia:

> *A physics engine is computer software that provides an approximate simulation of certain physical systems, such as rigid body dynamics (including collision detection), soft body dynamics, and fluid dynamics, of use in the domains of computer graphics, video games and film. Their main uses are in video games (typically as middleware), in which case the simulations are in real-time.*

Rigid bodies

A rigid body is indeed a hard object but it's a little more than that, as deformations to the object are not possible when set as a rigid body. The rigid body object will always maintain its shape without a mushy, gelatinous, or spring effect.

Rigid body prop examples would be a bowling ball, wall, floor, or any object that is solid and would not oscillate when a collision occurs. If it shakes or quivers, then it's a soft body, as will be discussed in due time, otherwise, it's a rigid body as a rule of thumb.

Setting the state of the object

The state of the object is crucial in defining how the object will react to the simulation. What state you choose depends on what you need that particular object to do. Let's take a moment to discuss the various states and their uses. Once again Jason Lin at Reallusion was invaluable in getting this information for us to use:

Dynamic	For use with objects whose intent is passive, such as free fall or collisions.
Kinematic	Use with rigid body groups that you wish to key frame or puppet (animate) and for collision props linked to an animated character or object.
Static	Objects that do not allow penetration or reaction from another physics driven object, such as a floor or wall that will provide containment for the simulation instead of the objects passing through. Static objects are not moved by the collision effect.
Frozen	Objects that need to be held in place until dislodged or touched by another physics driven object, such as a group of dominoes, a stack of boxes, barrels, or cans.

Object properties

Mass	Weight and volume. The more mass something has, the more inertia and gravity it will experience.
Friction	A damping effect that can slow down or control spin in some cases.
Damping	Helps to reduce the effect of oscillations or jittery movement.
Elasticity	Bounce or lack of bounce.

Bounding settings

Bound Type	
Box	Surrounds the object with an invisible collision box and the default settings as of this writing.
Sphere	Surrounds the object with an invisible collision sphere.
Cylinder	Surrounds the object with an invisible collision cylinder.
Capsule	Surrounds the object with an invisible collision capsule.
Convex Hull	Surrounds the object with an invisible collision hull that would be like wrapping it with a plastic wrap as it fits to the object in that manner.
Bounding Mesh	Surrounds the object with an invisible collision Bounding Mesh, usually a simple low poly box.
Self Mesh	Surrounds the object with an invisible collision mesh based on the objects form.
Bound Axis	
Used with cylinder and capsule bounding type to set the orientation axis.	

We need to visualize what we are doing when working with bounding types as they have a dramatic effect on a simulation.

 Bounding a capsule prop with a box will negate the curves of the capsule when in contact with other physics props, so always check that the Bounding Type matches the objects shape as closely as possible.

Soft bodies

Soft bodies are deformable objects that can shake, quiver, and fold up, to name a few options.

Preset

General, leather, silk, softball, stress ball, and beach ball preset options are available in the drop-down menu to get us started. These presets, of course, mimic the items they are named after.

Property

Mass	Weight and volume.
Friction	Opposing force. Another dampening effect.
Damping	Reduce the jitters or vibrations.
Stiffness	Rigidity.
Lift	External lift.
Drag	External drag.
Pressure	External pressure.
Volume Conservation	Attempts to preserve shape.
Pose Matching	Attempts to preserve the structure of an object.
Bending Constraint	Along with Pose Matching attempts to preserve the structure of an object.
Solver Iterations	In simplified terms, it means firmness. Like a splat versus a rock.

Collision settings

Soft Vs Rigid Collision	Allows for Soft Body versus Rigid Body Collisions, when checked.
Soft Vs Soft Collision	Allows for Soft Body versus Soft Body collisions, when checked.
Self Collision	Allows for parts of the Soft Body object to collide with itself.
Collision Margin	The area of collision detection around the object.

Removing and clearing physics animations

We can use the right-click menu option **Remove All Animation** on individual objects, or we can use the **Clear Animation** button on the bottom toolbar to clear all the animations in the project.

Time for action – dropping the ball

Our first action section will be a very simple demonstration of gravity:

1. Open a new blank scene, select the **Set** tab and click on the **Props** button.

2. Double-click on **Ball_001** from the **3D Blocks** folder in the **Content Manager** on the left side menu.

3. With **Ball_001** selected, enter 100 in the Z axis input box of the **Move** area in the **Transform** section on the right side menu.

4. Click the **Physics Setting** icon (*Shift + F9*) in the top toolbar. The following image shows the physics section of the top toolbar:

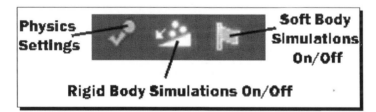

5. With **Ball_001** selected, click on the **Active Physics** checkbox to turn on the physics for the ball prop.

6. Click the **Realtime** button on the bottom of the playback area to change to By Frames mode, which will simulate physics more accurately than realtime.

The following image shows the **Realtime** button on the bottom toolbar of the workspace, when selected, it will turn to By Frames mode:

7. Time to play our simulation. Click on the play button and watch the ball drop.

8. Select the **Set** tab, click on the **Props** button and double-click on the **Infinite Plane** prop in the **Physics** folder within the **Content Manager** on the left side menu.

9. Return the time scrubber to the beginning, if you didn't do so before you added the infinite plane.

10. Press the play button and watch the change as the ball stops and slightly bounces onto the infinite plane we just added.

11. Return the time scrubber to the first frame.

12. With the **Ball_001** prop selected, change the **Elasticity** to 100. Change the **Bound Type** to **Self Mesh**.

13. Play the simulation again. Save the project.

What just happened?

We added a very simple primitive sphere, which was then raised on the Z axis, 100 units above the ground plane. We opened the physics setting panel and clicked active physics to turn on the physics properties of the ball prop, which will be included in the simulation. We also made sure that the rigid body simulation was active.

After the initial test, we needed to stop the ball from falling through the floor so we added an infinite plane from the physics prop folder. A subsequent playing of the simulation now shows the ball stopping and slightly bouncing on the infinite plane.

We then changed the elasticity to make it bounce more and the bound type to self mesh so it reacts like a ball instead of the default box bounding type.

Available physics props

Reallusion has provided several physics enabled props in the physics prop folder that have properties you can save and load into other objects for future use.

Have a go hero – setting up the physics

Save our project first, then experiment with the different settings available from the **Physics Object Settings** pop-up menu. Observe the behavior of each available setting.

Place a second prop underneath the first one, add the physics, and view the results. Move the second prop around and try again. Change the ball to a soft body by clicking on the **Soft Body** tab.

As you can see when we need a character to drop something all we have to do is use physics to animate the drop of the object. Changing mass and other settings will have a combined impact on the object.

Time for action – setting up the wall

There will be times when we want to knock things down, like a door or a wall. This can be done in many different ways. At the time of writing, to use an avatar for collision we would use an attached dummy for the physics settings. There are many great character developers in the Reallusion Marketplace already developing custom G5 characters with built-in collision mesh. This author will develop future characters with this trait in mind too:

1. Start a new blank project and select the **Set** tab then click on the **Props** button.

2. Double-click on the **Box_001** prop in the **3D Blocks** folder to load it into the workspace.

3. With **Box_001** selected, enter the following into the **Scale** input boxes on the right side menu: X=4.5, Y=457.7, Z=41.6.

4. Click the **Reset Transform** button.

    The following image displays the scale settings to turn our box prop into a board prop, as shown in the bottom half of the image:

    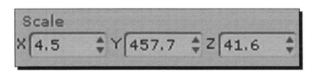

5. With the **Box_001** prop still selected, click on the **Multi-Duplicate** button (*Shift + D*) and enter the following:

    Duplicate: 4

    Move: X=0 Y=0, Z=43

    Rotate: X=0, Y=0, Z=0

    Scale: X=100, Y=100, Z=100

The following image details the settings to create multiple board objects:

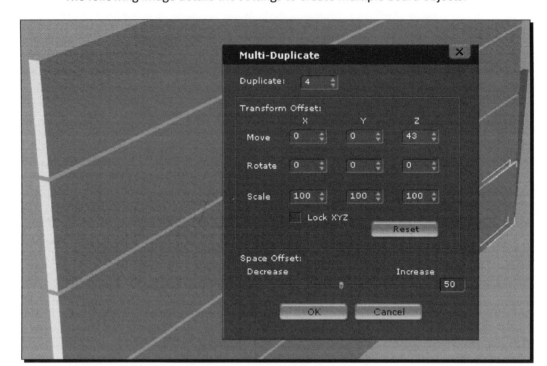

6. Select the **Set** tab and click on the **Prop** button.

7. Double-click on **Ball_001** from the **3D Blocks** folder to load it into the workspace.

8. Enter the following coordinates into the **Ball_001 Move** input box on the right side menu:

X=150.0

Y=0.0

Z=50

The following image shows the settings for the Ball_001 prop:

9. With the **Ball_001** prop selected, right-click on the prop and select **Timeline** to open the timeline for the ball prop.

10. In the **Current Frame** input box on the top toolbar of the timeline, input 50 or move the time scrubber to frame 50.

11. With the **Ball_001** prop selected, input the following into the props **Move** section located on the right side menu:

X= -215.0

Y= 0.0

Z= 50.0

12. Move the time scrubber back to the first frame. Save your project and press the play button to see the ball pass through the "board" props.

The following image shows the ball passing through the boxes:

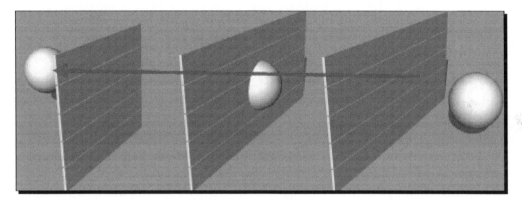

13. Double-click on the top board to select it.

14. Hold down the *Ctrl* key and click the other 4 boards until all boards are selected.

Multiple object selection

We could also use the select tool to draw a marquee around the objects while holding our left mouse button down. It is possible to change the physics settings on a group of objects by selecting them and then choosing the physics selection from the **Physics Settings** dialog box.

15. Click on the **Physics Settings** button on the top toolbar or use *Ctrl + F9*.

16. With the board props still selected, click on the **Active Physics** checkbox and set the boards to **Frozen** as the state.

17. Select the Ball prop, with the **Physics Object Settings** panel still open.

18. Click the **Active Physics** checkbox and select **Kinematic** as the state.

19. Click on the **Rigid Body Simulation** button on the top toolbar to turn on the iClone physics engine.

20. Save our project.

 It's a good idea to save our project after we set them up and BEFORE we actually run the physics to give a clean project to start over with, should you need to.

What just happened?

To this point, we have set up our simulation with the boxes acting as boards. Think of them as boarding up a passageway or tunnel entrance. Setting the boards to Frozen state holds them in place until our collision object, Ball_001, strikes the boards. The ball prop is our collision object to knock the boards down with.

We are now ready to actually start the physics simulation in the next action section.

Time for action – knocking down the wall – first run

1. With the **Rigid Body Simulation** button on, press the play button to run the simulation.

2. Stop the simulation whenever you desire after the simulated objects stop moving.

The following image shows the early seconds of the impact for the first run:

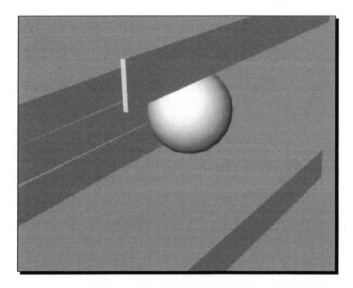

What just happened?

We ran the first simulation with the result being the following:

◆ The top board was frozen in place due its freeze constraint state as it was not impacted by the collision object (Ball_001).

◆ The other boards were either carried through with the impact object or fell through the floor as we did not have a static floor plane set up to catch them.

Time for action – fine tuning the first run

1. Set the time scrubber back to the beginning of the timeline.

2. Select the **Set** tab and click on the **Props** button.

3. Double-click on the **Infinite Plane** prop located in the **Physics Props** folder of the **Content Manager** to load it into place.

4. Save the project to a new file name and run the simulation.

The following image shows the result of the refined simulation with the boards scatted out across the infinite plane:

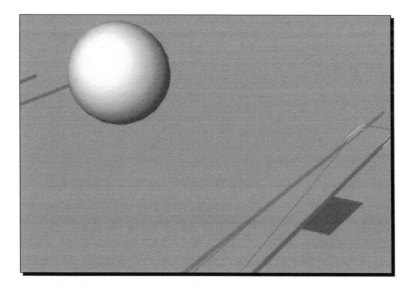

What just happened?

We added the infinite plane physics prop to stop the boards from falling through the floor and the change of state on the bottom board effected the entire simulation including the top board dropping down as well.

At this point, we can turn off the simulation and the objects retain the animation. This is also known as **baking** in animation. The props will always retain the last simulation animation unless you specifically select the prop or props and turn off the physics properties. Otherwise, the animation is overwritten with the next simulation. After we turn off the simulation we can observe the baked in animation segments on the timeline of the physics prop.

Have a go hero – finish the scene

Delete the ball prop or turn its opacity off and place a character in the scene or a prop such as a forklift and have it hit the boards at the same time as they start to fall. This will simulate using the prop or character to knock the boards down.

Better yet... use a character driving a forklift to appear to be knocking the boards down!

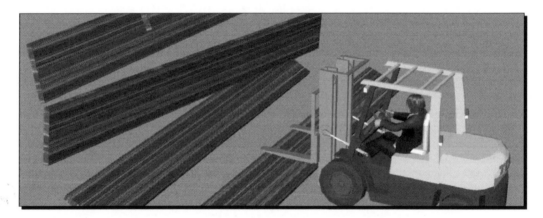

This is a very nice simulation at this point and we would be very hard pressed to keyframe this by hand so as you can see... physics rock!

Time for action – batting the ball

1. Load a new blank scene. Select the **Set** tab and click on the **Props** button.

2. Load the **Infinite Plane** prop in the **Physics** folder.

3. Double-click on **Ball_001** from the **3D Blocks** folder to load it into the center of the workspace.

4. Double-click on the **Cylinder_001** prop from the **3D Blocks** folder to load it into the center of the workspace.

5. Change **Cylinder_001** settings to:

   Move: X= -70, Y= -217.7, Z= 46.4

   Rotate: X=90, Y=0.0, Z=125.3

   Scale: X=18.7, Y=18.7, Z=293.6

6. With the cylinder prop selected, move the time scrubber down the timeline to frame 35.

7. To create the swing arc, change the cylinder settings to:

   Rotate: X= 90.0, Y= 0, Z=232.8 (this will create the swing arc).

8. Move the time scrubber back to the beginning of the timeline.

9. Load the **Arc_009** prop into the workspace from the **Arc** sub-folder of the **3D Blocks** folder.

10. Change the **Arc_009** settings to:

   Move: X= -2242.0, Y=2085.2, Z=0.0

   Rotate: X=0, Y=0, Z=45.0

   Scale X=600, Y=600, Z=600

11. Duplicate the **Arc_009** prop or load another copy of the prop.

12. Change the new **Arc_009** settings to:

   Move: X= -2594.0, Y=1564.8, Z=0.0

   Rotate: X=0, Y=0, Z=65.0

   Scale X=600, Y=600, Z=600

13. Save the project.

The following image shows the setup in the workspace to this point:

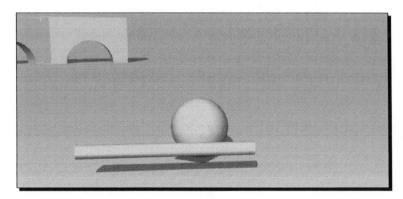

What just happened?

We loaded the object for the simulation into the workspace and set it up in terms of placement and scale. We also loaded the infinite plane from the physics props folder so the items would just fall away to the bottom of the workspace.

Time for action – setting up the physics

We've got our props in place so let's set up the physics and run the sim.

1. Click on the **Physics Settings** button in the top toolbar or use *Shift + F9*.

2. Select the ball prop. Check the **Active Physics** checkbox and set the state to **Dynamic (for interaction)**.

3. Select the cylinder prop. Check the **Active Physics** checkbox and set the state to **Kinematic (for collision)**.

4. Select both the arch props. Check the **Active Physics** checkbox and set the state to **Static**.

5. Set the **Bounding Settings** in the **Bound Type** section to **Self Mesh** in the drop-down menu.

6. Turn on the **Rigid Body Simulation** button on the top toolbar.

 We are now ready to run the physics simulation. You can save a copy to reload if you have trouble but you can always remove the animation from each object with the right-click menu. Just don't remove the animation from the cylinder as it is our collision object and that would remove the swing we built in.

7. Press the Play button to run the simulation. The ball may or may not make it through one of the arches.

 To rerun a simulation just slide the time scrubber to the first frame and press the play button again. Continue to re-run until you have the simulation you like then turn off the **Rigid Body Simulation** button on the top toolbar to preserve the animation.

8. Save your project once you have the simulation you like, such as getting the ball through the arch on the right.

9. Select the cylinder, right-click on it and choose timeline to open up the cylinder timeline.

10. Click on the **Transform** button of the timeline to see the keyframes.

11. The last keyframe is on frame 35. Move that to frame 15 to shorten the distance between frames which will speed up the swing.

12. Play the simulation and replay until you see the possible variations of the setup. Usually a pattern will develop not so much in a particular order but in the type of reaction the simulation produces. You will start to recognize similar results.

What just happened?

We used the built-in physics to simulate hitting a ball into, near, or through another target. By changing parameters, we can see how the force is multiplied when we shorten the swing time on the timeline.

The shorter distance between the key frame that starts the swing and the key frame that ends the swing will determine the speed and the force of the impact.

The further apart the key frames are, the slower the swing, and the impact will be less or none at all if the ball doesn't reach the target area.

Have a go hero – experimenting with the settings

Take the time to experiment with the various settings without moving any props until you get an idea of what is possible within that setup.

After testing the existing setup move the props around to see the reaction. Move the bat forward or back on the ball prop. Change the ball prop to Kinetic or other states and view the results.

Time for action – changing the impact object angle

We are going to modify the same scene and use the cylinder as a push object like a pool cue.

1. Save a copy of the previous action section under a new name.

2. Make sure the **Rigid Body Simulation** button on the top toolbar is turned off.

3. Click on the **Reset** button as shown in the following image and a pop-up dialog will ask if we want to reset all animation data in the project, which is exactly what we want to do, so answer YES.

The following image shows the reset button located on the bottom toolbar:

4. Select the cylinder and position around behind the ball facing the right side arch. The settings for this example are as follows:

Move: X= 112.4, Y= -108.0, Z= 49.1

Rotate: X= 88.7, Y=14, Z=51.1

Scale: X=18.7, Y= 18.7, Z= 293.6

The following image shows the cylinder setup:

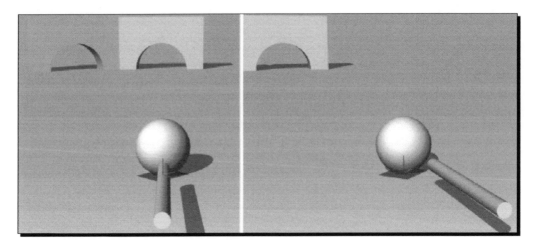

5. Move the time scrubber down to frame 35.

6. Set the cylinder parameters as follows:

Move: X= 42.2, Y=-35.7, Z= 44.2

Rotation: X= 88.7, Y= 13.9, Z= 51.1

Scale: X=18.7, Y=18.7, Z= 293.6

7. With the cylinder still selected, turn on the **Physics Object Settings** dialog located on the upper toolbar and check the **Active Physics** checkbox. Set the state to **Kinematic**.

8. Select the ball prop. Check the **Active Physics** checkbox and set the state to **Dynamic**.

9. Select both of the arches, active their physics and set them as **Static**.

10. Save the project.

11. Activate the **Rigid Body Simulation** by clicking the button on the top toolbar.

12. Run the simulation.

13. Select the cylinder, right-click on it and open its timeline.

14. Move the key frame from frame 35 to frame 15.

15. Rerun the simulation by pressing the play button.

What just happened?

Our first attempt was very weak and didn't generate enough force to power the ball down to the arches. We shortened the length between key frames and got more momentum but also got a small bounce in the ball and it's off target more than it's on, so let's see if we can add an aiming site to the simulation.

Time for action – adding the aiming site

We'll use the **Cross_003** prop located in the **3D Blocks** prop folder as our aiming site:

1. Double-click on the **Cross_003** prop in the **3D Blocks** folder to load it into the workspace and position the prop as in the following image:

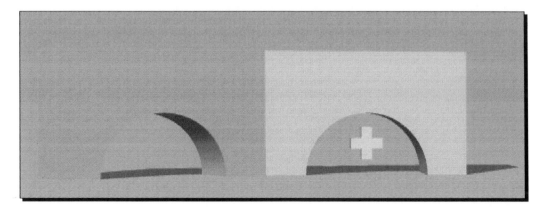

2. Attach the cross prop to the cylinder.

3. Rerun the simulation several times till you see a pattern develop then stop the simulation on one of those recognizable patterns as we are trying to get an aiming point set. Back up the simulation to a point where the ball is in front of the arches.

4. Select the ball prop, right-click on it and remove all animation.

5. Move the time scrubber back to the first frame.

6. Select the **Aiming Dummy** and move it over to the ball as shown in the following image:

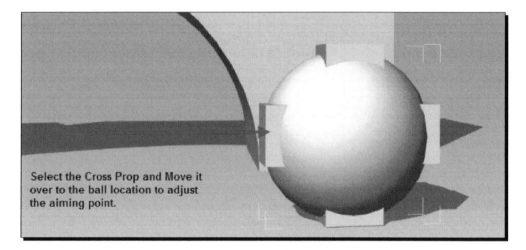

Select the Cross Prop and Move it over to the ball location to adjust the aiming point.

7. Select the ball prop.

8. Click on the **Reset** button located in the **Transform** section of the right side menu, as shown in the following image to place it back at its original location:

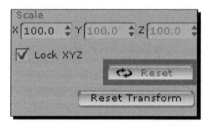

9. Select the cylinder, right-click on it and select the **Remove All Animation** option to remove all animation from the cylinder.

10. Use the rotate tool to move the cylinder till the **Aiming Dummy** is lined up as shown in the following image;

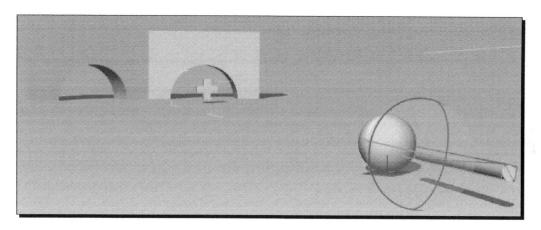

11. We lost our impact animation when we removed the cylinders animation so we need to move the time scrubber down to frame 20 and set the cylinder location as follows:

Move: X= -35.7, Y=42.2, Z=44.2

12. Save the project file and run the simulation.

The following image shows the best case result after aligning the **Aiming Dummy**. Depending on velocity the aim should be more accurate now:

What just happened?

We added a cross shaped prop for a crosshair. Then we attached that prop to the cylinder for aiming but we had to align the cross with the cylinder for the rig to shoot where the **Aiming Dummy** was located.

It wouldn't be that difficult to make a cannon or artillery piece fire using the same method as we just discovered.

Time for action – crashing the jeep

Car chases and crashes have long been a part of the moviemaking culture and iClone physics can help you simulate crashing into items:

1. Open a new blank project.

2. Double-click on the **Infinite Plane** in the **Physics** folder of the **Props** button to load the plane so our boxes won't fall through the floor.

3. Double-click on the **Box_001** prop located in the **3D Blocks** folder in the **Content Manager** to load it into the scene.

4. With the **Box_001** prop selected, open the **Multi-Duplicate** dialog by pressing the button on the top toolbar or using *Shift + D*.

5. Enter the following info into the input boxes.

    Duplicates: 10

    Move: X=105, Y=0, Z=0

    Rotate: X=0, Y=0, Z=0

    Scale: X=100, Y=100, Z=100

6. Click on **OK** to close the dialog box and create the duplicates.

    The following image shows the **Multi-Duplicate** dialog box:

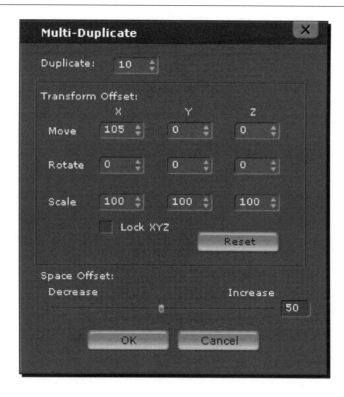

7. Select all the boxes either by using the **Select** tool and drawing a marquee around them, or by selecting them in the **Content Manager**.

8. Open **Physics Object Settings** by clicking on the button or using *Shift + F9*, if it's not already open.

9. With all the boxes selected, check the **Active Physics** checkbox on **Physics Object Settings**.

10. Choose **Frozen** as the state. Leave the mass and other settings as they are.

11. With all the boxes still selected, hold down the *Ctrl* key and move the stack of boxes up until a new set of boxes are created and place them on top of the original set using the move gizmo. Repeat the process until we have a stack of 8 boxes high by 11 boxes wide as in the following image:

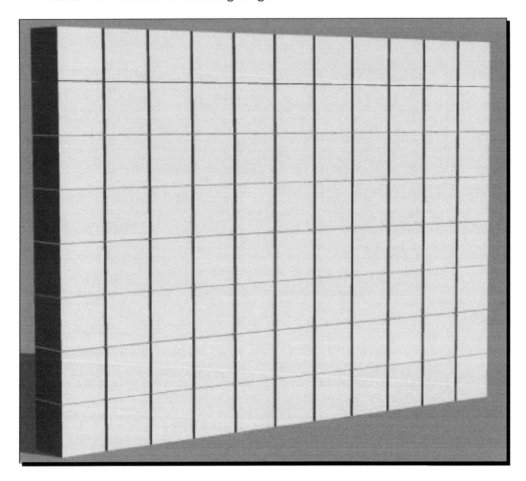

What just happened?

We multiplied one box out to eleven boxes then duplicated that row of boxes until we had a stack of boxes 8 high by 11 wide.

We set the state on the boxes to frozen to hold them in place, otherwise, they might topple in to a giant pile of boxes!

We can always change the state of the boxes by selecting them in mass to make the change.

Time for action – duplicating rows of boxes

1. Highlight the entire set of blocks with the mouse or select the boxes in the left side menu.

2. Hold down the *Ctrl* key and use the **Move** gizmo to create another set of boxes directly behind the original set. Repeat this step till we have at least 4 rows of boxes.

3. Double-click on the **Jeep** prop in the root directory of the props folder located in the **Content Manager** on the left side menu to load it into the scene.

4. Position the **Jeep** as in the following image:

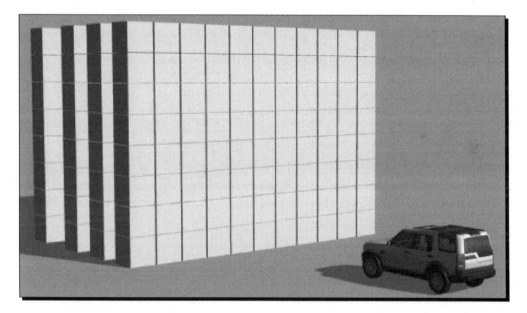

5. Select the **Jeep** prop.

6. Open the **Physics Settings** dialog if it is not already open.

7. Check the **Active Physics** box and choose **Kinematic** for the state.

8. Right-click on the **Jeep** prop and select **Move Forward** from the **Move** sub menu choice.

9. Click on an area on the other side of the boxes that will drive the jeep through the stack of boxes to the other side.

10. Return the time scrubber to the first frame and make sure **Rigid Body Simulation** is active.

11. Press the play button and let the simulation run its course till movement stops.

12. Turn off the **Rigid Body Simulation** button on the top toolbar to bake the sim.

13. Save the project.

The following image shows the jeep driving through the box, using the jeep as its own collision object:

What just happened?

We added our collision object, the **Jeep** prop, and set it to **Kinematic**. We also used the built in AML script to drive through the boxes to accomplish the goal of the scene.

Have a go hero – driving through again

Use the remove animation or the reset animation button on the bottom toolbar to remove existing animation. Move the **Jeep** prop to another area and have it drive through again or have the jeep hit the stack of boxes at an angle. Be creative!

Time for action – setting up an ejection sequence

Every once in a while we need to have a character launched upward from a sitting position, as would be used by a pilot ejecting from an aircraft. While this could be animated with key frames, it would be rather stale compared to letting physics handle it. This motion can be simulated using a simple see-saw technique. This simulation may produce differing results for you as simulations are dependent on a lot of variables including computer load at the time of simulation:

1. Create a new blank project. Select the **Set** tab and click on the **Props** button.

2. Double-click on the **Infinite Plane** prop in the **Physics** folder to load it into the scene, as we always need to do when we want a floor to stop objects during a simulation.

3. Double-click on the **Pyramid_005** primitive in the **3D Blocks** folder to load it into the center of the workspace.

4. Load the **Wall_001** prop from the **Wall and Floors** sub-folder of the **3D Blocks** prop folder.

5. Center the **Pivot Point** on the wall prop by clicking the center pivot icon in the pivot section of the right side menu.

6. Set the **Wall** attributes to the following:

Move: X= -11.3, Y= -11.1, Z=56.8

Rotate: X= 90.0, Y=14.7, Z=3.8

Scale: X=100.0, Y= 65.3, Z= 12.0

7. Load the **Box_004** prop from the **3D Blocks** folder and set its attributes to:

Move: X=138.5, Y=4.3, Z=20.8

Rotate: X=0.3, Y=14.7, Z=4.3

Scale: X=100.00, Y=100.00, Z=100.00

8. Load **Ball_001** from the **3D Blocks** prop folder into the workspace and set its attributes to:

Move: X= -115.0, Y=-30.1, Z=327.3

Rotate: X=0.0, Y=0.0, Z=0.0

Scale: X=100.0, Y=100.0, Z=100.0

The following images show the prop setup and location in the scene:

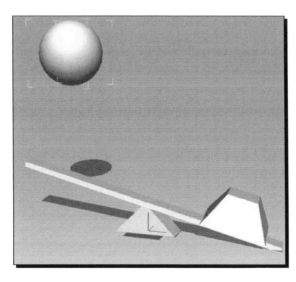

What just happened?

We laid out a basic see-saw just like in a children's playground with the pyramid as the fulcrum. The box simulates the ejection seat and the ball will be the impacting object that imparts the force.

Now we just need to setup the physics, which is very simple.

Time for action – setting up the eject physics

1. Open the **Physics Settings** dialog by clicking on its button in the top toolbar.

2. Select the ball prop and click the **Active Physics** checkbox then set the state to **Dynamic**. Set **Bound Type** to **Self Mesh**. Set the **Mass** to 400.

> In a simple simulation such as this, the type of impact object we use is not as important as the Bounding type since that will actually determine the effects of the contact. We used a ball to differentiate it from the other box in this example for the purpose of clarity of instruction.

3. Select wall prop (our board) and click the **Active Physics** checkbox then set the state to **Frozen** with the **Bound Type** to **Self Mesh**.

4. Select the **Box_004** prop and click the **Active Physics** checkbox, then set the state to **Frozen** with the **Bound Type** to **Convex Hull**. **Mass**=1, **Friction**=0, **Damping**=0, **Elasticity**=100.

5. Select the **Pyramid_005** prop and click the **Active Physics** checkbox then set the state to **Static** with the **Bound Type** to **Self Mesh**.

6. Save the project file in case you need to reload it and start over for any reason.

7. Turn on the **Rigid Body Simulation** (if it's not already on) by clicking the button on the top toolbar.

8. Run the simulation by pressing the play button.

    Though it doesn't look like much, the following image is the result of a simulation run (yours may and probably will vary). The end result isn't what we are after anyway. It's the arc up and then back down that we want to capture for use:

What just happened?

After selecting, activating, and setting the state of each object along with the type of Bound Mesh necessary, we ran the simulation to see if it was anything we could use. The box was launched upward into a nice tumbling arc that we would once again be hard pressed to animate ourselves.

Time for action – attaching the character

Let's get visual now and attach our character to the box dummy to inherit the motion we just created through the simulation:

1.   Using the same project, return the time scrubber to the first frame.

2.   Turn OFF the **Rigid Body Simulation,** otherwise you will overwrite it with another simulation run.

3.   Select the **Actor** tab and click on the **Avatar** button. From the **Special Character** folder drag-and-drop or double-click to load the **Dummy** character into the scene.

> Any character will work as this appendix was created during the beta testing phase of iClone 5 and stock characters provided may change by release date.

4.   With the **Dummy** character selected, click on the **Pick Parent** button in **Linkage** then click on the **Box_004** prop on the end of the board.

5.   Click on the small **Link To** button and select **Position and Rotation** then click **OK**.

6.   Rotate the dummy to face the ball prop.

7.   Click on the **Animation** tab then select the **Motion** button.

8. With the Dummy still selected, double-click on the **Idle_00** motion located in the **Idle** sub-folder of the **Mode_03** sub-folder of the **Male Motion** sub-folder of the **Male** folder located on the left side menu: Male | Male Motion | Mode_03 | Idle | Idle_00.

 Don't worry about the dummy disappearing or what happens on screen, just go to the next step. It will look like a mess!

9. Return the time scrubber back to the first frame. If the **Dummy** character is not selected then use the **Scene Manager** to select it.

10. With the **Dummy** character selected, click on the tiny **Link To** button (make sure you are under the **Actor** tab, **Avatar** button) on the right side menu and choose position to bring the character back into position.

11. Select **Box_004** and turn the opacity slider down to zero on the mid to lower right side menu to make the box invisible.

The following image shows the **Dummy** character repositioned then the **Dummy** with the **Box_004** opacity turned off:

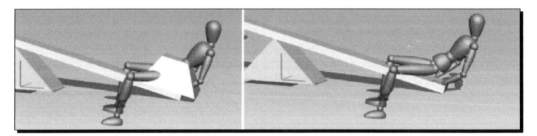

12. Save the project under a new file name.

13. Delete the ball, pyramid, and wall (board) props from the scene.

14. Play the scene.

The following image shows the character launched into the air during the early arc of the physics generated action:

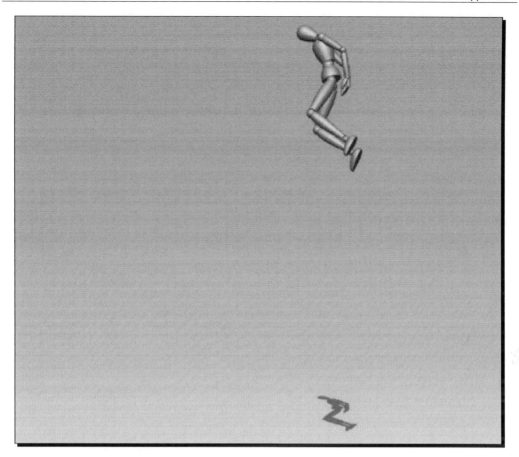

What just happened?

We attached and posed the character to Box_004 which was previously animated by the physics simulation run. We then deleted the other objects from the scene as they were no longer needed in the scene itself, set the Box_004 opacity to zero so it would not be visible.

To save the animation for use in another project turn the opacity back up to 100 percent for the box and save the box to attach to a character such as a pilot/ejection seat combination.

Saving physics animations

When using dummies the physics animation is stored in the dummy, NOT the attached object so we must save the dummy to save the physics animation. There may be times we will want to use the **Collect** feature to save animations if external key framed events are involved in addition to the physics animation.

Have a go hero

We got the basics of a good ejection start sequence with the physics generated animation to this point. Now take over and try to change the way the character will be ejected by changing various conditions of the simulation. Move a prop here or adjust a setting there.

Spend some time experimenting with this simulation as it's simple enough for a starting point but will still need some modification with the physics properties settings if you don't want the pilot to be spinning or rolling (which might be a good effect in itself).

Time for action – creating a chain action

There are times you may need a fluid chain action or possibly chains lining a wall or walkway and you'd like them to sway down naturally. We'll be using primitives for this quick and easy way to create a chain.

1. Open a new blank project and select the **Set** tab then click on the **Props** button.

2. Load the **Box_001** prop from the **3D Blocks** folder into the workspace.

3. With the **Box_001** prop selected, click on the top center icon, in the right side menu, to reset the pivot point to the top center and set its attributes as follows:

   Move: X= 0, Y=0, Z=0

   Rotate: X= 0, Y=0, Z=0

   Scale: X=25, Y=25, Z=80

   The following image shows the **Top Middle** pivot icon, which when clicked resets the pivot.

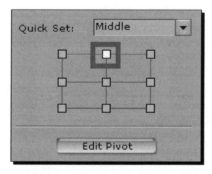

4. With the **Box_001** prop selected, click the **Reset Transform** button located in the **Transform** section on the right side menu.

The following image displays the **Reset Transform** button for the box prop which resets the scale to 100 percent:

5. Open the **Multi-Duplicate** dialog by clicking the button on the top toolbar or using the *Shift + D* shortcut and use the following settings:

   Duplicate:8

   Move: X=0, Y=0, Z=183

   Rotate: X=0, Y=0, Z=0

   Scale: X=100, Y=100, Z=100

   The following image shows the newly created chain of boxes with the **Multi-Duplicate** dialog:

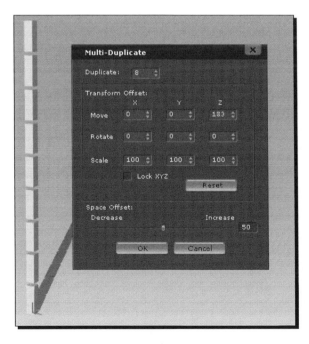

6. Select all of the boxes and open the **Physics Object Settings** dialog by clicking the button on the top toolbar or using the *Shift + F9* shortcut.

7. Click the **Active Physics** checkbox and set the state to **Dynamic**.

8. Set the **Bound Type** to **Capsule** with the Z axis.

9. Click on the first box at the **top** of the chain and set its state to **Kinematic** as it is our anchor object.

10. Use *Shift + Alt + R* to bring up the additional physics dialog as shown in the following image. Your dialog may look different as this was in beta testing at the time.

11. Click on the **Rigid Body** button in the top middle of the dialog.

12. Make sure the **Active** checkbox is checked.

13. With all the boxes selected, choose **Point To Point** as the type of constraint. Input the following attributes:

Rotate X: Min: -30, Max: 30

Rotate Y: Min: -30, Max: 30

Rotate Z: Min: 0, Max: 0

What is a constraint?

A simplified way to view it would be that a constraint holds (limits) or, otherwise, binds one object to another upon one or more of the axes. These constraints can be further constrained (limited) on each individual axis. If we need an object to move within a certain axis or limit the amount of movement on all axes we constrain it.

14. Select the bottom box and click the **Pick Target** button in the dialog then select the box directly above it.

15. Select the second box from the bottom and with the **Pick Target** button select the box directly above it.

16. Repeat this process until each box is constrained to the box above it, all the way to the second from top box. The top box has no object to be constrained to.

17. Save the project.

18. Move the time scrubber down to around frame 50.

19. Select the top block and move it a short distance to the right of the screen.

Only the top block will move until the simulation is started. Do not be alarmed by this as it is normal behaviour.

20. Make sure the **Rigid Body Simulation** button is on, located on the top toolbar.

21. Move the time scrubber back to the start and run the simulation.

What just happened?

We used several box dummies to simulate a chain, which can be used to attach props to including links from to form an actual chain! We reset the pivot point to top center initially so that all of the boxes move cleanly on their restraints. The bounding mesh capsules allow for more movement between boxes with the rounded corners.

Point To Point constraints also allow for more movement as a hinge constraint will only allow one axis to move. If you want some twist in the chain, then add some parameters to the Z axis of the constraints, which were set at zero for our example.

The most tedious part of the process was actually picking each individual box constraint, which was the box directly above it, in the order that we worked. It would have worked if we had started top down also.

 Horizontal chains

While writing this appendix, stuckon3d, an advanced 3D artist in his own right with television and movie experience, authored a chain tutorial for the beta testers and it was much like the one in this book, except that he reminded us that you can turn the chain horizontal and set the first and last boxes as kinematic to produce a hanging chain that sags when the simulation is run! Look for stuckon3d in the Reallusion forum.

The following image shows our chain with the animation removed, rotated, the first and last boxes set to kinematic and re-simulated:

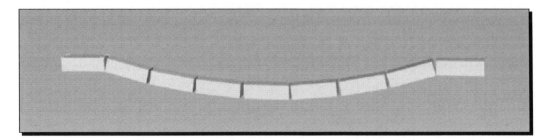

Applying physics to props that have been scaled, instead of resized, can produce unexpected results. Since, you can only rescale in iClone the **Reset Transform** button has been provided to reset the scale to 100 percent after rescaling an object, eliminating or reducing problems when working with physics.

Colliding with characters

An earlier action section prepared us for using characters for collision. At the time of writing, there was no collision detection built into the avatars, but Reallusion and several other developers including this author are working on characters with built-in collision mesh. Until fully developed physics enabled characters are released, we must rely on this technique of attaching dummies to characters for collision with items such as a car or a wall.

Attaching dummies

Using building block primitives for dummies will be standard practice when setting up the scene with characters. These dummies need to be low poly so they do not add to the overhead of the scene, which is why it is recommended to use the props provided in iClone.

Time for action – preparing a character collision

A car crash! Oh no! Oh Yeah! Let's have some fun with this one! We'll use the Benny character for this mayhem:

1. Load a new blank scene. Select the **Actor** tab and click on the **Avatar** button.

2. Double-click on the **Benny** character to load him into the scene. Any character will work.

3. Load the **Infinite Plane** from the physics props folder into the workspace.

4. Load the **Jeep** from the **Prop root** folder into the workspace.

5. Arrange the objects as in the following image:

6. Load the **Ball_001** prop from the **3D Blocks** folder into the scene and scale it up along its Z Axis to around 146.

7. Position the ball prop around Benny as shown in the following image. It doesn't have to be exact, just make sure the curve of the ball is outside of his body:

8. With the **Benny** character selected, click on the **Pick Parent** button in the **Linkage** section on the right side menu and select the ball to link Benny to the ball.

9. Load **Box_001** prop into the workspace.

10. Scale the box to X= 187.8, Y=207.4, Z=47.4 and place it as in the following image:

11. Use the **Pick Parent** button to attach the new box prop to the jeep.

12. Select the jeep, right-click on the jeep and choose **Move_Forward** from the **Move** command. Select a spot behind the Benny character that will cause the jeep to impact the character when it drives off.

13. Return the time scrubber to the first frame if it's not already there.

14. Click on the **Physics Settings** button or press *Shift + F9*.

15. Select **Ball_001**, activate the physics and set its state to **Frozen** and the **Bounding Type** to **Self Mesh**.

16. Choose the **Box_001** prop and click on the **Active Physics** checkbox and set the state to **Kinematic** and **Bounding Type** to **Self Mesh**.

The following image shows the meshes to this point:

17. Save the file.

18. Run the simulation.

Linking/Attaching tip

Remember to LINK to characters and ATTACH to props when using dummies for physics collisions.

19. Select the box and turn it's opacity down to zero to render it invisible. Do the same for the ball. The opacity slider is located in the right side menu when the prop is selected.

20. Select the **Ball_001** prop and change the **Bounding Type** to **Box** then rerun the simulation to see the difference.

The following image shows the Benny character colliding with the jeep when using a box bounding type:

What just happened?

We used the ball prop to act as a collision dummy for the character and used a box prop for the same purpose on the jeep. While props can act as their own dummy, we needed to use the built-in Move feature of the Jeep, so using a dummy allowed us to animate the jeep while having an impact object on the front of the jeep without cancelling out the built-in move scripting.

We pushed the collision dummy out and down low on the jeep to force the Benny character into the air. If you find that the character is crashing through the top of the jeep, then add another box to that part of the jeep, size it to cover the area of penetration, set it up like the other box, then attach it to the jeep. Use as many dummies as necessary.

Summary

In this appendix, we covered a lot of information and examples concerning the new physics capabilities of iClone 5.

Specifically, we covered the following:

- Rigid and soft bodies
- How to set up the physics objects and simulation
- How to rig dummies for collisions
- General object collisions and how to set them up
- Force driven collisions
- Many different action sections for physics applications

C

Exploring New Features

Version 5 brings a lot of new features and tools to the animator's toolbox, besides physics and new animation methods. iClone's upgrades have always been dramatic for the sheer number of new features and this version delivers as well. There are several new tools and toys that can put a smile on the face of any iCloner.

In this chapter, we shall do the following:

- Explore new visual enhancements, such as ambient occlusion and toon rendering
- Discuss improved performance features, including Level of Detail (LOD) and height map terrain among other improvements
- Explore the new post effects, such as blur, color adjust, and color filter
- Learn about enhanced usability features, such as multi-duplicate along with other time and labor saving new additions

So let's get started...

Discovering new visual enhancements

Some of the self-evident upgrades and improvements have to do with the lighting and rendering, which are two extremely important parts of the iClone process. Reallusion has not only given us more control over lighting but they have also given some wonderful new tools that will improve the real-time look and final render of our videos.

Understanding ambient occlusion

Ambient Occlusion (AO) is a major leap forward in the improvement of real-time and final render of a scene.

From Wikipedia:

> *Ambient occlusion is a shading method used in 3D computer graphics which helps add realism to local reflection models by taking into account attenuation of light due to occlusion. Ambient occlusion attempts to approximate the way light radiates in real life, especially off what are normally considered non-reflective surfaces.*

Ambient Occlusion (AO) makes a dramatic and instantly recognizable improvement to the look of the video but can, like all tools, be overused. The best way to describe AO is to look at the difference it makes in scene.

The following image demonstrates the difference in no AO (left image) to exaggerated AO (right image). Notice the depth of shadows on the edges of objects and how more defined the objects are, like the books and candle wax. Glare was also reduced. This exaggerated setting is far from optimal and for demonstration purposes only:

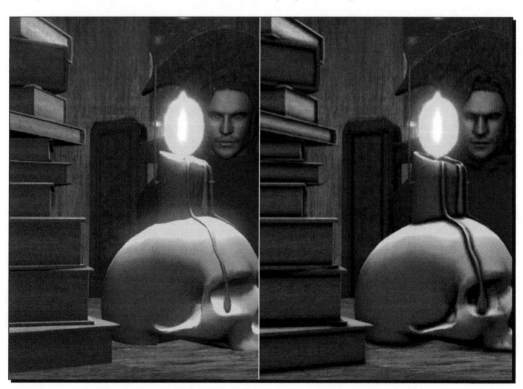

Time for action – using ambient occlusion

To further demonstrate this tool, we'll create our own simple scene to view the dramatic difference that Ambient Occlusion provides:

1. Open a new blank project. Select the **Set** tab and click on the **Water** button.

2. Double-click on **Water 9** to load it from the **Still Normal** sub-folder of the water folder in the left side **Content Manager.**

3. Set the water's **Height** to 0 in the **Basic Water Parameters** of the right side menu and change the color to black, which will actually change the water to a light blue for the moment.

4. Select the **Stage** tab and click the **2D background** button.

5. Set the background color to white and uncheck the **Active** box so we can see the white background. The workspace will appear white at this point.

6. Select the **Set** tab and click on the **Props** button. From the **Architecture** folder in the left side **Content Manager,** double click on **Deckhouse_B** to load it into the workspace.

7. Double-click on the **Jeep** prop located in the prop folder to load it into the scene.

8. Pull the camera back to see the prop. Position the camera and the jeep as in the following image:

9. Select the **Stage** tab and click on the **Atmosphere** button.

10. Check the box for **Ambient Occlusion** within the **Ambient Occlusion** section of the right side menu.

11. Change the AO parameters as follows.

> **Strength**: 30
>
> **Range**: 62
>
> **Distance**: 4

12. Save the file.

What just happened?

We set up a light colored scene with light colored objects to make a quick test of the AO features and then made changes in the parameters to demonstrate the differences.

Have a go hero – experimenting with ambient occlusion

Turn the **AO** checkbox on and off to view the difference AO makes. Focus on sections of the house and jeep, then click the box on and off.

Change the three parameters that affect AO so you can really get an idea of what depth this great tool brings to the overall look of iClone generated footage.

 Post effects and atmospheric changes can be animated on the timeline.

Exploring the toon shader

The **Toon (cartoon) Shader** was a much requested feature and came about mostly at the insistence of a particular Reallusion community member and fellow developer named Paumanok West, a dedicated toon head and all around great artist in many disciplines. It also helps that he is a perfectionist who constantly strives to improve his work so he will most likely be one of the go-to members of the community for future information about this shader.

 To achieve a cartoon look, it can take more than just the Toon Shader. It's a combination of Toon Shader, Post Effects, Templates, if needed, and matching the sky or terrain colors to the scene.

Time for action – enhancing the existing scene

We will not know this shader's complete capabilities until it has been fully explored by the community, so we will take a look at the basics and do some exploring! We'll use the same scene we just created to explore the toon shader tools and options:

1. With the previous scene loaded, select the **Set** tab and the **Sky** button.

2. Double-click on **Clear Day 05** to load it into the workspace.

3. Set the sky **Height** to -2000.

4. Select the **Terrain** button while under the **Set** tab and double-click on **Grassland** to load the terrain.

5. Remove the water.

6. Click on the **Tree** button under the **Set** tab and plant a couple of trees to fill up space. This example used American Elm A and American Elm.

What just happened?

We needed a scene to explore our Toon Shader options, so we used our previous scene and added a few items so we would have more objects to view as visual reference for our toon shading.

Toon shading involves more than just setting the Toon Shader parameters in the Atmosphere controls. There are also templates and an effect filter (NPR) available to enhance the look.

The following image shows the scene as we've set it up for this demonstration. You may place as many trees and objects as you wish:

Time for action – setting up the toon shader

We've created the scene and now we need to toon it:

1. Select the **Stage** tab and click on the **Atmosphere** button.

2. Make sure that **Ambient Occlusion** is on.

3. Check the **Toon Shader** box in the **Toon Shader** section towards the bottom of the modify menu when the **Atmosphere** button is depressed.

4. In the **Silhouette Edge** section change the selection to **Texture Color**.

5. Click on the **Effect** button at the top.

6. Double-click on the **NPR** effect to load it into the workspace.

What just happened?

You will notice, when we added the NPR effect, it gave us dark edges similar to the Silhouette Edges, which is why we changed those to color instead of black to cut back on the dark edges in the scene unless that is what you are looking for.

The sky and terrain have been affected by the NPR post effect too. They now have more of a cartoon look to them. The following image shows the effects of the Toon Shader with minimal adjustment and the NPR post effect at its default value:

Time for action - exploring the NPR post effect

Let's take a look at the NPR effect first then we'll get into the Toon Shader settings next. We get into the entire selection of post effects in another section of this appendix:

1. Select the **Stage** tab and click on the **Effects** button.

2. Highlight the NPR effect by clicking on its name.

3. Select the **Paint Weight** slider and move it back towards the left to 30.

4. Select the **Colorful** slider and move it back towards the left while observing the difference it makes in the workspace.

5. Move the **Colorful** slider all the way back to the right to restore the color.

6. Double-click on the NPR post effect on the left side **Content Manager** menu and load another NPR effect into the workspace.

7. Reduce the **Paint Weight** and **Colorful** sliders to view the changes they create. Restore them back to their original positions after you are finished experimenting.

8. Highlight the second NPR effect and press on the **Delete** button above it to delete it from the project.

What just happened?

We adjusted the NPR post effect to discover its parameters and what we can do with it. We also discovered that we can load more than one version of the effect and stack effects until we run out of slots.

Time for action – exploring the toon shader

Now let's tinker with the Toon Shader parameters:

1. With the **Stage** tab selected, click on the **Atmosphere** button and scroll down the right side menu to the **Toon Shader** section.

2. Click on the left side color selector in the **Paint** section of the **Toon Shader**. Change its color to orange as shown in the following image:

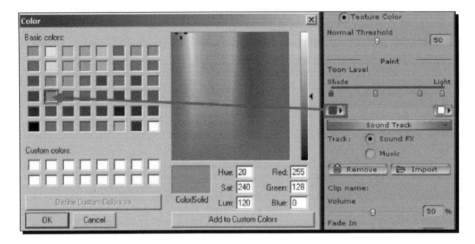

3. Select **Sky** from the **Content Manager**.

4. In the **Adjust Color** section on the right side menu change the **Brightness** to 10, the **Contrast** to 59 and the **Hue** to -14.

What just happened?

We added bit of warm color to the scene by replacing the dark color with orange, then jumped over to the Sky modify panel and changed the parameters to give the sky more of a cartoon look and to better match the scene colors.

The following image shows our toon work:

Removing skin color

According to the research notes provided by Jason Lin, another method for using characters with the toon shader is to remove the skin color diffuse images and use the color channels for the skin color. This alters the interaction with shading.

Time for action – tooning the characters

Time to prep some characters for "tooning":

1. Open a new blank project. Select the **Actor** tab and click on the **Avatar** button.

2. Double-click on the **Violet** character to load her into the scene and move the camera in towards the character until she fills the workspace so we get a better look at what we are going to do.

3. Select the **Stage** tab, click on the **Atmosphere** button and check the **Toon Shader** box.

4. Select the **Violet** character and click on the **Animation** tab then click the **Motion** button.

5. Double-click on the **Idle_001** motion in the **Idle** sub-folder of the **Mode_01** sub-folder of the **Female Motion** sub-folder within the **Female** folder: Female | Female Motion | Mode_01 | Idle | Idle_00.

6. Let the motion play until it stops then return the time scrubber to the first frame.

7. Save the file.

8. Select the **Violet** character and move the character to the left of the screen or input -75 into the X axis input box in the **Transform** section on the right side menu.

9. Deselect the **Violet** character.

10. Double-click on the **Violet** character from the **Actor** tab, **Avatar** button to load a second **Violet** character into the scene.

11. With the newly loaded Violet character selected, click on the **Animation** tab, then the **Motion** button and load the same **Idle_00** motion into the character.

12. Return the time scrubber back to the first frame. Save the file.

13. The following image shows the two characters in basic toon shade:

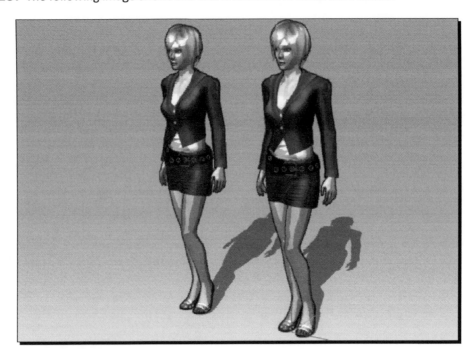

What just happened?

We created a new scene, started up the Toon shader and loaded two characters into the scene for comparison. We are now ready to skin a toon!

Time for action – skinning the character for tuning

Let's take a look at removing the diffuse skin images and using just color for the skin:

1. With the second Violet character selected, click on the **Actor** tab and then click the **Skin** button.

2. In the **Materials & Texture Settings** section of the right side menu, select **Face** from the drop-down menu under **Select Material**.

3. Instead of deleting the skin diffuse map, click on the diffuse channel and slide the strength slider back to zero to turn the face white.

4. Make sure the time scrubber is on the first frame or we will have a character that changes colors as the animation plays out!

5. With the **Head Material** still selected, click on the **Diffuse Color** selector and choose a flesh tone. R=206, G=150, B-125 was used for this example.

6. Repeat the process with the **Upper**, **Lower**, and **Shoes** sections of the skin till all the skin matches the new color.

7. Move the **Toon Level** sliders in the **Paint Section** to match the following image or to match your taste:

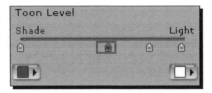

8. To give the newly colored Violet character a little more definition, we can adjust the **Normal Threshold** back to around 26, which will define the character a little more.

9. Save the project and play it to review the differences in the characters as they move through the short motion we added.

The following image shows both our Violet characters with the original diffuse skin on the left and the color only skin on the right:

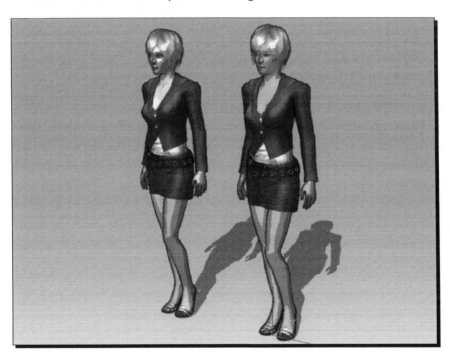

What just happened?

We changed the diffuse skin image to a standard color making the character into even more of cartoon while adjusting the **Toon Level** to control the painting features of the Toon Shader. This will give us a choice of characters and looks for future projects.

Using post effects

We've briefly discussed the use of a Post Effect so let's take a look at this new feature of iClone that brings controllable effects to the iClone Interface.

What is a Post Effect anyway? This is after the video is rendered when an effect or effects are added to the video, usually with another application. The reference to Post concerns the fact that the effect was applied post (after) render.

iClone 5 gives us five of these effects within the iClone 3D workspace **before** the render of the video which gives us a chance to see our effects sooner and have more control over how they interact with the iClone environment.

The following image displays the new Post Effects:

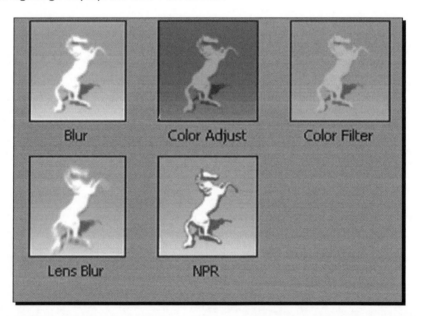

Time for action – applying blur

The best way to understand these effects is to demonstrate them:

1. Open a new blank project. Select the **Stage** tab and click on the **3D Scene** button.

2. Double-click on the **Flood** project to load it into the workspace.

3. Select the **Set** tab and click on the **Water** button.

4. Remove the water from the scene by clicking on the **Remove** button at the top of the right side menu.

5. While still under the **Set** tab, click on the **Sky** button and double-click on the **Cloudy_02** sky to load it into the workspace.

6. Select the **Actor** tab and click on the **Avatar** button.

7. Double-click the **Dylan** character to load him into the scene.

8. With the Dylan character selected, rotate the camera to the right and pull back till you have a view that is similar to the following image:

9. Save the file.

10. Select the **Stage** tab and click on the **Effect** button.

11. Double-click on the **Blur** effect in the **Content Manager** on the top left menu.

12. Click on the **Blur** effect that has been added to the **Post Effect** section of the right menu as shown in the following image:

13. Notice the Blur Range slider that appears when you select the **Blur** effect. Move the slider to 8 or type 8 into the input box. Next, input or move the slider to 50 to view the difference.

 To easily gauge what the effect you are currently working with is having on the video, click the **Eye** icon (located next to the effect name in the right side menu) to toggle the effect on and off to see the difference.

14. With **Blur** highlighted, click on the **Delete** button located above it to delete the effect.

What just happened?

We set up a simple scene with buildings, sky, and character so we can demonstrate the various **Post Effects** starting with the **Blur** effect. The slider that appeared after selecting the blur effects allowed us to control the amount of blur and demonstrated how the effects controls will appear when an individual effect is selected in the right side control panel.

The order of post effects is very important!

The order of the Post Effects "stack" is important or Reallusion wouldn't have given us a way to move individual effects up or down the stack. This is similar to a modifier stack in applications like Studio Max. Moving an effect up or down in the stack can affect the overall look of the combined effect. You are encouraged to experiment in this area.

Time for action – testing the other post effects

Let's move on with the other post effects so we can get a handle on what they can accomplish for us.

1. With the previous scene still loaded, double-click on the **Color Adjust** effect, then click on the effect in the right side menu to access its controls.

2. Move the **Brightness** slider to 15.

3. Change the **Contrast** to 8.

4. Move the **Gray** style slider to the maximum of 20.

   At this point, your image should look similar to the following image:

5. Click on the **Eye** icon to the right of the **Color Adjust** filter to turn off the filter for now.

6. Double-click on the **Color Filter** effect to load it into the workspace and select it from the right side menu to see its controls.

Animating the Post Effects

Post effects generate key frames and are, therefore, controllable within the timeline for starting and stopping or fades.

7. Move the Red filter to zero and the Blue filter to the maximum to get a dark blue tint to the scene.

8. Move the Green slider to 6. Leave this effect on.

9. Double-click on the **Lens Blur** effect to load it, then select it in the right side menu.

10. With the time scrubber on the first frame (which you were at anyway right?) change the **Position X** slider to 0.

11. Move the time scrubber to frame 500 and change the **Position X** slider to 100.

12. Return the time scrubber to the first frame and play the animation to review our work to this point. Turn the effect off (click on the **Eye** icon) and save the file.

What just happened?

We explored the Post Effects, which we have not already seen, and now have a good idea of what they can do. The **Color Adjust** effect is very useful for brightening the entire scene with the proper combination of Brightness and Contrast. The **Gray Style** slider can achieve a range of looks from full color to full grayscale.

The **Color Filter** is a very simple Red, Green, Blue slider setup that can achieve different colors with different combinations of the sliders. We changed the scene to blue then warmed it up a little by adding some color from the green slider.

The **Lens Blur** is a very cool effect that we will probably find many uses for as projects come and go, but for now we explored the basics of it, including key framing it to move from the left to the right of the screen.

The following image shows our scene to this point with an active blue color filter:

Time for action – adjusting the overall post effect

Now that we've looked at the basics let's apply our effects to this particular scene:

1. Make sure the time scrubber is on the first frame. Click on the **Eye** icon to turn the **Color Adjust** effect. Select that effect and change the **Gray Style** slider to 10.

2. Change the **Brightness** to the maximum 20.

3. Set the **Contrast** to 10.

4. Turn on the **Lens Blur** effect and set it to 5.

5. Double-click on the **NPR** filter, located in the **Content Manager** on the left side menu, to load it into the workspace.

6. Set the **Paint Weight** slider to zero.

7. Set the **Colorful** sider to zero.

8. Move the time scrubber down to frame 500.

9. Move the **Colorful** slider to the maximum of 20.

10. While still on frame 500 select the **Lens Blur** effect and set it to 5.

11. Move the time scrubber to frame 550.

12. Select the **Lens Blur** effect and set the **Lens Blur** to zero.

13. Return the time scrubber to the first frame and save the file.

14. Play the animation.

What just happened?

We used the combination of Post Effects to create a fade in from white while leaving a blue tint to the look. We also used the tools within the Color Adjust effect to brighten the scene for easier viewing.

Have a go hero – experimenting with the scene

It's time for you to experiment with the Post Effects in this project but be sure to save a copy first as we will use this project to expound on the Light Multiplier in the next section. Don't just change the parameters within the effects themselves but also move the effects up and down the Post Effects stack to visibly demonstrate the results of such moves.

Setting the light with the multiplier

One of the great new features of iClone is the **Light Multiplier** control that gives us control over the amount of light generated by the light source. This could very well be the simplest to use tool that has the greatest impact on a scene.

The following image shows the easy to use but highly effective new Light Multiplier control:

Time for action – using directional versus spotlight

We'll use our previous scene to experiment with the **Multiplier** control.

1. With the previous scene loaded, click on the **Reset** button in the bottom timeline and answer Yes to the pop-up dialog to reset all of the animation in the scene.

2. Select the **Stage** tab and click on the **Effect** button.

3. Turn off or delete the **NPR** and **Lens Blur** effects from the right side menu.

4. Select **Light01** in the **Dir/Spot Light** section of the **Content Manager** located on the left side menu.

5. Change the **Multiplier** to 2.00 to view the change in light.

6. Now change the **Multiplier** to .25 to view the difference in darkening it.

 Hold down the top or bottom arrow with our left mouse button to roll the selector up and down, however, the changes are not viewable until the left mouse button is released from the control.

7. Now click on **Spotlight** to change the light from directional to spot.

8. Change the **Angle** to 174 under **Spotlight Beam** and change the **Falloff** to 4.

9. Change the **Multiplier** to 1.50.

10. Save the file.

The following image shows the results of our Light Multiplier action section:

What just happened?

We demonstrated how to dial the light power up and down using the Light Multiplier. This simple tool in combination with the other lighting and atmospheric tools gives us a lot more control over the intensity of our lights.

Pop quiz

1. The Post Effect filters are permanent and have no adjustments available in this release.

    a. True

    b. False

2. The Light Multiplier creates as many lights as the user specifies.

    a. True

    b. False

3. Which of the following is not related to Toon Shading:

    a. NPR post effect.

    b. Toon Shader Atmospheric Templates

    c. Tone Map

    d. Silhouette Edge

    e. None of the above.

    f. All of the above.

Discovering the performance enhancements

Reallusion has also provided us with a handful of performance enhancements in version 5. These enhancements help with the overall performance of iClone as they strive to reduce the load on the real-time engine while maintaining the quality of the preview and render.

Height Map Terrain	This is an amazing feature still under development that uses information from an Earth Sculptor (as of the beta version) created terrain and texture images along with an `ini` file to present four levels of detail from close up to distant to reduce the load on the realtime engine. The `ini` file calls up the appropriate detail map for the terrain depending on distance.
LOD – Level of Detail	Height Map Terrain Only – Four levels of detail as referenced above switched on by default. Use the *Ctrl + L* shortcut to toggle it on and off.
Instance	An instance is a method of duplicating objects by sharing the same source of data. Any change to one object changes all the objects that are instanced from that object. A Reallusion research note stated that a project with 100 balls is almost the same size as a project with 1 ball. The instancing is taken care of by iClone when duplicating objects.

Alpha Threshold	This is a long awaited addition for those of us that have fought with the problem of the top residual line left when using opacity masks on a plane or billboard or multi-layer cloth. This little jewel is a threshold tuner that determines which part to pass through depending on the gray (alpha) level. Increase or decrease the Alpha Threshold if you are having transparency problems. Experimentation is highly encouraged.

The following image displays two planes using opacity maps to cut out the sky area. The right side plane shows the result of having the **Alpha Threshold** slider moved up to increase the alpha threshold based on grayscale transparency:

Improving usability features

Reallusion has also added several features to improve the usability of the program. These features comprise a list of "wants and needs" of the iClone user community and have been under development for some time now.

Camera Gizmo	Now available with visible bounding boxes to depict the Clipping Planes, Depth of Field, and 3D Stereoscopic rendering so the director can see just what is framed by the camera from an external view.
Camera Mini-Viewport	A much requested feature that opens a mini-view window that can be docked in three different corners of the workspace (Left Top, Left Bottom, Right Bottom). The view is selected from the available scene cameras or you can create a camera specifically for it. There is also a size slider for the Viewport that enlarges up to fifty percent of the main workspace size. This can make scene setup much more intuitive and help new users navigating the 3D workspace.
Merged Motion Track	Another DRAMATIC improvement to the timeline system. In the past, if you had a motion, a movement and a perform action it was difficult to blend them as they appeared on different timelines and it was impossible to blend across timelines. This solves that problem by placing all the motions on ONE TIMELINE! We can then blend to our heart's content to smooth out the motion. No more uncontrolled jumps or lurches in animation!
Path Enhancement	New path controls include the ability to change the color of the start and end control point. Hotkey TAB jumps to the next point and we now have a close path option.
Model Snap	Another great time saver that snaps objects (models) together on their edges. Makes quick work out of creating a wall and many other uses. Can turn it on or off in the preferences or use the shortcut *Ctrl + M*.
Align/Center	Yet another great time saving tool that aligns and centers multiple selected objects. Also has uniform spacing. Both work along the X, Y, Z axes.
Instant Texture Update	No more pressing the update button when working with textures via a third-party image editor. As soon as the file is saved, the texture is updated in iClone so it's ready when you switch back to it.
Enhanced Scene Manager	An already great scene manager made better with filter, sort and search features to handle those complicated scenes with lots of objects.
Multi-Duplicate	We have already seen and used this wonderful tool. It is worth the time taken to place a building block into the workspace and experiment with the different controls on the Multi-Duplicate pop-up menu so you can have a grasp of the time saving features this powerful tool offers.

Using the tree brush

This is a feature that this author, for one, is very glad to see. We have been able to "plant" Live Plants such as grass and flowers with a resizable tool that speeds the process. The trees, however, were another story as those had to be planted one at a time and was very tedious.

In fact, this author found it so tedious that he created Trees that worked as Live Plants and could be planted with the Planter too. They are not as good as regular trees, in that they are animated billboards that always face the camera and give the illusion of a tree.

Using an actual three dimensional tree is easier and the **Tree Brush** gives us that ability.

Time for action – planting and felling trees

We will use a new project for this action section so let's get started:

1. Open a new blank project.

2. Select the **Set** tab and click on the **Terrain** button. Double-click on the **Grassland** terrain to load it into the workspace.

3. While still under the **Set** tab click on the **Tree** button.

4. Double-click on **American Elm A** to load it into the workspace.

5. Pull the camera back to see more of the terrain and the tree.

   The following image shows our terrain and the elm tree:

6. Click the **Tree Brush** button as shown in the following image:

7. Click on the **Feller** tool, place the square tool indicator over the tree and click to remove it.

8. Click on the **Planter** tool and make sure the **Brush Preview** is checked.

9. Set the **Brush Size** to 500 and the **Tree Number** to 4. Keep the **Height** and **Angle Variation** at 50 each.

10. Click a couple of times on the screen to plant the trees in any location you desire.

This example uses two plantings of trees on the left and right of the screen towards the back of the terrain as shown in the following image:

11. Pull the camera back so we can see the entire terrain as in the following image:

12. Go back to the **Tree Brush** by selecting the **Set** tab and clicking on the **Tree** button. Select one of the **Elm Tree** groups or select an **Elm Tree** in the **Scene Manager**.

13. Click on the **Tree Brush** button to activate it.

14. Change the **Brush Size** to 5000 and the **Tree Number** to 50. Fill the terrain with trees. This example only took two clicks of the mouse to accomplish, one on the left side and one on the right side of the terrain as shown in the following image:

What just happened?

We just created an entire forest with two clicks of the mouse! Now that is a time saver as we can now go back and cull out our trees for paths, building locations, or any other use. Some people plant trees around their structures or you can use a combination of both before and after planting and felling to get that just right scene of trees with little time or effort.

Have a go hero – cutting paths in the forest

Use the tree feller tool in combination with the size of the tool to cut paths, roads, or walkways through our forest, or clear out an area for a building with paths. Clear the entire forest and build another one if you don't like what you have.

You can plant different tree types to get familiar with them and experiment with the variation settings for the trees when planting. Combine the trees with Live Plants such as grass, rice, and flowers and you can create some lush, beautiful landscapes.

Using soft cloth

Soft Cloth is a great way to have soft items like curtains, tarps, tablecloths and even ocean waves to a certain extent. The tool is physics driven but is included in this appendix for fear it would get lost in all the other physics eye candy and toys. Soft Cloth stands out on its own as it is very versatile for hanging, swaying, or rolling motions and fits a niche for most people. However, enterprising users are always coming up with innovative ways to use Soft Cloth.

 Soft Cloth can be a standalone cloth or a cloth with built-in pinning points that hold the cloth in place. At the time of writing, it was not possible to add our own pinning but there are several pinned and unpinned cloths available as props. As iClone evolves Soft Cloth is a candidate for clothing such as skirts and other soft garments.

Time for action – testing a cloth

We'll use **Soft Cloths** in the **Cloth** sub-folder of the **Physics Props** folder.:

1. Open a new blank project. Select the **Set** tab, click on the **Props** button.

2. Double-click on the **Capsule_033** from the **Capsule** sub-folder of the **3D Blocks** prop folder to load it into the workspace.

3. Click on the **Physics Props** folder in the **Content Manager** and load the **Infinite Plane,** then click on the **Cloth** folder within the physics folder and double-click on the **Cloth_64X64** prop to load it into the workspace.

4. With the **Cloth** selected, input the following parameters:

Move: X=0.0, Y= -312.2, Z=125

Rotate: X=270.0, Y=0.0, 0.0

Scale: X=500, Y=500, Z=500

The following shows the setup to this point:

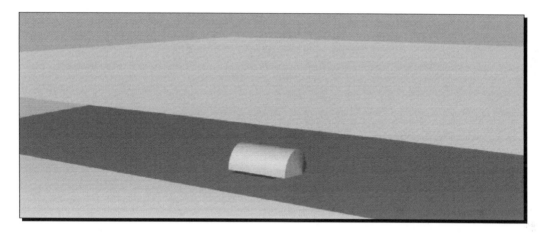

5. Select the capsule prop and open the **Physics Setting** window by clicking on the button in the top toolbar or using *Shift + F9*.

6. Click the **Active Physics** checkbox. Set the state to **Kinematic** and set the **Bound Type** to **Cylinder** on the X axis.

7. Select the cloth and change the **Damping** to 10 and the **Solver Iterations** to 40.

8. VERY IMPORTANT! Click on the **Realtime** button in the bottom toolbar to change it to **By Frame** or the cloth may fall through or be otherwise unstable.

 If a simulation just stops working even after removing the animation then save the file and restart iClone for a fresh session.

9. Make sure the **Rigid Body** and **Soft Body Simulation** buttons are on.

10. Save the project and press the play button. The following image shows the result of the cloth dropped over the capsule:

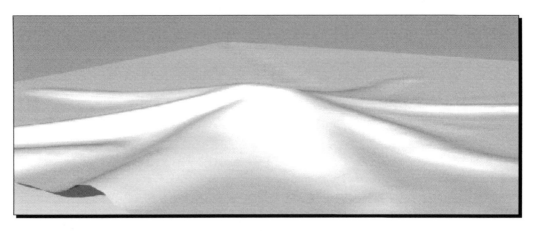

What just happened?

We set up a simple soft cloth simulation where the cloth falls on the half capsule as the capsule is vaulted up from contact with the infinite plane. The result is a draping of the cloth over the capsule. The Damping and Solver Iterations slowed the descent of the cloth. It is recommended that you save your project and experiment heavily with these controls.

With a little imagination we can see other uses for this technique. Just as I was about to send off this chapter I saw a great use for this trick by Cricky, one of the Beta Testers and a skilled iClone veteran in his own right, who covered the ground with a soft cloth textured with the same grass texture as the terrain. When the dummy under the cloth moved it looked like something was burrowing underground as it travelled across the screen. The effect was very dynamic and eye opening for this author!

According to Bigboss, we can also attach a physics enabled prop to the head of a character and drape a soft cloth to act as a veil. There will be many uses for this unique tool.

Time for action – creating a ghost effect

Let's have a little fun with the soft cloth and create a children's cartoon ghost:

1. Open a new blank project and select the **Set** tab then click on the **Prop** button.

2. In the **Physics Props** folder, load the **Infinite Plane** into the workspace.

3. Double-click on the **Ball_001** prop in the **3D Blocks** folder to load it into the center of the workspace.

4. Scale the ball to 50 percent on the X, Y and Z axis.

5. Double-click on the **Cloth_64X64** prop in the **Cloth** folder to load it and set its attributes at:

Move: X=0, Y= -157.8, Z=55.2

Rotate: X=270.0, Y=0, Z=0

Scale: X=150.0, Y=150.0, Z=150.0

6. Open the **Physics Settings** dialog by clicking on the button or using *Shift + F9*.

7. With the ball prop selected, click on the **Active Physics** checkbox and set the state to **Kinematic**.

8. Set the **Bounding Type** to **Sphere**.

9. Move the time scrubber to frame 100.

10. Select the ball prop and move it up or type in 150 in the Z axis to raise the ball.

11. Select the cloth and set the **Damping** to 10 and the **Solver Iterations** to 40.

12. Save the project and play the simulation until around frame 150 to 160 then stop the simulation at that point.

13. Select the ball prop and move it to the right of the screen or input 178.6 in the X axis of the ball prop.

14. Return the time scrubber to the first frame, and press the play button. Save the project.

The following image shows our ghost setup from start to finish:

What just happened?

We used the physics and the soft cloth together with the ball prop to fill and raise the sheet, then used key frames to move the ball which in turn moved the sheet object when played back. This tool is simple but effective. Soft Cloth is a nice addition to the toolbox.

Have a go hero

The general idea of this action section is to reproduce one of those little childhood ghosts made from a floating sheet that are popular in cartoons and comics. You've now been given a general idea of how to make the soft cloth work with the ball prop, so experiment with the soft cloth settings and the texture of the cloth. Try different sizes of cloth and ball props. Refine the prop as much as you wish or use a different Bounding Type but at the time of writing the Self Mesh, Bounding Mesh and Convex Hull did not always work with Soft Cloth.

Mass along with other settings creates a stronger cloth

We didn't use mass earlier so we could experiment with other methods of keeping cloth from passing through an object. You can also increase the mass of the cloth but you may have to make up for that increase in other settings. It is a combination of all the settings we have reviewed to this point that can create stronger cloth

We can also experiment with the settings of the physics parameters panel. These settings can have a dramatic impact on a simulation.

Exploring soft cloth options

There is a stock project file that demonstrates curtains. You'll certainly want to open that project and see how it's set up. Save the curtains as props because they are set up very nicely and work great to achieve the effect of curtains or drapes.

You can use spider web opacity maps to create spider webs to hang or drape over objects with Soft Cloth. An indoor flag on a pole, the rigging on a tall ship and many other uses come to mind for this fantastic prop. You can also use a simple Soft Cloth to cover a vehicle or use as a tablecloth as shown in the following image with a Soft Cloth draped over the jeep prop:

As was stated earlier, the Soft Cloth is in its infancy at the time of writing and there may be more improvements in the official release but there are still plenty of uses for Soft Cloth in its present form as we will see when the iClone community embraces the tool and pushes it to the limit.

Summary

There are many new features in iClone 5 and we have tried to touch on most of them but this upgrade is so feature packed that we couldn't cover every single item even though we came close.

Specifically, we covered the following:

- ◆ Ambient occlusion and the toon shader along with the light multiplier to improve the look of the video
- ◆ Using post effects and how to manipulate and stack them
- ◆ Important performance enhancements including Level of Detail and instancing of objects
- ◆ New usability features and tools including camera gizmo, mini viewport, merged motion track, path enhancements, and many other new features.
- ◆ Planting and felling trees with the new tree brush tool.
- ◆ Basic soft cloth operations and usage.

We discussed many new features, tools, and enhancements that will make iClone 5 another breakthrough upgrade and quite possibly a game changer among its few direct competitors. This release certainly shows us that for its price point iClone is more than competitive as version 4 leapt ahead of the pack and version 5 has increased the lead to where iClone is truly getting into a class of its own, filling a niche between the starter animation programs and the high-end applications costing thousands of dollars.

We've been through most of the new features and next we will turn our attention to the exciting new animation tools and features that are packed into the iClone 5 upgrade.

D

Discovering New Animation Tools

iClone 5 ushers in so many new animation features that you may confuse one with the other, but they are different tools and welcome additions to the animation toolbox.

In this chapter, we shall do the following:

◆ Cover the new MixMoves animation library

◆ Use the Motion Puppet feature

◆ Explore and use the newly incorporated Human IK technology.

◆ Animate via the Direct Puppet feature.

◆ Use Mocap – Motion Capture - using the Kinect and iClone 5.

◆ Prop Puppet and Prop Look At

So let's move on.

Exploring the modified timeline

Timeline has been modified in Version 5 to improve our ability to control key framed events The **Perform Timeline** has been eliminated and combined under the **Motion Timeline**. No longer will there be an uncontrolled jump from a perform action to a motion, as it can now apply curves or blend them on the same timeline.

The Timeline has grown huge if you open all the available buttons and channels. In order to get a grasp on the new Timeline, we will break it down into sections, they are as follows:

◆ **Project Timeline**: This is new for version 5 and holds the various generic timelines, such as the camera switcher and IBL parameters.

The upper-left corner of the **Timeline** holds the new **Track list** that toggles various tracks on and off and the **Object-related track** has moved to this location. This is where you can select the **Timeline** of specific objects:

◆ **Collect Clip**: There is nothing new here. Open the **Timeline** and highlight the area you wish to save and right-click to invoke the save motion (**Add**) menu:

◆ **Transform**: This is basically the same as in version 4. Transforms, movements, rotations, and other changes are recorded here:

The different control points of the characters now have their own timelines for precise control over body parts, right-click on the motion to invoke the contextual menu for that motion:

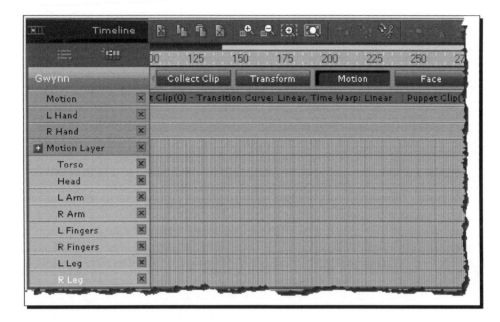

◆ **Face**: Direct lip-sync modification is now available in version 5. No more switching between CrazyTalk and iClone to tweak the lip movement. We can simply double-click on a **Lip** key and the **Lip Synching** dialog will pop up presenting us with choices of phoneme mouth positions. **Phonemes** are universal representations of certain sounds that are used with lip-synch to make the character appear to be talking.

We can delete or change the phoneme and we can move the phonemes up and down the timeline to modify the timing. The iClone lip-sync engine does a great job and with this new feature we can tweak it to make it even better, if we so desire:

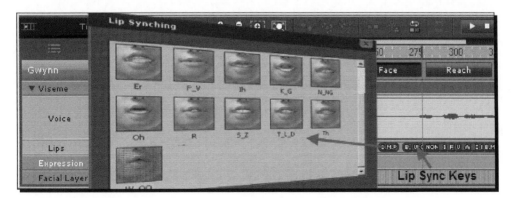

◆ **Reach**: This is a great new feature in iClone 5 that allows certain body parts, neck, hip, hands, and feet to actually reach for a target. Any usage of the **Reach** feature is displayed here:

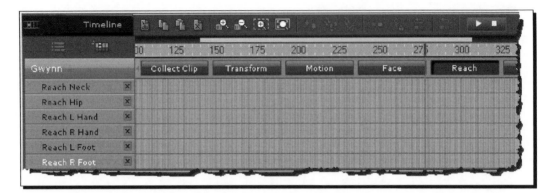

◆ **Constraint**: This tracks links, including constraints to paths and **Look** At timing:

◆ **Material**: Changes in color and material are recorded here. If, for example, we wanted an electric stovetop burner to light up, we could turn the glow off in the first frame and turn the glow on further down the timeline. The object gradually starts glowing as the animation is played:

◆ **Visible** and **Sound**: These are not changed from version 4 and each have a single timeline reflecting their on or off state.

Mixing moves the easy way

iClone 5 brings us a fantastic new way to add and control the animation of a character in the **MixMoves** feature. According to information received from Reallusion, this will be a library of over 200 common motions that mix seamlessly without any interaction on the part of the user.

As of the beta version, there were only a limited number of motions available for the male character but they do blend in seamlessly. In fact, it is a very impressive and extremely easy to use feature to animate everyday motions and filler motions.

When you select a MixMove, the highlighted character will start using that motion until we either stop the motion or choose another MixMove. We do not have to stop the playback, as we can double-click on another MixMove and it will transition seamlessly from the last MixMove to the newly chosen MixMove, as it plays.

 MixMoves contains 200 motion clips with 40-50 visible motion templates, which automatically generate natural transitions between previously selected motions - Reallusion.

The following image shows the new **MixMoves** button that is available in the animation section of the right side control panel:

Time for action – using MixMoves

We'll use the Jana character to demonstrate MixMoves:

1. Open a new blank project. Select the **Actor** tab and click on the **Avatar** button.

2. Double-click on the **Jana** character.

3. With the Jana character selected, click on the **Animation** tab and then click on the **Motion** button if it's not already selected. With Jana still selected, click on the **MixMoves** button on the right side menu. The following image shows the **Edit Action List**:

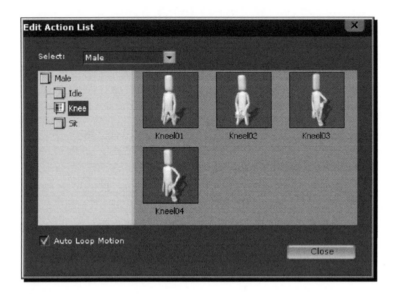

4. Check the **Auto Loop Motion** checkbox, if it's not already checked.

5. Make sure the time scrubber is set to the first frame and the Jana character is selected.

6. Click on the **Idle** folder.

 In this case **Idle01** is all that was available. If you don't have that motion, select another motion. Any motion will do.

7. Let the motion play for a short while, then click on the **Knee** folder, and choose a motion from it. In this case, we used **Kneel03**.

8. Let it run for few seconds and select the **Sit** folder. Click on a sit motion, in this case, it was **SitG01,** where the character sits on the floor.

9. Let it run for few seconds then click on the **Idle** folder again and load an idle motion.

10. Press the stop button when you are ready to stop the animation.

What just happened?

Congratulations, you just learned the ins and outs of MixMoves! You can add the movements as the animation plays or you can stop at the end of each movement and choose another one. It's really just a matter of preference at this point.

I'm guessing, you noticed how smooth the transitions were between added MixMoves. That would be difficult and time consuming to animate. Once again iClone does the heavy lifting and we reap the benefits.

Using the motion puppet

Motion Puppet is another exciting new addition that brings us several animation tools and allows us to practice (preview) our work before we record it. This dialog panel contains many controls, including slides to change parts of the motions included on the panel.

The following image shows the **Motion Puppet** dialog window:

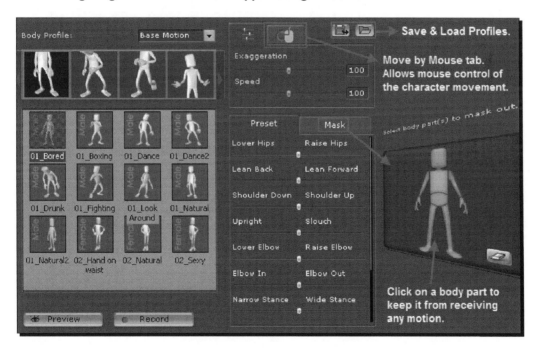

Type of Motion	Idle, Move, Mood, and Talk are the four types of motion categories available at the time of this writing.
Motions	There are various motions, such as, 01_Bored, 01_Dance, or 01_Natural.
Move by Mouse	This overrides the automatic movement and allows us limited control via the mouse within the confines of the chosen motion.
Mask	Click on a body part to prevent it from receiving any animation data. To select a body part or parts, masks those parts from the generated animation. This is done to save either the already existing animation for those parts, or for later animation of those parts.
Save or Open Body Animation Profile	We can save our custom created profiles here and load them for use later.
Face Puppet Button	Opens the **Face Puppet** feature, as introduced in version 4. This works as described in Chapter 4, *Animating the Characters*.
Preview vs Record	A great feature that allows us to practice the movement before we record it. Even when using a stock motion, it lets us see how that motion looks with the scene before we record it.
Preset	An extensive group of slider controls that allows us to modify certain elements of the character's motion. We can narrow or widen the stance, lower, or raise the elbows and shoulders, or alter the character's lean forward or backward along with many other parameters. A wide range of customization is available and experimentation is encouraged to get a grasp of the range of these controls.

Time for action – animating Gwynn

Let's test the **Motion Puppet** on **Gwynn** in an empty scene so we can focus on how the Motion Puppet works without any distractions:

1. Create a new blank project. Select the **Actor** tab then click on the **Avatar** button.

2. Double-click on the **G5 Gwynn** character, located in the **G5** character folder, to load her into the workspace.

3. Click on the **Home** button on the top toolbar to bring her closer to the camera.

4. Select the **Gwynn** character, then select the **Animation** tab and click on the **Motion** button.

5. Click on the **Motion Puppet** button to invoke the **Motion Puppet** dialog.

6. Click on the **02_Natural Female** motion. Click on the **Preview** button and watch the motion for a few seconds to preview it.

7. Now click on the **Mouse Control** tab in the upper-right side of the dialog, then click the **Preview** button and press the *Spacebar* to preview. The character's movements are controlled by our mouse movement and within the confines of the character's chosen movements.

8. Click on the **Slider Control** tab to deactivate the **Mouse Control** mode.

9. Make sure the **Gwynn** character is selected and right-click, then choose **Remove All Animation** from the menu.

10. Select the **Gwynn** character and click the **Motion Puppet** button to open the dialog again.

11. Click on the **02_Natural** pose again and this time click the **Record** button, then press the *Spacebar* to record. Record 3 to 5 seconds of this motion.

12. Now select **02_Sexy** motion. Press the **Record** button then the *Spacebar* to record a few seconds of this new motion.

13. Save the project. Return the time scrubber to the first frame and play the project.

What just happened?

We animated several seconds of idle movement for Gwynn, but we do have an abrupt jump in the animation when it moves from one motion to the next.

Time for action – smoothing the transition between motions

Let smooth out the jump between motions before we go any further in modifying the motions themselves:

1. Select the **Gwynn** character and press *F3* to show the **Timeline**.

2. Click on the **Object-related track** button to select **Gwynn** or select **Gwynn** from the **Scene Manager** on the lower-left menu.

3. Adjust the lateral slider bar at the top until you can see all of the motions.

4. Click on the **Motion** button located on the top of the **Timeline**.

5. Grab the transition handle and pull it a little to the left, then right-click on the motion and from the **Curve** menu select **Ease Out** and **Ease In**.

6. Save the project and press the **Play** button to review our work.

The following image shows the adjustment made to the transition and applying the curve:

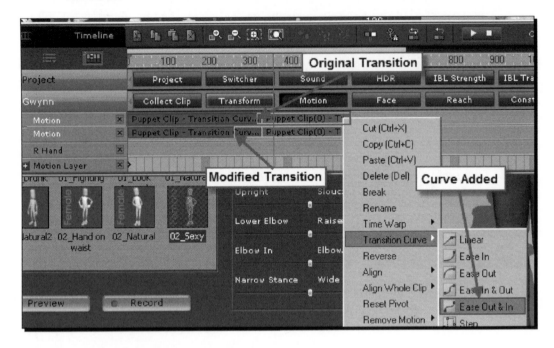

What just happened?

We modified the transition from one motion to another by pulling out the transition handle on the clip and adding an Ease Out and Ease in curve.

Have a go hero – adjusting the presets

Now that we've animated a couple of motions for Gwynn and set the transition, it's time to add another motion or two. Open the **Timeline** with **Gwynn** selected, and place the time scrubber at the end of the last motion then add two more **Motion Puppet** motions. Adjust the sliders on the motions until you get what you like, then record them. Then adjust the transition handles to smooth out the transition between motions.

Time for action – walking with the motion puppet

We tried out a stationary motion, so let's create a walking motion next:

1. Open a clean blank project and load the **Gwynn** character into the project.

2. With the **Gwynn** character selected, click on the **Animation** tab then select the **Motion** button.

3. Click on the **Motion Puppet** button to open the window.

4. Click on the **Move** profile in the upper-left part of the **Motion Puppet** dialog.

5. Select the **02_Basic Walk** and click on the **Preview** button, then the *Spacebar*, to see the walk cycle.

6. Click on the **Time Setting Panel** (little clock icon) on the bottom toolbar to invoke the **Time Setting** menu and set the length to 500 frames. Click **OK**.

   The following image shows the **Time Setting** button and panel:

7. Select the **02_Basic Walk**, then press the **Record** button and the *Spacebar* and let it run until the end of the timeline.

8. Close the **Motion Puppet** dialog window.

9. Save the project file and play back the project. Can you tell if she is walking in place or actually moving?

10. Select the **Set** tab and click on the **Terrain** button. Double-click on the **Community Stage** terrain to load it into the scene for reference.

11. Play the scene again and you will see she is not moving anywhere just walking in place.

12. With the time scrubber at the beginning, select the **Gwynn** character and move her up to the upper-right corner of the workspace.

13. Move the time scrubber to the last frame.

14. Move the Gwynn character to the lower-left side of the screen.

15. Save the project and play the animation.

The following image shows the character at frame one and the last frame:

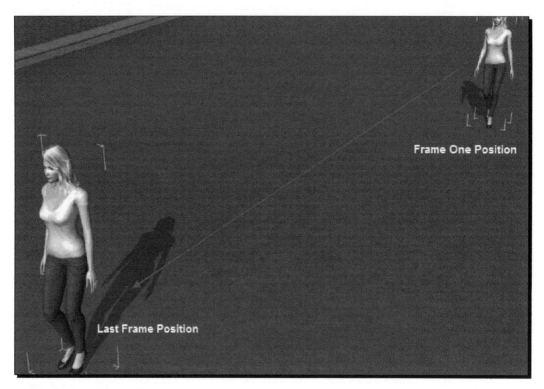

Frame One Position

Last Frame Position

What just happened?

We used the walk cycle to cover the 500 frames and then we positioned the character in the front in the first frame, and back in the last frame, walking across the screen. Chances are, you now have a terrible problem known in animation as foot sliding. We will correct that next.

 Foot Sliding is affected by speed versus distance. If the distance is too great or too little for the amount of keyframes in the span (500, in this case) we will get foot sliding. Either decrease the distance or move the final key frame to change the speed.

Time for action – stopping the foot sliding

It won't take much to work the foot sliding out of this project. We will move the character in this case. If we needed the character to move further off the screen, we could do another walk sequence or move the key frame on the timeline instead of moving the character. In this case, moving the character is easily visualized to demonstrate the concept:

1. Move the time scrubber to the last frame.

2. Select the **Gwynn** character and move her down and a short distance towards the left, then play the animation.

3. If foot sliding persists, then adjust the distance again until the foot sliding decreases.

   The following image shows the correction in the character's position:

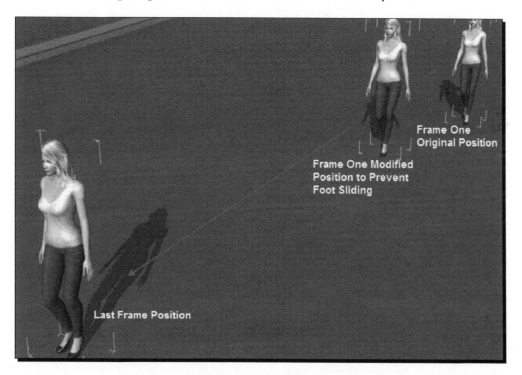

Correcting foot sliding problems will be hit and miss until you practice with it enough. Move the character or the key frame up and down the timeline until you hit that sweet spot where the feet do not appear to be sliding. Once you have experience with several walk or run motions, the foot sliding will be quickly worked out each time you apply the motion. Keep in mind that this is only one method of walking in iClone 5.

What just happened?

We discovered the problem most animators face at one time or another, like foot sliding due to bad timing. We chose to modify the character's physical position by shortening the distance, the character traveled instead of moving a key frame to change the time.

Understanding Human IK (pose and reach target)

Human IK is a fascinating technology licensed from Autodesk, the heavyweight of 3D animation tool companies that develops leading animation applications like Studio Max and Maya. They also produce MotionBuilder, which is a phenomenal high-end (and high priced) animation tool. Some of the technology that MotionBuilder is built upon is now incorporated into iClone 5 and we get to use it making our task easier and better yet... making us look like great animators!

Time for action – setting up a two-handed rig with Human IK

Using the **Reach Target** feature, we will build a two-handed rig utilizing Human IK:

1. Create a new blank project. Select the **Actor** tab and click on the **Avatar** button.

2. Load the **G5** male character into the workspace by double-clicking on it.

3. With the male character selected, click on the **Home** button to frame the character closer to the camera.

4. Select the **Set** tab and click **OK** on the **Props** button. Double-click on the **Box_001** prop in the **3D Blocks** prop folder to load it into the workspace.

5. Set the box parameters as follows:

    Move: X=0.0, Y=0.0, Z=0

    Rotate: X=1, Y=1, Z=0

    Scale: X=160, Y=5, Z=3.5

6. With the box selected, use the **Move** gizmo to duplicate the box by holding down the *Ctrl* key and moving up on the axis then releasing it or load another **Box_001** prop into the scene and set its parameters as follows:

    Move: X=0, Y=-15, Z=10

    Rotate: X=0.0, Y=0.0, Z=0.0

    Scale: X=5.0, Y=5, Z=3.5

7. Rename this new smaller **Box_001** prop to **Dummy Right**.

8. Duplicate the prop, either by selecting the prop and dragging it in one direction while holding down the *Ctrl* key, or load another **Box_001** prop from the **Content Manager** and set its scale to the same as the **Dummy Right** box.

9. Rename this box prop to **Dummy Left**.

The Box_001 prop, and the two smaller dummy box props, are shown in the following image:

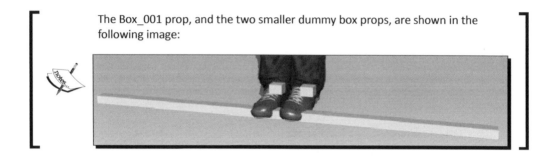

10. Move one small dummy block to each hand. Exact positioning is not critical at this point.

11. Move the **Box_001** prop to just below the dummy boxes.
The following image shows the positioning of the props:

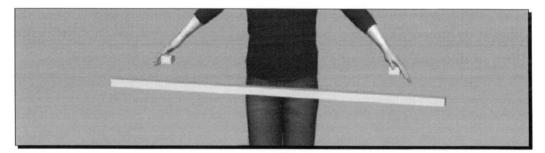

What just happened?

We loaded a character, then box props and scaled the box props for our needs. The longer Box_001 prop will be our two handed object like a weapon or tool. We then positioned our props near the area of the hands. The location or position of the props is not as important as the scale at this point, as we will be attaching them in the next action section.

We will use the new **Reach Target** feature along with the two dummies to position the hands on the elongated Box_001 prop.

Time for action – hooking up the dummies

We need to call up the **Edit Motion Layer** dialog so that we can access the **Reach Target** section:

1. Select the male character, right-click and choose **Edit Motion** from the right-click **Motion Menu** sub-menu or select the **Animation** tab, click on the Motion button then click on the **Edit Motion Layer** button on the right side menu panel.

2. Click the **Reach Target** button at the top of the **Edit Motion Layer** dialog window as shown in the following image:

3. Click on the large dot on the figure's right wrist in the **Edit Motion Layer** dialog box then click on the **Eyedropper** tool under **Target Setting** on the right side of the dialog.

4. Select the **Dummy Right** box with the **Eyedropper** tool. Click the small button next to the **Eyedropper** tool and check the **Reach Object** option.

5. Repeat the process targeting the left hand to the **Dummy Left** box and don't forget to check the **Reach Object** checkbox from the **Reach to Sub-Node** popup.

The following image shows the **Reach to Sub-Node** dialog triggered from the **Reach Target** popup dialog menu:

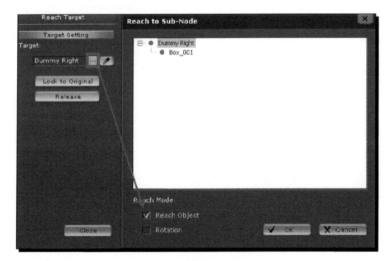

6. Select the **Dummy Right** prop and attach it to the **Box_001** prop.

7. Repeat the process for the **Dummy Left** prop attaching it to the **Box_001** prop too.

The following image shows the results of our targeting. The circle targets on the **Edit Motion Layer** dialog, which shows a symbol in the circle when the target is locked, as the left and right hands do in this example:

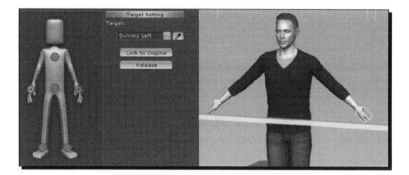

8. Select the **Dummy Right** prop and move the prop until the hand intersects with the **Box_001** prop.

9. Select the male character, right-click and open the **Edit Motion Layer** dialog if it's not still open and press on the **Pose** button to the left of the **Reach Target** button on top of the dialog window.

10. Select the right wrist, then click on the **Rotate** button on the top toolbar and rotate the hand into a proper position for gripping the box. You can also adjust the dummy block, if needed. The following image shows the hand positioning:

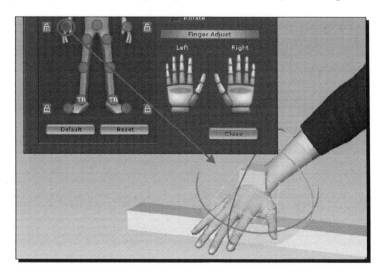

11. Repeat the previous three steps for the left hand and line it up on the left side of the **Box_001** prop.

> Please note that the beta version used for this research had a bug that kept the hands from holding their position, so we will jump over posing the hands but this can be done manually via the finger controls or more easily with the hand motions such as a grip or hold motion continuously looped.

12. Click off the show checkbox in the **Scene Manager** for the **Dummy Right** and **Dummy Left** props to hide them or you can turn them off with the off button under visibility in the right side menu or use the opacity slider set to zero.

13. Save the project.

The following image demonstrates the **Show** box unchecked to hide the dummies:

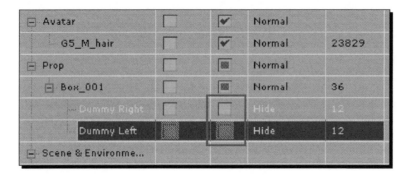

What just happened?

We used the character's Reach Target feature to constrain the hands to the left and right dummies, which were then attached to the long Box_001 prop at the desired locations. We now have a two handed rig in which we can move the character to do certain things or to mimic things like fighting with a two handed staff, carry a weapon, pull up on an exercise bar, or using a tool like a shovel.

Time for action – using the two handed rig for movement

Now that we've got the rig, let's do a quick section on how to move the character with it to fully demonstrate the Human IK feature:

1. Select the male character and press the **Home** key to center the character.

2. To give us something for reference, double-click on the **Floor_001** prop located in the **Wall and Floor** sub-folder of the **3D Blocks** prop folder to load it into the scene. Set its parameters to:

    Move: X= 0.0, Y=0.0, Z= -15

    Rotate: X=0.0, Y=0.0, Z=0.0

    Scale: X=100.0 Y=100.0, Z=100.0

3. Save the project.

4. Select the **Box_001** prop and choose the rotate tool from the top toolbar.

5. Press *Ctrl + Q* to toggle on the gizmo, if it's not already visible. If the **Rotate** gizmo is not visible in the viewport then zoom out until the gizmo is visible.

6. Select the green axis and roll the axis up and down with the rotate tool to view the interaction of the character with the scene and the floor.

7. Press the **Undo** button or use the *Ctrl + Z* shortcut to undo our movement.

8. Select the character, right-click and choose **Edit Motion** from the **Motion Menu**.

9. Click on the **Reach Target** button at the top left to make sure you are looking at the **Reach Target** section of the popup **Edit Motion Layer** dialog.

10. Click on the circle of the right ankle then press the **Lock to Original** button. Select the circle on the left ankle and click the **Lock to Original** button. Both ankles should now have an "L" in the circle, showing they are locked in place.

    The following image shows the ankles locked in place:

    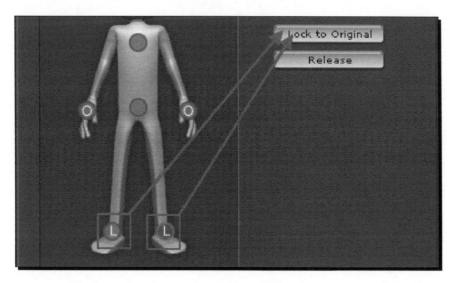

11. Select the **Box_001** prop with the **Rotate** tool and rotate the box to the top on the green axis just like we did before.

12. Press the **Undo** button or use *Ctrl + Z* to undo the last operation and save the file for future reference or use, should you ever need it to refresh your memory to use as a starting off point.

The following images shows the result of Human IK constraints when parts of the body are locked and properly targeted:

What just happened?

We used the Box_001 prop to move parts of the male character's body, but the feet were forced through the floor due to the Human IK constraints which pushed the body down. To eliminate this problem we used the Lock to Original feature of the Reach Target system to lock the feet in to place, making the body move as a human body would were we in a similar situation.

Time for action – using locking dummies

We can also use dummies to help us animate. Let's use dummies to control the foot movement of the character:

1. With our existing project, double-click on the **Box_001** prop in the **3D Blocks** folder to load it into the scene.

2. Rename the prop to **Foot Left.**

3. Scale the prop down to 20 on the X, Y, and Z axes in the **Transform** section of the right side menu with the prop selected.

4. Position the Foot Left dummy near the left foot.

5. Select the character, right-click and choose **Edit Motion** from the **Motion Menu** section.

6. Click on the **Reach Target** button at the top of the **Edit Motion** Layer dialog window.

7. Select the circle on the left ankle, click on the **Eyedropper** tool and select the **Foot Left** dummy. The foot will snap to the dummy.

8. Select the **Foot Left** dummy and using the **Move** tool (from the top toolbar) slide the foot back which will straighten the leg, then slightly up to bend the leg to a more natural pose. We may need to slide the foot slightly forward to close the stance.

9. Save the project.

   The following image shows the progression of moving the Foot Left dummy:

| Attached | Move Back | Move Up Until Knee Bends | Move Slightly Forward |

10. Repeat steps 1 through 7 to rig a dummy named Foot Right to the right foot of the male character so we can easily control that foot in the next few steps.

11. After rigging the right foot, like we did the left foot, select the **Box_001** prop in the character's hands, select the rotate tool from the top toolbar.

12. Move the time scrubber down to frame 100. Select the green axis and roll it up as shown in the following image:

What just happened?

We set up two dummies, one for each foot, to use as control and anchor points. The Reach Target feature was used to target the ankles and hands to the dummies. They not only anchor the character in place, but they can also be moved with Move and Rotate tools allowing the Human IK constraint to keep the body in a reasonable position. The following image shows a battle created with the above technique using two characters with the same rig:

 Load the bicycle demonstration project included in the iClone installation for another example of using Reach Target with IK constaints.

Have a go hero – experimenting with the three way rig

To practice animating with a rig like this, you can move the timeline scrubber down 25 or so frames and move one or more of the dummies, then move down the timeline again and move the dummies once more.

The foot dummies will hold the character in place while giving us a simple way to grab the foot and move it should we need to. The Human IK structure will keep the body in a proper position as it moves with the dummies. While we can move body parts by direct manipulation, this method is easy to visualize and anchors the character in place when needed.

You may find it necessary to open the Edit Motion Layer dialog and adjust the limbs or hands depending on how radical you get when moving the dummies.

We could also use the current rig to make the character look like he is climbing a large fence, or scaling a building wall, or have him hanging off a building, like the following image:

Time for action – setting up the unicycle

We'll explore the **Reach Target** feature further by hooking up a character to the unicycle iProp, which already has built-in dummies. The unicycle has been rigged with a control panel to control speed and rotation (direction):

1. Start a new blank project.

2. Select the **Actor** tab and click on the **Avatar** button. Double-click the **G5 Female** character to load her into the scene (was located in the G5 characters folder as of the beta version).

3. Select the **Set** tab and click on the **Props** button. Double-click on the unicycle iProp located in the **Outdoor** sub-folder of the **iProp** folder.

4. Select the female character and right-click on the character. Choose **Edit Motion** from the **Motion** Menu to open the Edit Motion Layer dialog.

5. Select the **Reach Target** button at the top of the **Edit Motion Layer** dialog.

6. Select the circle on the right ankle. With the **Eyedropper** tool choose the right side pedal.

7. Click on the small button next to the **Eyedropper** button. Double-click on the **R_ treadle** sub-node to open it, then double-click on the **R_treadle_dummy** sub-node to open it. Finally select the **R_treadle_dummy** sub-node and click **OK**.

The following image shows the sub node connection sequence:

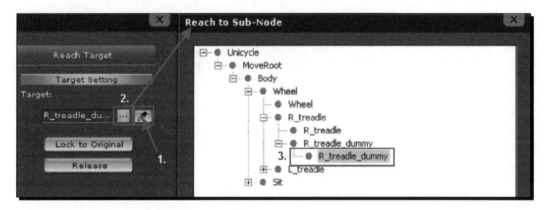

8. Repeat the last two steps to Reach Target the left ankle to the left pedal.

9. Select the circle in the lower torso area of the dummy and use the **Eyedropper** tool to select the seat of the unicycle. The character will jump to a very unnatural position which we will correct.

10. Click on the small button next to the **Eyedropper** button to open the sub-node dialog again.

11. Select the last **Sit_Dummy** as the target and click **OK** to properly place the character.

12. Close the **Edit Motion Layer** dialog and with the female character selected click on the **Actor** tab then click on the **Props Avatar** button. Link the character to the unicycle by clicking on the **Pick Parent** button in the right side menu, then selecting the seat of the unicycle. The character is now linked and targeted.

13. Move the camera in so we can see the feet and pedals.

14. In the **Scene Manager** open the levels of the unicycle until you get to the **R_treadle_ dummy**, or use the new search feature by clicking on the search button at the top of the Scene Manager and input **R_treadle_dummy**. Move the dummy up then forward to fit the pedal, as shown in the following image:

15. Repeat the last step for the left foot using the **L_treadle_dummy**. Save the project.

The following image shows the character's feet at the proper location on the pedals along with the **Unicycle** control panel used to move the unicycle:

What just happened?

After loading the character and unicycle, we targeted the feet to the pedals and the lower torso to the seat. We then linked the character to the seat creating a complete rig of the character to iProp. We then selected the treadle dummies to move the feet into the proper positions. This girl is ready to roll!

Have a go hero – operating the unicycle

Use the **Unicycle** operating control panel to drive the prop around. The unicycle animation drives the targeted parts of the character and imparts the motion to the character.

To use the control panel, select a slow speed around 40 for the first attempt and press the **Driving** button. Move the **Rotate** slider to turn the unicycle while it's moving. You can also change speeds with the speed slider. Press the stop button to stop the action.

If you really want to test your unicycle skills, load some of the barricade cones from the **Physics** folders then set them up in a course to steer through (remember to load the Infinite Plane too). If you wish you can turn on the physics, add a collision dummy to the unicycle, and knock around any cones you come too close to. See the physics appendix for information on using dummies in this manner.

Attaching the unicycle to a path creates very smooth and impressive animations.

The following shows the unicycle and character going through a simple course of cones:

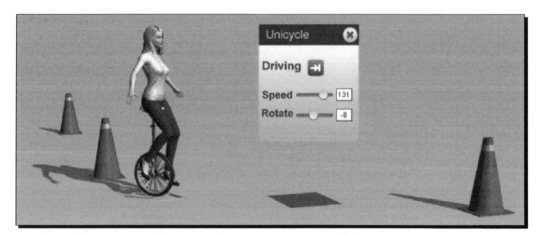

Manipulating Direct Puppet

The new **Direct Puppet** feature is a simple to use tool that moves or rotates the character within the limits of the human skeleton. Direct Puppet allows screen based movement by Camera View or Rotation or there is a Simple Mode available which has Horizontal, Vertical, and Rotate movement separated for easy control.

Time for action – puppeteering the character's movements

We'll test some basic movements with the G5 Female character:

1. Load a new blank project. Select the **Actor** tab and click on the **Avatar** button.

2. Double-click on the **G5 Female** character (was located in the G5 characters folder as of the beta version).

3. With the female character selected, click on the **Animation** tab then click the **Motion** button. Select the **Direct Puppet** button from the right side control panel.

4. Unlock the two hands and the upper torso control points by clicking on the lock icon next to each one control point. When unlocked the icon should appear as unlocked.

5. Make sure the **Move by Camera View** and **Screen Based** are selected.

6. Select the circle on the upper torso (near the head), press the **Preview** button at the bottom of the **Body Puppet** dialog window, then press the *Spacebar* and move your mouse side to side to see the result.

    The following image shows the order of steps:

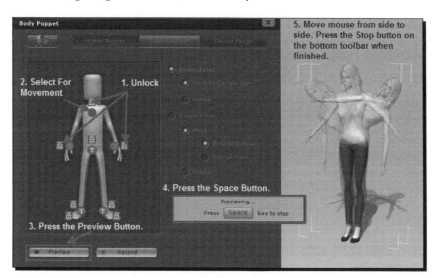

7. Click on the lower torso lock icon to unlock it and select the lower torso circle to use as the control point.

8. Click on the **Preview** button then click on the *Spacebar* and move the character up and down with the **Move** tool, like doing a deep knee bend exercise:

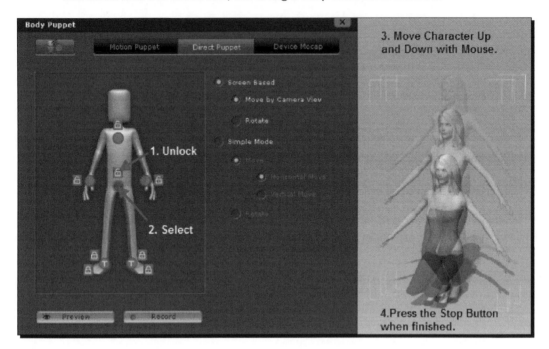

What Just Happened?

We used the new Direct Puppet feature in combination with the lock and control points map to lock parts of the character in place and force the body to move in the proper manner, when using a control point such as the upper or lower torso to invoke movement.

After selecting the preview mode, we then used our mouse to move the character in a fashion similar to the athletic deep knee bends one would use for exercising, bending down, or kneeling.

Have a go hero – experimenting with Direct Puppet

Use **different** combinations of lock and control points to experiment with the **Direct** Puppet feature and become familiar with its capabilities. Test the **Rotate** feature under the **Screen Based** section and test the **Simple Mode** movements.

To record your movement you simply select the **Record** button instead of the Preview button, then once you press the *Spacebar* you are recording the motion.

Time for action – climbing with Human IK

Now we are going to put into action one of the basic uses of Human IK, like animating a character climbing up a pipe on the side of a building. This is going to involve some hit and miss work on your part until you get used to how the Human IK works, keep this in mind as we go through these steps:

Use a combination of the **Move** and **Rotate** tools along with the **Pinning** and **Lock To** features when necessary.

Move a series of limbs and torso sections then re-pin, re-lock, or unpin and unlock for the next logical step in the climb.

1. Open a new blank project.

2. Load the Box_002 prop from the Props folder into the workspace and set its parameters as follows:

   Move: X=-55.3, Y=19.8, Z=0.0

   Rotate: X=0.0, Y-0.0, Z=67.9

   Scale: X=662.8, Y=662.8, ZZ=662.8

3. Load the **Pipe_001** prop into the workspace and set its parameters as follows:

   Move: X=147.7, Y=-67.6, Z=0.0

   Rotate: X=0.0, Y=0.0, Z=0.0

   Scale: X=30.0 Y-0.0 Z=400.0

4. Load the **G5 Chuck** character into the scene and place him next to the pipe.

5. With **Chuck** selected, right-click and choose **Edit Motion Layer** from the **Motion Menu**.

6. Using the **Edit Motion Layer** dialog place **Chuck** into a position on the pipe similar to the following image. Use the **Move** and **Rotate** tools to reach the proper position. Don't worry about exact positioning.

7. Unpin all the control points on the body so we can move them freely. Unclick the **Realistic Shoulder** checkbox too:

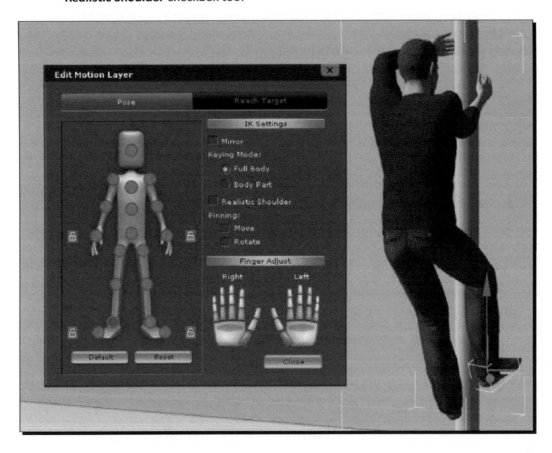

8. Move the time scrubber down to frame 20.

9. Select the character's right hand in the **Edit Motion Layer** dialog box, and with the **Move** tool move it up the pipe to its limit to just before it starts to pull the character out of place. Do not pull it so much it moves his body. Click the **Move** and **Rotate** checkboxes under **Pinning** to lock them.

10. Select the left ankle circle in the **Edit Motion Layer** dialog. Move the leg up the pole and check the **Move** and **Rotate** boxes in the **Pinning** section to lock them.

11. Select the left wrist control point and click the **Move** and **Rotate** checkboxes to lock them.

12. Move the time scrubber to frame 40.

13. Select the upper torso selection point and use the move tool to move his torso up the pipe, but do not move the character too high as we do not want to straighten his lower leg too much as we don't want it to look un-natural.

The following image shows the character climbing up the pipe:

 Pinning holds a control point in place just as **Lock To Original** holds a targeted limb in place with the Reach Target feature.

What Just Happened?

We positioned our character on the pipe with a starter position. Then we moved down the timeline and repositioned an arm and a leg, then moved down the timeline again where we locked the arms and legs into place, then moved the upper torso upward finishing the move making it look like our character is climbing up a pipe. By using the pinning feature to either lock or unlock certain parts of the character, we were able to move the character up the pipe.

Have a go hero – moving the character further up the pipe

Finish our animation scene by having the character climb up to the top of the pipe or at least move him up one more revolution. If you find you can't move the character or the entire, or part, of the character is moving when you don't want it to, then check the pinning. Be sure to pin and unpin each limb as you go.

Pop Quiz – Pinning versus Lock To

1. Pinning refers to:

   a. Locking a character control point to a reach target.

   b. Locking a character control point of a target.

   c. Locking a character control point from moving or rotating.

   d. None of the above.

2. We can pin a character's hand to another prop.

   a. True

   b. False

Understanding device Mocap (Kinect)

This is certainly one of the most anticipated additions to version 5, but it is also one of the most misunderstood at this point. **Motion Capture**, for those unfamiliar with it, is a very complicated and until now, an expensive undertaking that required special suits, lighting, and large areas to work in.

The advent of the **Kinect** sensor from Microsoft has been a boon to the fledgling amateur Mocap movement that was seeking an inexpensive device to capture with. The Kinect fits the bill due to its ability to interpret body movement but it has its drawbacks, in that the capture is one dimensional, since only one Kinect is used. Complicated moves, quick turns, and walking will be very difficult to produce until more skill is achieved and perhaps more tuning up of the Kinect to iClone interface in the future.

These types of drawbacks will disappoint those users that are thinking this will be an easy way to get quality animation. While it can produce quality motion, they will usually be very simple, everyday motions, or simple moves that can be captured with a one camera system. This is still extremely useful and worth the effort and extra expense for those that understand what they will be getting. Need to draw a pistol from a holster, answer a phone, put something away, push some buttons, run a keyboard, and so on then the Kinect can deliver those captures.

Two factors overlooked by almost everyone adopting, or thinking of adopting, the Kinect for Mocap are as follows:

♦ You need to be a good actor. This is no joke. Your physical acting needs to be good, consistent and pronounced almost to the point of overacting. Sluggish movement and bad posture will transfer to the character.

♦ This setup is limited in what motion it can capture. It cannot capture facial expression or motion, hand or foot motion. It captures the basic motion of the skeleton then we can add, edit or break out the parts we don't want or like.

♦ Try to maintain a clean capture environment, free of too many objects, and as lighted as possible.

There is no need for an Xbox (sorry) as the Kinect sensor, when purchased alone, contains the USB plug-in and power supply that is needed. If, however, you got your Kinect with the Xbox then you will need to purchase a power supply to use it with your computer.

There are also other solutions out there from open source Kinect applications to Ipisoft, which uses a Kinect with its software to produce Mocap, that is currently a bit better than iClone's new implementation and very susceptible to the body type of the actor. It is a middleware as you record the movements (free application) then run that video through their commercial software which then interprets the movements. The nice feature is that it has smoothing capabilities and captures action a little cleaner. The not so nice feature is the price tag of $395 for the Express addition, which is considerably more than the iClone Pro software package costs!

The additional cost for the Kinect plug-in software from iClone had a suggested retail price of $99.95 at the time of this writing.

Time for action – installing the Kinect plugin

Once again Reallusion has provided us with a professionally packaged installer that will get your Kinect sensor up and running with iClone 5:

[Before I ran the installation, I had my Kinect sensor already plugged into the computer's USB port with the power on.]

1. Click on the **Mocap_plug_in** installer icon to start the installation.

2. Click **Next** to continue.

3. Accept the License Agreement to continue.

4. Enter your name, company name, if applicable, and your serial number. The computer name should already be entered by the installer.

5. Click **Next** to continue.

6. Follow the onscreen instructions until installation is complete:

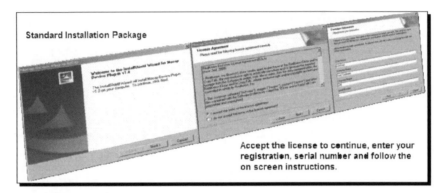

Accept the license to continue, enter your registration, serial number and follow the on screen instructions.

What just happened?

We followed the on screen instructions to install the Mocap software package onto our computer for use with the Kinect sensor and iClone. We are now ready to test the device plug-in.

Time for action – starting the Mocap Device Plug-in

Now that we have installed the plug-in we will start it up and connect it to our Kinect sensor. Make sure the Kinect is plugged into the computer's USB and the external power source is plugged into an outlet:

1. Start the **Mocap Device Plug-in**.

2. Click on the **Connect** button.

3. Stand in front of the sensor from around 2.5 to 5.5 meters according to Reallusion documentation. The green dummy appears when the sensor detects you.

4. Assume an "H" pose with feet apart and hands up, arms bent at the elbows with a slight bend at the knees until calibrated.

5. Maintain the pose until the countdown is over, or the skeleton appears, and the four indicators on the upper-left corner turn green. If you lose calibration, the top left indicators will turn red and the green pose dummy will appear again. Assume the "H" pose again to recalibrate.

Changing actors

We can click the **Calibration** button if we need to change the person doing the Mocap acting. This will trigger the green pose dummy to come on screen when the new actor is detected.

6. Once all four indicators are green the green dummy will disappear and motion capture data is now being passed to the character in iClone.

    The following image shows the process just before the calibration is successful and after successful calibration in the inset:

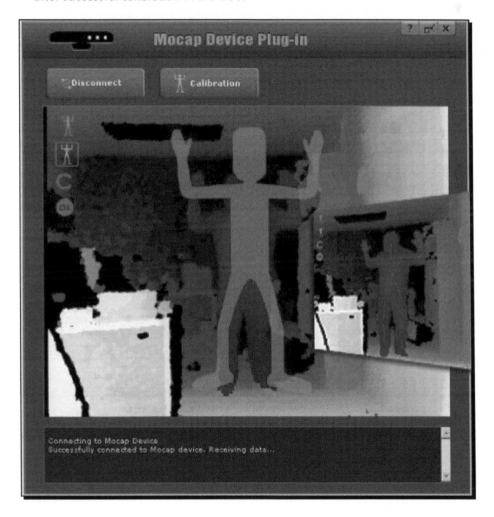

7. Start iClone.

8. Load a character. Preferably the same type of character you will actually be using the Mocap for. In this case, we loaded the new G5 male character.

9. Select the character and click on the **Animation** tab then the Motion button.

10. Select the **Device Mocap** button to bring up the **Device Console** window.

The following image shows the **Device Console** window for **Mocap**. Click on one or more of the body parts to mask them out from receiving Mocap data:

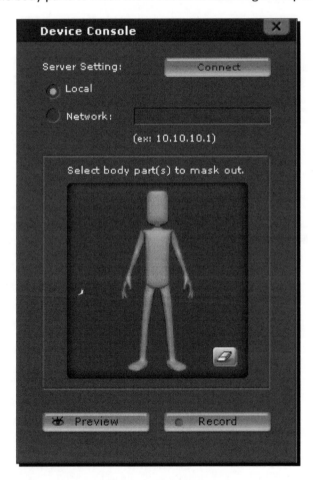

11. Click on **Connect** to link iClone to the Mocap plugin software.

12. Click on **Preview** to practice and test the animation.

Please note that you may lose calibration from time to time. Go back to the Mocap Device Plug-in and recalibrate then return to iClone.

13. When you are ready to record motion, press the *Spacebar* to stop the preview, then press the **Record** button and the *Spacebar* to start recording.

14. Now... act! What to do? Do anything. Make an idle motion. Look around. Record long enough so we can have a motion to use later when we learn how to clean them up.

15. Save the project file.

Most people I've worked with instinctively start moving their arms then their legs. It's actually quite fun to watch a person linked up to the system for the first time as they watch the avatar they are animating move within the 3D workspace.

What just happened?

We recorded our very first motion capture animation! The set up that used to take a lot of time, effort, and money, can now be accomplished in our offices, living rooms, basements, or anywhere else.

The sensor inputs the motion directly into iClone and the feedback is instantaneous.

Use the mask feature for twitchy legs

If you are having trouble with the legs twisting or jumping, then use the mask feature to lock the legs from receiving any Mocap data by selecting them with the mouse in the **Mask** section of the **Mocap Device** dialog.

Time for action – cleaning up the Mocap

We've captured our motion and now we are ready to clean it up as we almost always capture more motion than we need and motions we don't want to keep:

1. Using the Mocap we just generated, select the character, right-click and choose **Timeline** from the right-click menu to open the **Timeline** for the character.

2. Click on the **Motion** button to open the motion timeline.

3. Move the time scrubber to a point on the **Timeline** that starts the motion you want to keep. This will be past any junk motion or bad motions that can appear at the start of any Mocap session.

4. Right-click on the motion and choose **Break** from the menu to cut (break) the motion at the location of the time scrubber, as shown in the following image:

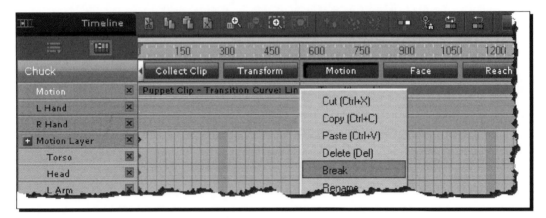

5. Select the first part of the motion and delete it.

6. Move the motion forward to the beginning of the Timeline.

The following image shows the steps taken with the **Motion Timeline**:

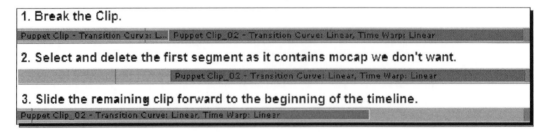

7. Repeat this process at the end of the motion to trim off unwanted Mocap data. Break the motion at that point and discard the last motion segment as we want to keep the middle motion segment.

What just happened?

Congratulations again as you just successfully edited out the parts of our motion capture that we didn't want or need. By breaking the motion at the start and end of the motion section, we were then able to delete those unwanted sections and move the main motion segment up to the first frame.

Using motion capture effectively

While Mocap is a great tool, it is not the final solution for iClone animation as the one sensor capture is limited, as described earlier it is a great leap forward and provides us with a method of capturing, recording, and editing those everyday motions that make a movie special such as driving a car, eating a meal, writing a letter or note, using a keyboard, talking on the phone, and many other uses.

You have been shown the basics of Mocap including how to capture and how to edit. This feature is new to all of us, and the well informed iClone animator will join in and keep up with what is going on in the iClone community in regards to Mocap and other new features to what develops as the future is bright for this great tool.

Using the Prop Puppet

The new **Prop Puppet** tool is another example of Reallusion giving us tools to make our life as animators much easier. This tool allows for direct manipulation of a prop either through constrained axes, general movements, or specific supplied movements.

In a great example of using the Prop Puppet, duchess110, another very talented iClone/3DS Max user and developer, manipulated a jump rope motion with the Prop Puppet. The action the puppet imparted fitted the needs of the situation very well.

We will create a tank turret out of 3D building blocks to demonstrate the power and ease of use this tool brings to our animation process.

Time for action – building the tank turret

The props for this action section will come from the **3D Blocks** folder:

1. Double-click on the **Box_004** prop in the **3D Blocks** folder to load it into the workspace. Set its parameters as follows:

   Move: X=0.0, Y=102.7, Z=87.6

   Rotate: X=0.0, Y=0.0, Z=0.0

   Scale: X=130.2, Y=130.2, Z=60.4

2. Double-click on the **Box_002** prop in the **3D Blocks** folder and set its parameters as follows:

Move: X=0.0, Y=102.7 Z=16.6

Rotate: X=0.0, Y=0.0, Z=0.0

Scale: X=187.8, Y=435.9, 118.4

3. Double-click on the **Pipe_001** prop in the **Pipe** sub-folder of the **3D Blocks** folder to load it into the scene and set its parameters at:

Move: X=0.0, Y=128.3, Z=100.7

Rotate: X=90.0, Y=0.0, Z=180.0

Scale: X=32.5, Y=32.5, Z=193.9

4. Double-click on the **Ball_002** prop in the **3D Blocks** folder and set its parameters to:

Move: X=1.9, Y=107.8, Z=135.1

Rotate: X=90.0, Y=0.0, Z=0.0

Scale: X=35.6, Y=35.6, Z=7.4

5. With the **Pipe_001** prop selected use the **Pick Parent** button in the **Attach** section on the right side menu panel to attach it to the **Box_004** prop (our turret).

6. Select the **Box_002** (our turret base) and attach it to the **Box_004** prop.

7. Uncheck the **Rotate** checkbox under the **Inherit** section as we do not want the base to rotate with the turret.

8. With the **Ball_002** prop selected (our radar dish) use the **Pick Parent** button to attach it to the **Box_004** prop.

9. Save the project.

The following image shows our primitive turret and base. It looks almost like a very simple hover tank from a science fiction adventure:

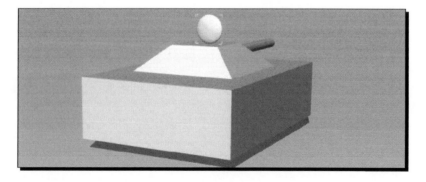

What just happened?

We have created our primitive tank from the 3D Block which was then attached to the turret prop (Box_004) as the master prop, except we didn't have the base inherit the turrets rotation.

With our current rig, we can hold down the left mouse button (when the move button is selected) to turn the turret, but to actually make a useful animation, we would have to move down the timeline, turn the turret, move down the timeline, turn the turret back, move down the timeline, turn the turret again, and so on and so forth.

With our prop puppet feature, we will not be moving down the **Timeline** manually, as this will be recorded for use using the **Prop Puppet** feature.

Time for action – animating the radar

1. Position your preview camera so it is viewing the tank from the back, similar to the following image, which also shows a side view of the camera orientation. We can't see the gun barrel because of the radar:

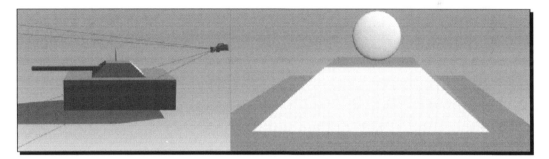

2. Select the **Set** tab and click on the **Terrain** button. Double-click to load the **Combat Stage** terrain into the scene.

3. Click on the **Sky** button at the top and double-click on **Cloudy 02** to load it into the scene.

4. Using the **Scene Manager** select the **Ball_002** prop that is attached to **Box_004**.

5. Click the **Puppet** button located on the right side menu to open the **Prop Puppet** dialog as shown in the following image:

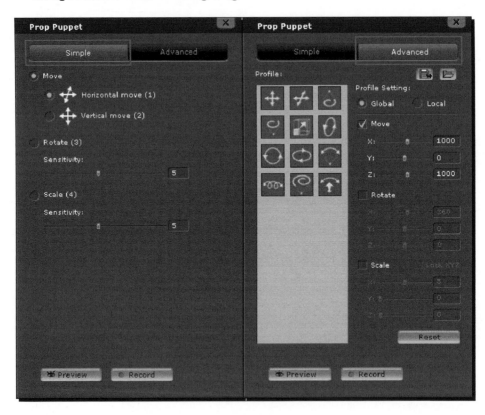

6. Let's skip the **Simple** interface and click on the **Advanced** button at the top to jump over to the advanced interface, as it has just what we need to animate our radar and our turret.

7. Select the **Rotation** as shown in the following image:

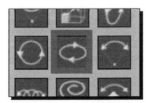

8. Click on the **Record** button, position your mouse behind **Ball-002** (radar) then click the *Spacebar* to start the session. If you wish to preview (practice) first then please do, but remember to record your action before you move on.

9. As the scene plays slowly, pull your mouse towards the bottom-right corner to make the dish rotate. Make at least one complete revolution or continue to drag the mouse towards the corner until you either run out of room to drag, or press the stop button to stop playing, or it stops due to running out of available frames.

10. Save the project and play it back.

The following image shows the radar rotating with the puppet supplied movement:

What just happened?

We use the **Prop Puppet Advanced** section to find the rotation we needed which was applied to the radar prop to spin it around. Since the radar is attached to the turret, the turret does NOT inherit its rotation. So far so good!

Time for action – animating the turret

1. Make sure the time scrubber is back to the start of the **Timeline**.

2. Select the **Box_004** prop (the turret). Click the **Prop Puppet** button on the left side to open the **Prop Puppet** dialog.

3. Select the same motion as we used in the previous action section to rotate the radar.

4. Select the **Preview** or **Record** button (remember to record before leaving this section) and place the mouse behind the turret just as we did with the radar.

5. When you are ready, press the *Spacebar* and move your mouse to the right of the screen then pause a few seconds (the turret will rotate left).

6. Move your mouse to the left of the screen then pause a few sections.

7. Make a few more random back and forth movements with a pause each time, then press the stop button if you have not run out of frames by now.

The following image shows the turret swivelling back and forth with the puppet motion:

What just happened?

We, again, used the built-in rotate motion from the **Advanced** section of the **Prop Puppet** to animate the entire prop. We now have two motions recorded for the turret! The radar is rotating and the turret is moving back and forth traversing the terrain as a mounted gun would do.

 The **Prop Puppet** generates multiple key frames when used, so any corrections, curves or other adjustments are addressed in the **Transform** timeline instead of the **Animation** timeline using the same methods as discussed in this book when dealing with key frame animation.

Customizing the transition and time warp

In version 4, we got a good curve system with **In**, **Out**, **Out-In**, **In-Out**, **Step** and **Linear**. In version 5, Reallusion took it one step further and gave us a custom user interface to edit the curve. More control is always a good thing in animation when done properly, or least done in a manner that most people can understand, and Reallusion didn't let us down.

The following image shows the **Transition Curve** editor that allows us to use more or less of the selected transition curve:

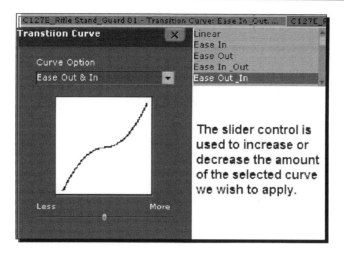

The **Transition Curve** is used on timeline keyframes and clips. This controls the manner in which the clips interact with each other as it transitions from the end of one clip to the beginning of the next clip. With exception of this new control panel, the Transition Curves are the same as was discussed in Chapter 4, *Animating the Characters*, for version 4.31.

The following image shows the **Transition Curve** and new **Time Warp** curve features:

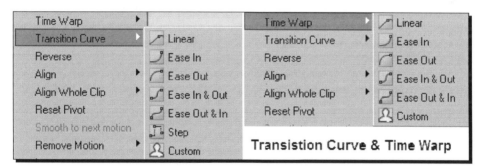

The **Time** Warp feature has been added and works just like it sounds. The different curves change the timing of the clip it's applied to. The same clip can give a hesitant, quick action, or a smoother, slower action depending on the time warp curve selected.

Have a go hero – using the transition and time warp curves

This works the same as version 4.31, covered in Chapter 4, *Animating the Characters*. Add a character to a new project. Load two different motions from the motion library and load them back to back, meaning, let one play out then load the second one. Set the curves to various combinations of in and out, then set the time warp curve and go through the various curves available to see how they affect the clip.

For transitions, watch as one clip ends and the other begins. For **Time Warp,** watch how it affects the clip it's been applied to as compared to its original (Linear) behaviour.

Using the Prop Look At

The **Prop Look At** feature is another great new tool, that once again reduces the amount of work we have to do to accomplish our animation tasks. We no longer have to manually move every item, such as a security camera prop tracking a subject, as the **Look At** feature with the proper settings can do this for us. It will track the subject based on the subject's movement, so in that case we would only have to animate the subject, not the subject and the security camera prop.

To explore this new feature, we'll use some simple building blocks to cover the basic parameters then we'll create a funny little creature to put this training to practical use.

Time for action – grasping the basics of Prop Look At

1. Load a new blank project. Select the **Set** tab and click on the **Props** button.

2. Double-click **Box_002** in the **3D Blocks** prop folder to load it into the scene.

3. Double-click on the **Ball_001** prop in the **3D Blocks** folder to load it into the scene. Set its parameters as follows:

    Move: X=230.0, Y=-100.0, Z=100.0

    Rotate: X=0.0, Y=0.0, Z=0.0

    Scale: X=25, Y=25, Z=25

4. Select both the box and ball prop, then press the **Home** button on the top toolbar to center the shot (select one prop then hold the *Ctrl* key and select the other prop).

5. Select the **Box_002** prop and click on the **Pick Target** button located within the **Look At** section on the right side menu panel.

Notice how the box prop rotated into a new position when the **Look** At feature is used to look at the ball prop:

6. With the box prop selected, change the **Look At Axis** to X.

7. Move the time scrubber down to frame 150.

8. Select the ball. Move the ball from the right to left of the screen.

    The following image shows the box prop tracking the ball prop as it moves across the screen:

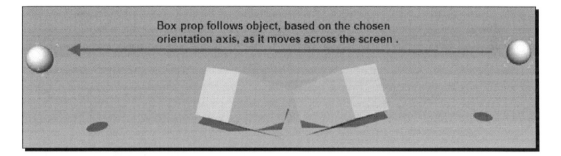

Box prop follows object, based on the chosen orientation axis, as it moves across the screen .

What just happened?

As a simple demonstration of the feature, we loaded two objects with one object looking at the other object as it moved. When the **Look At** was first created the box was turned long side toward the camera. We used the **Look At Axis** feature to re-orient it to the end of the box looking at the object instead of the side of the box.

Time for action – using a practical example of the Prop Look At

We are going to use some stock flex props along with a 3D block prop to create a nonsensical character for use with the feature. This type of character could be background or filler for other scenes in a fantasy or magical setting:

1. Start a new blank project. Select the **Set** tab and click on the **Props** button.

2. Double-click on the **Soft_Ball** prop in the **Spring** props folder to load it into the scene.

3. Double-click on the **Eye** prop in the **Spring** props folder to load it in to the scene.

4. With the **Eye** prop selected use the **Pick Parent** button to attach it to the top of the soft ball.

5. Double-click on **Antenna01** in the **Spring** props folder to load it into the scene.

6. Use the **Pick Parent** button to attach the **Antenna01** spring prop to the top of the **Soft_Ball** prop.

7. Double-click on the **Tail01** spring prop to load it into the workspace and attach it to the back of the **Soft_Ball** prop.

   The following image shows our nonsensical creature created from spring props:

8. Double-click on the **Ball_001** prop in the **3D Blocks** prop folder to load it into the scene. Set its parameters as follows:

   Move: X=125.0, Y=55.0, Z=80.0

   Rotate: X=0.0, Y=0.0, Z=0.0

   Scale: X=25.0, Y=25.0, Z=25.0

9. Select the **Eye** prop and click on the **Pick Target** button of the **Look** At section on the right side menu. Select the ball prop as the target.

10. Move the time scrubber to frame 100.

11. Move the ball prop slightly towards the left of the screen enough to see the **Eye** prop move as it tracks the ball prop.

12. Move the time scrubber to frame 200 and select the **Soft_Ball** prop.

13. Use the **Pick Target** button in the **Look At** section on the right side menu panel to select the ball.

14. Move the time ball towards the opposite side of the screen until it is almost off screen.

15. Save the project and press the play button.

    The following image shows the progression of the scene as the **Look At** feature forces the **Soft_Ball** and **Eye** spring props to follow the target **Ball_001** prop:

What just happened?

We created a creature out of spring prop parts and used the Prop Look At feature to make the Eye and Soft_Ball props track the target. The combination of the movement generated by the Prop Look At feature, plus the inherit spring properties add a lot of movement to the scene with very little animation on our part.

This author predicts there will be some very creative and even mind blowing uses of this tool when the iClone community has had time to work with it.

Applying iClone 5 techniques to Chapter 4, Animating the Characters

Chapter 4, Animating the Characters, was written before the release of version 5 and those techniques still apply to iClone 5, but there are some changes as mentioned throughout this appendix.

For one, the **Timeline** has been altered but its usage remains basically the same. Other actions, such as, idle and motions were on two different timelines. These are now combined into the single **Motion** timeline, which simplifies transitions from an idle, to what we used to refer to as a **Perform** action.

One good example is animating the grill closing, so let's take a look at doing that in iClone 5 instead of iClone 4.31.

Time for action – animating the grill with new features

For us to better understand how to apply some new techniques we will animate the closing of the grill as referenced earlier:

1. Load the "Version 5 Close Grill" project found in the code bundle. This is a version 5 project file:

2. Select the male character. Right-click and choose **Edit Motion Layer** from the **Motion Menu** option.

3. Click on the **Reach Target** button at the top right of the edit **Motion Layer** dialog.

4. Click on the selector circle on the right hand.

5. Use the **Eyedropper** tool and click on the **Box_001** prop on the grill handle.

6. Click on the **Reach To** button and check the **Reach Object** checkbox at the bottom then click **OK** to continue. Close the **Edit Motion Layer Dialog**.

7. Select the grill prop.

8. Right-click on the grill prop and select **Close Top** from the **Perform** menu. You'll notice it looked great until he went through the floor at the end of the motion.

9. Move the time scrubber back to the first frame.

10. Select the male character and check the **Foot Contact** checkbox in the **Avatar** section of the upper-right menu.

11. Replay the animation and you will see that our character now bends at the knees instead of going through the deck.

12. Return the time scrubber to the first frame.

13. Select the **Box_001** prop and turn its visibility off by unchecking the **Show** checkbox in the **Scene Manager** or by clicking the **OFF** button in the visibility section of the right menu panel.

14. With the box still selected, position the hand to fit the grill handle.

15. Save the project:

What just happened?

We used the Human IK system combined with an invisible dummy to allow the built-in prop animation to drive the character's movements. The dummy was used as a means to control exact placement of the hand. The grill prop did an excellent job of animating the hand and body. All that is left for us to do now is clean it up, with some adjustment of the hand and body position.

Have a go hero - adjusting the hand position

Using the **Box_001** dummy adjust the hand position on the handle as it the top closes. Add the **Fist** or **Grab** hand motion to the right hand and extend it to play until the grill top is closed. Move the time scrubber back and forth stopping and correcting the hand position of the handle.

Use the **Move** and **Rotate** tools with the **Edit Motion Layer** dialog to straighten up his final stance if you don't like the look of the knees bending. This could also be corrected by creating a new motion after closing the grill, that releases the character's hand from the handle and straightens him up into a better standing position.

This was a lot easier and smoother than we were able to accomplish in version 4.31. As you go through the 4.31 exercises, think about how to apply the new methods to animating the main project, as well as using the existing methods outlined in Chapter 4, *Animating the Characters*.

Summary

iClone 5 has so many new tools and features that it's taken us this long just to cover their basic usage. As you can see, Reallusion has brought iClone development forward in a huge leap in terms of bringing animation to the masses:

Specifically, we covered the following:

- MixMoves, how to use them and mix them as we play the animation.
- Puppet Motion: Letting iClone do the work with sliders and options that can customize almost any motion.
- Discussed and used Human IK technology licensed from AutoDesk that allows us to animate a character with body part movement aided by natural motion of the bone structure.
- Explored installing and using Mocap animation along with how to clean it up for easier usage.

- ◆ Discussed and worked with the Prop Puppet which allows us to control any prop with a preview before we record option.

- ◆ We covered topics such as customizing the transition curves and time warp of multiple motion clips.

- ◆ Used the Prop Look At feature to point props at certain objects using the proper orientation axis.

It's an exciting time to be an iClone animator. All of these exciting new animation features and tools give us more power than ever to animate a great story, highlight a fantastic concept, or sell a wonderful idea.

The tools and features covered in this appendix can only get better as the software matures. Most of us that have been with iClone since its first release couldn't be more pleased with the newest version of our favorite animation software.

iClone is the little animation engine that has grown up and is maturing into a full-fledged movie making package. This release puts it in a class of its own with its great price, fantastic content, and wonderfully supportive community.

Let us not forget the people at Reallusion! These people have worked very hard to bring us this wonderful software and they've taken their fair share of grief from would be animators that want a one button does all solution. In their favor, they have always acted professionally and strived to resolve any problems to the satisfaction of all concerned.

As a group of users, this community asked for a lot of improvement over the already powerful version 4. A lot of it was pie in the sky dreaming but low and behold... Reallusion delivered all that we asked for and then some.

Now it's up to us to learn the improvements and push them to levels of usage that will awe even the Reallusion engineers.

E
Pop Quiz Answers

Chapter 5, Enhancing Animation with Particles

- iClone particles are a billboard type of particle based on what type of images?

    - **Answer:** Diffuse and Opacity Maps

    These control the look of the particles

- Particles can be altered by which of the following actions?

    - **Answer:** All of the above

    All of the above are methods to alter the appearance of the particles.

- The following screenshot shows an iClone particle interface button. Identify the button.

    - **Answer:** Attach To button

This button invokes a sub-node window when attaching objects to other objects. It also contains the position and rotation options. The following screenshot shows the Attach To button within the Attach section of the right panel.

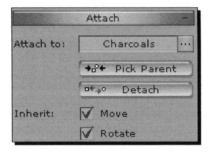

- ◆ Particles in general can be attached to:
  - ❏ **Answer**: All objects except skies and terrains

Particles can be attached to all objects except Skies and Terrains.

Chapter 6, Working with Cameras

- ◆ Which of the following cameras is not a smooth cam as it inherits its motion from the parent?

Answer: Actor Cam

- ◆ How is a follow cam actually converted to a permanent camera?

Answer: Create a new camera from the follow cam view and link the camera to the root.

- ◆ Which lens is the default lens of for the iClone cameras?

Answer: 50 mm

- ◆ The 200 mm lens would place the focal point further away than a 35 mm lens.
  - ❏ **Answer**: False

The focal point would be closer

- ◆ The lens size and focus can be animated with the timeline.
  - ❏ **Answer**: False

Only the lens size can be animated.

Chapter 7, Enhancing Scenes with Images and Videos

- ◆ To properly use a billboard or image Plane which of the following image maps are required?

    - ❑ **Answer**: Diffuse and Opacity

- ◆ An image Plane always faces the camera.

    - ❑ **Answer**: False

    A billboard always faces the camera.

Chapter 8, Rendering our Work

- ◆ A codec is:

    - ❑ **Answer**: A program that compresses/decompresses an audio/video file.

- ◆ Which of the following would be a codec?

    - ❑ **Answer**: VP8

- ◆ MP4 for PC is:

    - ❑ **Answer**: A codec.

Appendix C, Exploring New Features

- ◆ The Post Effect filters are permanent and have no adjustments available in this release.

    - ❑ **Answer**: False

    Post Effect filters can be deleted or edited via their individual parameter interface.

- ◆ The light Multiplier creates as many lights as the user specifies.

    - ❑ **Answer**: False

    The light Multiplier tool increases or decreases the amount light generated (brightness) by a single light.

- ◆ Which of the following is not related to Toon Shading:

    - ❑ **Answer**: Tone Map

    The Tone Map has been part of iClone since version 4 so it predates Toon shading.

Appendix D, Discovering New Animation Tools

◆ Pinning refers to:

❑ **Answer**: Locking a character control point from moving or rotating.

◆ We can pin a character's hand to another prop.

❑ **Answer**: False

Pinning concerns motion not attachment.

Index

I

iClone
  3D stereoscopic rendering 271
  about 18, 19
  accessories, attaching 95
  accessories, using 95
  animation tools 411
  cameras 189
  characters, customizing 81
  community, interacting with 19-21
  facial mapping feature 84
  formats 261
  iClone physics 338
  image sequences 258
  installing 8, 9
  Light Multiplier 396
  particles, exploring 168
  props, attaching 95
  Puppeteering panel 122
  rendering 252, 253
  storyboarding 291
  version 5 337, 379

iClone 5
  about 411
  grill, animating 460, 461
  hand position, adjusting 462
  techniques, applying to 459

iClone bakes
  about 339
  physics activated props, duplicating 340
  saving simulations 340
  testing simulations 340

iClone installation
  bonus content, installing 10
  display information, controlling 13, 14
  options, exploring 11, 12
  steps 8, 9

iClone particles. *See* **particles, iClone**
iClone particles, attaching to props
  loading 174, 175
  manipulating 174, 175
  torch, creating 174
  torch handle, creating 174

iClone physics
  about 338, 339

  animation, clearing 340
  frames vs realtime 339
  iClone bakes 339
  menu 340
  rigid body object 342
  simulations, working with 339
  soft body object 342, 343

iClone user interface. *See* **user interface, iClone**
iCloneWiki
  tabular description 319

IK Constrain option 125
Image button 292
Image Layer
  about 232
  Animated Clouds prop, adding 239
  cameras/objects attaching, dummy object used 235
  image 235
  layer control menu 237
  multiple image layers, using 236-238
  using 233-236

image sequences
  about 258
  exporting, to own folder 259
  first sequence, exporting 259
  formats, in iClone 258
  images 259, 260

installing
  iClone 8

Instance 398
Instant Texture Update 400
interactive props. *See* **iProps**
iProps
  about 51, 330
  adjustments 331
  AML 51
  beer, grabbing 99, 100
  characters clothing, altering 100
  door, using 332-334
  event sequence 52
  home iProps folder, exploring 330-332
  interacting with 98
  linking, link feature used 53
  placing 51
  scene viewing 53
  working with 51-53

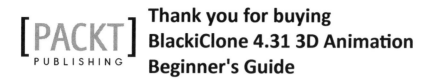

About Packt Publishing

Packt, pronounced 'packed', published its first book "Mastering phpMyAdmin for Effective MySQL Management" in April 2004 and subsequently continued to specialize in publishing highly focused books on specific technologies and solutions.

Our books and publications share the experiences of your fellow IT professionals in adapting and customizing today's systems, applications, and frameworks. Our solution-based books give you the knowledge and power to customize the software and technologies you're using to get the job done. Packt books are more specific and less general than the IT books you have seen in the past. Our unique business model allows us to bring you more focused information, giving you more of what you need to know, and less of what you don't.

Packt is a modern, yet unique publishing company, which focuses on producing quality, cutting-edge books for communities of developers, administrators, and newbies alike. For more information, please visit our website: www.PacktPub.com.

Writing for Packt

We welcome all inquiries from people who are interested in authoring. Book proposals should be sent to author@packtpub.com. If your book idea is still at an early stage and you would like to discuss it first before writing a formal book proposal, contact us; one of our commissioning editors will get in touch with you.

We're not just looking for published authors; if you have strong technical skills but no writing experience, our experienced editors can help you develop a writing career, or simply get some additional reward for your expertise.

ImageMagick Tricks

ISBN: 978-1-904811-86-2   Paperback:232 pages

Unleash the power of ImageMagick with this fast, friendly tutorial and tips guide

1. Complete tutorial and a gallery of tricks and techniques

2. Create impressive image manipulations and animations on-the-fly from the command line or within your programs

3. Complete PHP-based sample applications show how to use ImageMagick to add pizzazz your web site

SketchUp 7.1 for Architectural Visualization: Beginner's Guide

ISBN: 978-1-847199-46-1   Paperback: 408 pages

Create stunning photo-realistic and artistic visuals for your Google SketchUp models

1. Create picture-perfect photo-realistic 3D architectural renders for your SketchUp models

2. Post-process SketchUp output to create digital watercolor and pencil art

3. Follow a professional visualization studio workflow

4. Make the most out of SketchUp with the best free plugins and add-on software to enhance your models

Please check **www.PacktPub.com** for information on our titles

Blender 2.5 Character Animation Cookbook

ISBN: 978-1-849513-20-3   Paperback:308 pages

50 great recipes for giving soul to your characters by building high-quality rigs

1. Learn how to create efficient and easy to use character rigs

2. Understand and make your characters , so that your audience believes they're alive

3. See common approaches when animating your characters in real world situations

4. Learn the techniques needed to achieve various setups, from IK-FK blending to corrective shape keys and eyes controllers

Learning VirtualDub: The Complete Guide to Capturing, Processing and Encoding Digital Video

ISBN: 978-1-904811-35-0   Paperback: 212 pages

Get started fast, then master the advanced features of VirtualDub, the leading free Open Source video capture and processing tool

1. This book is available as a free download, scroll down for more information

2. Capture and process broadcast, digital, home, streaming video

3. Cut, paste and edit ads, trailers, clips

4. Demos and walkthroughs of processing sample videos

Please check **www.PacktPub.com** for information on our titles

Printed in Great Britain
by Amazon.co.uk, Ltd.,
Marston Gate.